The Opening Country

The Opening Country

A Walk through France

John Micklewright

Matador
9 Priory Business Park,
Wistow Road, Kibworth Beauchamp,
Leicestershire. LE8 0RX
Tel: 0116 279 2299
Email: books@troubador.co.uk
Web: www.troubador.co.uk/matador
Twitter: @matadorbooks

ISBN 978 1800461 277

British Library Cataloguing in Publication Data.
A catalogue record for this book is available from the British Library.

Printed and bound by CPI Group (UK) Ltd, Croydon, CR0 4YY
Typeset in 11.5pt Adobe Garamond Pro by Troubador Publishing Ltd, Leicester, UK

Matador is an imprint of Troubador Publishing Ltd

To the memory of Alasdair, Jon, and Tony,
who contributed in different ways,
and my father, David, whose contribution was fundamental

La liberté alors, c'est une bouchée de pain, une gorgée d'eau fraîche, un paysage ouvert.

Frédéric Gros, *Marcher, une philosophie*, 2009

So many architectural masterpieces, so many varied countrysides, so many distant prospects of the world – villages, towns, flowers, birds, human contacts, and sun. But my main enjoyment has consisted of sitting at café tables or on benches in parks or under plane trees, gently absorbing the visual impressions and watching the French at work and play, and listening to the blackcaps singing in the poplars of the north, or the cicadas in the mulberry trees of the south, in fact, just being in France.

Letter from my father to his father, August 1975

Contents

Prologue   1

1   Landing   14
2   Walking alone   38
3   Town and forest   72
4   Heading upstream   100
5   Rich and poor   128
6   Heat   156
7   Mountains   184

Envoi   216

Notes   222
Bibliography   232
Acknowledgements   241
Index   243

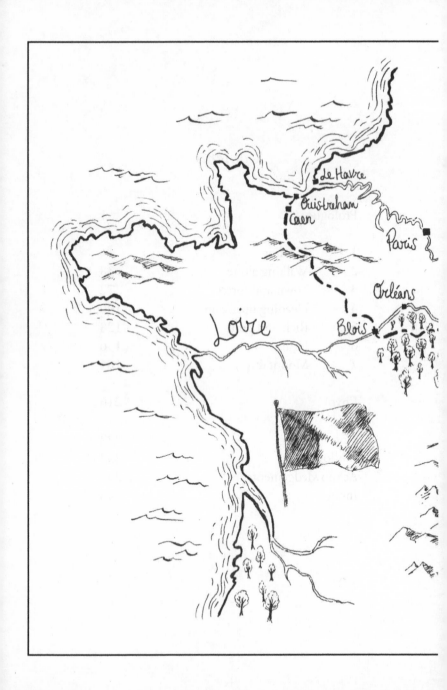

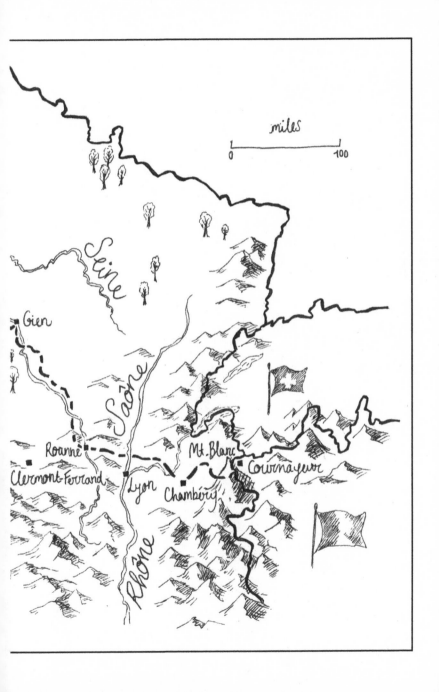

Prologue

Marcher – to walk; to travel on foot.

I first went to France as a child in the 1960s, for just a day – an excursion during a family holiday on the Channel Island of Alderney. My parents, my sister, my brother, and me, the youngest. A dim memory stays of the small ferry arriving in Cherbourg and – unbelievably, given our parents' usual frugal habits – of going to a restaurant for lunch. I did not want to eat what was offered. Father would have been keen to introduce us children to the France he loved so much. His own first visit was as a young man in 1939 and it was always the country to which he wanted to return; the chance of doing so for even a day would have been impossible to resist. The landscape, the mountains, the natural history, the architecture, the people, the food, the feeling rural France evoked in him of a different pace of life, of a quieter, slower world – all drew him back time after time.

For the next twenty-five years after that Cherbourg lunch, France was the default for my own travel outside Britain. No cheap flights to the rest of Europe or further afield. My generation, like our parents, looked across the Channel to France as the first place abroad, the nearest source of another culture. A couple of visits with my parents before I left school and a first holiday without them when

I was sixteen, trying and often failing to hitch-hike my way around with a friend. More holidays with friends when a student plus a day trip on a hovercraft to Boulogne for lunch again, which this time I ate – an enormous blow-out of seafood. Walking twice with my father in the Pyrenees in my twenties and skiing in the Alps with my future wife. Going to France felt natural.

Then for another twenty-five years, France became the opposite: a country to ignore, a country to hurry through. Or to fly over and avoid entirely. This new state of affairs arose when I went with my young family to live in Italy, settling in the hills north of Florence. France was now an obstacle, somewhere to get across quickly. Father had never been to Italy. He came with my mother to visit us willingly but I always had the feeling that he would have been happier had we moved to France instead. Italy absorbed us and adopted us, and Italian quickly pushed out my schoolboy French. We moved back to England a dozen years later but kept a part of our Italian life, returning at every opportunity. France, Britain's closest continental neighbour, was now foreign.

That foreignness unsettled me. I felt European – I wanted to know the country across the Channel. To feel, if not at home as in Italy, at least an easy familiarity. The time had come to rediscover France, to fill in what had become an uneasy void in my mind. To do so I would cross the country, back to Italy, slowly, on foot. 'Walking causes absorption... The body becomes steeped in the earth it treads,' argues the French writer Frédéric Gros in *A Philosophy of Walking*. In walking through France, I would absorb the country – its geography, its nature, its history, its language and culture, all those things that had captivated my father down the years.

I would also at last be realising an idea I'd had on leaving school of doing exactly this, of crossing France on foot. The seeds for that included a passage in a John Buchan novel that enthused my teenage self. The hero of *The House of the Four Winds*, Jaikie Galt, has just left university and is walking alone on the Continent. Buchan conjures up landscapes and sensations with prose that seems a bit overblown now but it portrayed such an adventure as bliss to my young imagination:

> [His journey] had led him through vineyards grey at the fringes with dust, through baking beet-fields and drowsy cornlands and solemn forests; up into wooded hills and flowery meadows, and once or twice almost into the jaws of the great mountains… He had walked and walked, seeking to travel and not to arrive, and making no plans except that his face was always to the sunrise… He began to rise whistling from his bed in a pine wood or in a cheap country inn, with a sense that the earth was very spacious and curious.

After a month on the road, puffing at his pipe after a fine supper, Jaikie feels that 'he had walked himself into contentment'. (I think the pipe was part of the attraction for me.) I thought the world of Buchan at the time and I remember asking Father whether he was one of England's great writers. He smiled gently and, without pouring on too much cold water, managed to convey that he did not see him in quite that light.

I hadn't always liked walking. As a child it annoyed me, often. Why did our parents, and especially our father, always insist on walking? We walked everywhere during that holiday in Alderney, criss-crossing the island. Going to the beach always meant a walk to get there, we children grumbling. But the day of childhood walking that stands out from others was during another family holiday, my first proper visit to France. We got off a train at the stop before our destination for the day so that we could walk the last two or three miles across the hills. My siblings and I seethed – it was just incomprehensible. Why on earth would one want to do that? But I have another memory from the same holiday, of following a path marked every now and again with red and white horizontal flashes of paint, one below the other, daubed on rocks, on trees, on the corner of old farm buildings. Of eagerly seeking out these marks, a treasure hunt threading through the landscape. Of walking as a mystery, never knowing what's ahead. As I grew older I slowly caught the bug. It infected me, thoroughly, and never left. And the idea of walking across France kept coming back.

Buchan's Jaikie tramped across France into Germany. My teenage plan had been to walk to Spain; this was long before the Camino de Santiago became the draw that it is today but I had heard of the paths to Compostela. Now, for this journey, I would have to plot a route to Italy instead.

* * *

Where to start in France and where to cross into Italy? Had he still been alive, my father would surely have urged me to consult *The Path to Rome*. Written by one of his favourite authors, Hilaire Belloc – sometime Liberal MP and prolific man of letters – it is the account of a journey on foot to Italy in 1901. But Belloc started from Toul, where he had spent time in the French army, and Toul is in north-east France, well away from the Channel. Belloc's path to Rome also took him into Switzerland along the way. Another possibility leading to the same destination would be to follow the Via Francigena, a recently revived pilgrim way from Canterbury to Rome, now a 'cultural route' of the Council of Europe. But again, this passes through Switzerland and anyway the idea of following a named path with its associated infrastructure for walkers did not appeal. I wanted something anonymous, something personal. Something to work out myself and then to deviate from if I had a better idea. My start and finish in fact needed little thought; the obvious choices were where we had always come into and out of France in our car-bound hurry across the country. Our standard entry was a ferry from Portsmouth to the little port of Ouistreham, in Normandy. And our usual exit was the Mont Blanc tunnel through the Alps, although this time I would go over the mountains rather than under them.

How to get between these start and end points? The days are long gone when you could walk on dusty, unpaved country roads, like Belloc or Buchan's hero, just heading where you would, picking your way across the country. Twelve years after Belloc's journey, on the eve of the First World War, France still had only a thousand kilometres of metalled road – just three per cent of the network of main *routes nationales*. Even in 1939 when my father first walked in France, there would have been many unsealed minor roads for him to follow. But now, as in England, country roads in France are almost all tarred. I quickly came to learn the French for such a road when asking the way or discussing progress, *une route goudronnée*. Tarmac or its modern replacement, asphalt, is unforgiving on the feet, unremittingly hard and too hot in summer. And it brings with it the traffic something any journey on foot should try to escape. As far as possible, I meant to walk on footpaths and tracks.

France is blessed by a huge network of long-distance paths, the *sentiers de Grande Randonnée* (GR), marked by those flashes of red and white paint splashed across my childhood memory. In practice, the paths often involve some stretches of asphalt road. But that is a small price to pay for what they offer most of the time: green lanes through the interior. I stared long at an Institut Géographique National map of all of these paths, spread out on our kitchen table. A map of dreams, for poring over on winter evenings. Just looking at it fired a thousand thoughts, unimpeded by reality – it is so much easier to walk on the map than on the ground. A thin strip of southern England is included at the top and my home town in Hampshire just makes it into the final millimetre. Courmayeur, at the Italian end of the Mont Blanc tunnel, is near the right-hand edge in the bottom half. After the blue of the Channel, the green of France is criss-crossed by red lines of the GR paths. One path starts right at Ouistreham and heads inland to nearby Caen. Another runs up to an 8,000-foot pass into Italy, the Col de la Seigne, an old trade route around the southern flank of Mont Blanc, and then drops down the other side to Courmayeur.

Most of the way I could trace a promising route across the map that linked the two, my finger moving from path to path in a broad south-easterly direction. From Caen, down through Normandy and beyond, to reach Blois, on the Loire. Then east, cutting off the great Orléans bend in the river, to reach the Loire again at Gien. Up the Loire, for a long way south, to Roanne, to the east of the main highlands of the Massif Central, which I would avoid, and roughly level with Lyon. Next a stretch where the paths marked on the map did not join up, over the hills to the southerly flowing Saône just above its junction with the Rhône at Lyon where their combined waters head on for the Mediterranean. And, finally, east out of the Rhône valley towards Chambéry and into the Alps where the best way forward to get through the mountains to that path up to the Col de la Seigne and the Italian frontier was again unclear. The uncertainties were a spur. In all, the distance would be not far short of Land's

End to John o' Groats if you keep off the roads. Perhaps a thousand miles.

* * *

Preparation… After working out a rough route, I realised to my surprise that I had never been to any of the places I would be likely to see. Our car journeys to and from Italy may have started and ended at the same points. But they were confined to *autoroutes* radiating out from Paris with overnight stops here and there – or even none as we battled on to get through France as quickly as possible. It was as if they had been in a different dimension. Nor, as far as I could remember, had earlier French holidays taken me to anywhere I would now go. Even in this narrow geographical sense, the journey would be one of discovery rather than rediscovery. Should I mug-up on the route in advance? That great Edwardian naturalist and walker W. H. Hudson started his classic *Afoot in England* with a chapter titled 'Guide-books: An Introduction'. 'If pleasure be the main object,' he wrote, 'it will only be experienced in the highest degree by him who goes without book and discovers… the "observables" for himself.' Learning as I went along would match the spirit of the adventure, increasing surprise and delight in what I found. And it would help the gods of chance to push me serendipitously off my chosen road. The map and accompanying gazetteer were largely blank in my mind, bar the main rivers and mountain ranges, to be filled in as I progressed. Even the Loire, which I now saw I would follow upstream for many miles, was a river I had known only for the chateaux in its lower reaches. I had never really thought about from where the river came.

My father could have told me much. But he also left behind a mine of written information. Throughout his life he kept a nature diary that doubled up as a travel journal in middle age and his later years. I read his diaries properly for the first time only when starting to write this book. He wrote at length about his time in France. He had visited many of the areas I passed through and stopped in some of the very towns and villages where I stayed. But it had been better to go in ignorance. He wrote after one of his last visits of the thrilling power of 'the unadvertised – unheralded and unexpected'. His diaries would have taken on the nature of a guide, spoiling the surprises.

Had I read these diaries before starting out, the entries from his early trips to France – the first one in 1939, and subsequent visits after the war and into the 1960s – would in fact have been of little help. At this time, his diary was restricted to observations on the natural world. The first volume starts as a fifteen-year-old in 1931 and is headed 'Nature Notes' in a rounded teenage hand. He recorded flowers and trees – an early ambition was to be a botanist although he eventually trained as a doctor, becoming a country GP – together with insects, reptiles, butterflies and birds. By the time of the fortnight in the Massif Central in the spring of 1939 that was his introduction to France, the diary had become firmly focused on birds. 'May 2nd – the upland between Le Puy and Monistrol d'Allier was full of linnets, goldfinches, larks, kestrels, serins, treesparrows. Saw a shrike – v. dark eyestripe, light above it... May 6th – heard golden oriole in the poplars by the Bave at Bretenoux... May 9th – hordes of nightingales and blackcaps while walking down from Martel to the Dordogne.' There is no comment on the landscape, the towns and villages, the farms, or the French.

By the 1970s, he was writing about a far wider range of subjects, especially when on holiday. The birds were still recorded but his entries for visits to France, usually made with our quiet mother in their little red, open-topped Triumph Herald, began to note also geography, farming, architecture (especially that of churches), the little hotels and campsites in which they stayed, walks, meals eaten and coffee and beer drunk, picnics, people spoken to – indeed how each day was passed. His diaries became vastly more informative about rural France, at that time.

But it was a much-changed countryside compared to that of his first visit, and it is frustrating that the diary entries for his introduction to France contain so little general observation of the country at the end of the 1930s. Writing in 1976, the historian Tony Judt commented: 'A French Rip Van Winkle who fell asleep in 1815 and awoke today would recognise very little... But had he woken some forty years earlier, it would have been very different... Once out of Paris he would have felt strangely at home.' Ten years earlier, another observer wrote that most French peasants in 1930 'probably had more in common with their predecessors of Balzac's time than with their successors of today'. The urban population of France only reached a half of the total in 1931, eighty years after Britain and thirty after Germany. A third of the French workforce was still working on the land on the eve of the Second World War. There were just 35,000 tractors at this time, one for every seventy farms. Subsistence farming was still hugely important – a quarter of all agricultural production never reached the market and was consumed in the home. This was the country my father would have seen, but did not record.

Rural France transformed from the 1950s onwards during *les trente glorieuses*, the thirty-odd years of modernisation and economic growth that followed the Second World War. Rapid mechanisation of farming resulted in nearly a million tractors in use by 1963. Average farm size rose as the number of farms fell. By 1975, agriculture accounted for only a tenth of the working population. Father noted in his diary for that year seeing some oxen still working in fields in higher farms in the Cévennes, in the southern Massif Central, but he also wrote about the change in the area since his first visit before the war and another in the late 1940s. Monastier had 'no old ladies sitting crocheting at their doors any more… all the roads now tarred – they were grit and mud in 1939'.

And the rural France that I would find had changed again from the one he recorded in the 1970s and early 1980s, or the one I would have seen had I realised my teenage ambition of walking down through France to Spain. Farm sizes have continued to rise and the average today, a hundred and fifty acres, is the same as in Germany and nearly two thirds of that in Britain. The popular image of the small French farm is outdated. Employment in farming has fallen substantially again: only three per cent of the French workforce is now on the land. Life for the great majority of people in *la France profonde* is no longer dominated by agriculture. A big growth has taken place in commuting to work from country areas and in second homes – the economic life of a half of all rural France is now formally classified as mainly 'residential'. More employment in rural areas is now in manufacturing than in farming. Taking France as a whole, the long exodus from the countryside, in progress since the mid-nineteenth century, came to a halt in the late 1970s. In the first decade of the twenty-first century, the population actually grew more quickly in rural areas than in urban areas. But the picture varies. I would see well-to-do, growing villages and towns. Here the turnaround has sometimes been spectacular. But I would also pass through areas where the population is still falling and where the villages are full of closed shops and houses for sale, the areas where rural France is still emptying out.

* * *

Preparation for a journey on foot includes choosing kit – and discarding it. The weight of your rucksack greatly affects the pleasure to be had; nothing is worse than trudging along bowed down by things that go unused. I chose a target of about eight kilos, a weight well within the conventional definition of 'lightweight' backpacking. Compromises had to be made but they did not require the extremes of what is known as 'ultralight' hiking, such as cutting an inch off your toothbrush handle. Hilaire Belloc, however, appears to have been a true ultralight walker. 'Weight counts,' he wrote, 'every ounce counts… Weight counts all the time.' He even advised against taking a rucksack at all on a walking holiday and reported leaving Toul on his way to Rome with just 'a small bag or pocket slung over my shoulder, [containing] a large piece of bread, half a pound of smoked ham, a sketchbook, two Nationalist papers, and a quart of the wine of Brulé'. For his walk across Europe some thirty years later, described in *A Time of Gifts* and its sequels, Patrick Leigh Fermor was more generous in his packing and included 'an aluminium cylinder full of Venus and Golden Sovereign pencils' and a couple of white linen shirts 'for best'. I took a single pencil and chose to forego the smart. On the other hand, Leigh Fermor had no phone charger or backup battery to remember.

Packing also gave me a chance to lay something to rest. Visiting my parents one weekend when in my twenties, I told Father proudly that I was reading *War and Peace* and loved it. 'What translation?' he asked, looking up over his gold-rimmed, half-moon glasses that were an almost permanent fixture. What translation! I checked – it was by Rosemary Edmonds, from the 1950s. 'Oh, not the one by Louise and Aylmer Maude,' he said flatly. This was the version published in 1922 and endorsed by Tolstoy, with whom the Maudes had a long friendship. End of conversation. I had always wanted to re-read *War and Peace* and now I would. And this time I would try the Maude translation; I had Father's little three-volume hardback edition, printed on fine India paper like an old bible, each volume smaller and lighter than a modern paperback. I packed the first volume, which would keep me going for a while.

Another decision was not to take a tent. In general, I would try to sleep in a bed each night, looking for them as I went along, armed with mobile phone and a link to the internet – too risky to just rely on coming across a B&B or Jaikie Galt's cheap country inns, ubiquitous no more. But if no bed were to be found, or if the urge took me, I would sleep under the stars. I was setting out in mid-May and this promised conditions at least nearer to the balmy evening in 'the very beginning of June' when Belloc left Toul than the December landscape 'hushed by snow' in which Leigh Fermor started his journey from the Hook of Holland. On one of the walking holidays with my father in the Pyrenees, we had slept out with no tent every night beneath fresh, clear mountain skies, when sleeping in the open seems that it simply cannot be bettered. However, on another outing together we had been caught under-prepared. I had joined him for a couple of days when he walked westwards along the South Downs one July, by then in his seventies. He had booked nowhere to stay, confident in the belief that he could find beds in pubs and B&Bs as he progressed. The night I spent with him we had no luck and after turning down the offer of the Wendy house in a pub garden at the foot of the chalk escarpment, we walked back up onto the down – he, as usual, in old tweed breeches and a Guernsey sweater – and spent a cold night huddled in a hollow just below the brow of the ridge trying to get some sleep, covered only by our jackets. His diary entry reads tersely: 'legs were very cold – frequent waking – dawn beginning 3.30 – cockcrow – finally.' A couple of nights later, after I had returned to London and work, he repeated the performance, writing triumphantly to me afterwards of lying in the grass looking down on fireworks at Goodwood racecourse as a full moon rose, although in his diary he noted 'another cold night and not much sleep'.

To avoid this fate, I needed a sleeping bag. My old one, companion of walking trips since my twenties, weighed nearly two kilograms, a quarter of my target total. I bought an encouragingly named down-filled 'Minimus' bag as replacement. Just half a kilo and it squeezed into a tiny stuff sack. I then decided to get a new, very thin, insulation mat to sleep on. Made in the USA by 'Gossamer Gear' – the name alone almost sold it to me – there was no British importer. An old American friend was due to visit not long before my departure and offered to bring me one. Jon sent an email after the mat arrived at his apartment in the post: 'Gad – if I'd realised it was going to be that thin I could have brought you over a couple of sheets from the New York Times instead.'

The day before leaving, I went into a local wood and cut myself a modest-lengthed stick from a pollarded hazel tree. Protection against dogs. Something to propel myself along with when I flagged. And for swishing at nettles or brambles, for sounding the depth of mud or water, or just for fiddling with. Light, slender but strong – more like a wand than a staff, in line with the hazel's reputation as a magical tree that wards off the evil eye.

I was ready, or as ready as I was ever going to be. One morning I stepped out of our front door, hoisted on my rucksack, and walked across the hills to catch the night ferry to France.

1

Landing

'How am I going to get to Cayenne?' demanded a fellow passenger of a patient crew member. Not the capital of French Guiana, but Caen, just inland from Ouistreham (pronounced 'cong' without the 'g'). Easy to smile knowingly. But I too would stumble over the pronunciation of place names in the weeks ahead. Blank looks when I said where I'd come from that day or where I was heading next. How do we manage to mangle this beautiful language so easily?

And it was a good question. The ferry had arrived not at Ouistreham, the little town with its tiny harbour at the mouth of the modest River Orne, but thirty miles up the coast at the city of Le Havre on the other side of the great estuary of the Seine. Explanation, a port strike. With our ship riding high on the top of the tide, the switch in landfall at least gave a chance to look out over Le Havre and admire the redesign after the city's destruction in the Second World War. Early-morning sunlight picked out the clean lines of the buildings beside the harbour basin: a long, five-storey concrete block of flats, floor to ceiling windows with broad surrounds, arcades of shops and offices below, the block punctuated by short square towers themselves broken up by periodic bands of balconies. The proportions were perfect. Close behind was the three-hundred-foot octagonal tower of Le Havre's main church, built in the same pre-cast concrete. The rest of the city stretched beyond to an escarpment of hills, surprisingly harmonious.

The answer to the question was a minibus, laid on to take us foot passengers to Ouistreham. I was joined for this first week by an old friend, Andrew, who had walked with me several times in Scotland in the past. Tall, craggy Andrew who had once pulled out of a cycling holiday down the Loire that he had suggested – I and the third member of the party promptly took a car instead. We squeezed in next to a couple of cheerful Australians who had just brought several dogs to England for a charity from a rescue centre in Thailand, our puzzled reactions mirrored in theirs as I explained my plan to walk across France. A drive up the Seine for several miles before we soared high over the river on another triumph of modern design, the mile-long Pont de Normandie built in the 1990s, a sinuous elongated coat hanger supported by twin slender, seven-hundred-foot towers. And so after another half hour to Ouistreham, where we were deposited with our rucksacks on the quay.

The port lies on the edge of town, standing almost alone. Not much more than a single quay in the river mouth and a couple of small breakwaters, together with a lock at the entrance to the ship canal that runs down from Caen next to the Orne, the Canal de Caen à la Mer. The humblest of entries into France. A tall white lighthouse stands next to the lock, topped with a broad red band below the lantern.

This little patch of land – the quay, the lock, the harbour master's house, and a bar – was the setting for one of Georges Simenon's Maigret novels from the 1930s, *Le Port des Brumes*, which I read after my return home, struggling along in the original to try to hold on to my French. It is the murder of the harbour master, poisoned with strychnine, that Maigret must solve amid the mists, *les brumes*, for which Ouistreham is famed.

A much more recent book also revolves around the quay. The title of *Le Quai de Ouistreham* by the journalist Florence Aubenas gives only the location of the main action. That of the version published in English, *The Night Cleaner*, reveals more. Aubenas wanted to investigate the lives of unskilled workers at the bottom end of the labour market after the financial crash of 2008. She chose Caen ('neither too far north nor too far south, neither too big nor too small') and looked for work, posing as someone with no qualifications or experience. Eventually she found some hours with a firm that cleaned the Portsmouth to Ouistreham ferries. Aubenas stuck at it for six months, documenting the precarious life of a cleaner, under constant pressure to keep up with the tightest of schedules, rushing from one part-time job to another. Her account is in the tradition of *The Road to Wigan Pier*, which must have influenced her choice of title – the French translation of Orwell's polemic is published as *Le Quai de Wigan*.

But on a brilliant, late-spring morning with no hint of *les brumes*, we were not thinking any more about the ferries, the cause of the strike that had diverted us, or about the conditions of local employment. We were looking landward, eager to be off and to stretch our legs up the Orne. The adventure had begun. I was at last setting out, full of expectation and excitement, all of France before me. As we started inland, past the lighthouse, a repetitive, purring 'turr, turr, turr' of birdsong came across the canal. The sound that gives the bird its name, something Father labelled in his diary as 'a hot summer sound'. A turtle dove, all too rare in England now. A good omen, a sign of new or unfamiliar things to come.

* * *

My father's arrival at Ouistreham over seventy years earlier, on his second visit to France, was very different. He got no further than the seashore before turning around and going back to England. Ouistreham is at the eastern end of Sword Beach, one of the five sets of beaches used in the Allied landings on the Normandy coast in June 1944 – *le débarquement* as I came to hear it referred to in conversations or on plaques and anniversary posters. June 6, D-Day, was his birthday and he was a ship's doctor on a huge tank landing craft. His diary, still focused at this time just on birds, is silent about the main events of the day. A single entry covers two months: 'June-July. The Channel. Very few birds – an occasional gannet – a few flocks of black duck on the Normandy coast.' But his collection of little black and white photos, marked 'Ouistreham D-Day' or 'Sword D+1', 'Ouistreham D+3' and so on, are more revealing. They record what must have been a birthday marked by the highest tension, followed by a growing realisation that the landings had gone well as his ship ploughed back and forth across the Channel through the rest of June and July. His photos of D-Day itself show the invasion fleet streaming across the Channel, ships everywhere, all heading purposefully in the same direction; the battleship HMS *Warspite*, a veteran of the First World War Battle of Jutland, shelling shore batteries near Le Havre; thick black smoke rising from the fighting on the coast; and his own tank landing craft, looking down from the open bridge at the stern onto rows of lorries on the deck ahead. These ships, some three hundred and fifty feet long, were the forerunners of the roll-on roll-off ferry that brought Andrew and me to France, the deck sinking into the ship after the load from the hold had been disgorged through the massive bow doors. Flat-bottomed, they were run up onto the beach and then winched off or waited for the tide to rise. Father had taken one photo standing on the beach, looking back up at the ship above, the bow doors yawning.

What was a doctor doing on such a ship? The short voyage over from England would have generated few calls on his skills. His real work began on the return leg when the tanks and lorries of equipment had gone. Other photos show ambulance lorries lined up on the wet sand outside the bow doors, soldiers hurrying with stretchers up the ramp, and the hold full of the wounded in rows waiting to be shipped back to England.

The wounded might be seen as the lucky ones. Andrew and I walked up the Orne, across the Pegasus Bridge, the scene of a famous glider-born attack in the early hours of D-Day, to Ranville, the first French village to be liberated. Here, by the church still pockmarked with bullet holes, is a war cemetery. Row upon row of graves, mainly British but also some German, the combination underlining the common suffering of war. The headstones each a simple slab, all with flowers planted at their feet – pinks, whites, yellows. Immaculately mown lawns. We wandered the rows reading names, ages – some only eighteen or nineteen, some over forty – regiments, dates of death. The dates bring home the intensity of the struggle to establish a bridgehead and then move inland: their sudden start on June 6 and then the seventh, the eighth and on into the rest of June and July. In places runs of half a dozen or more graves, one after another, of men from the same regiment, all killed within a couple of days. And occasionally just the bleak descriptions: 'A Soldier of the 1939-45 War' or '*Ein Deutscher Soldat*'. We moved through the rows separately, each with our own thoughts, and on leaving walked on in silence for a while.

We pressed on up the Orne and the ship canal towards Caen – only three or four more hours on foot but it took the Allies a month in 1944. Poor Caen took an immense pounding from Allied bombers in the meantime and guidebooks are not kind to the modern-day city. But the mix of old and new has some charm. And when you are puffed and hungry, as we were after long, straight stretches of canal and riverbank with tarmac paths, it all looks good.

Caen was the seat of a successful invasion across the Channel in the opposite direction – Duke William of Normandy built the great castle just a few years before 1066. The keep is long gone but its vast ramparts remain, still dominating the city centre, and we skirted round them as we roamed out from our hotel to find somewhere to eat, passing bars full of students. We settled into a crowded little restaurant with a rather off-hand *patron*, ordered, and toasted the walking ahead. My mind went back to another time that I had come with a friend on the night ferry to Le Havre. It had been my first visit to France without my parents, the rather unsuccessful hitch-hiking holiday aged sixteen, the lack of success eased only by my companion, Walid, being a fluent French speaker. My parents had driven us to catch the ferry and, wishing us goodbye, Father could not stop himself adding a last word, with a slight smile: 'Don't drink too much.' Of course we were going to drink too much. That was one of the purposes of the trip and we started in the ship's bar, finishing the night asleep on its benches. Our first day in

France was a lot less rewarding than the one I had just had with Andrew. Hitching proved harder than we had expected and instead of getting to Paris we ended up surreptitiously pitching a tent after dark in a field outside a little village somewhere near Rouen. We awoke to the farmer kicking at the tent, a situation saved only by Walid's quick speech and natural charm.

The castle in Caen and a few other sights could easily have occupied Andrew and me the next morning. But we were itching to get out into the countryside proper. We wound our way through the streets back towards the river. Underneath the overhead wires of Caen's modern trams. Past the immense, open green space of the hippodrome on the edge of the old centre, lined with plane trees, a tractor raking the sandy track for the next trotting races. Past the joggers returning from their early-morning run. We crossed a bridge over the Orne, turned inland, and quickly picked up our path out of the city.

* * *

If you go for a walk in the country, your route may often be a loop taking you back to where you started. Or if you walk along the coast, you might just walk for a while, turn around, and then go back the way you came.

Returning to a starting point brings its own sense of satisfaction. But think of walking from A to B rather than back again to A. That's a journey with a purpose, other than the enjoyment of the exercise, the scenery and what you come across along the way: you are trying to get to B. Of course, you risk becoming too focused on doing just this, so best of all perhaps is to set off from A with no set destination, 'seeking to travel and not to arrive' like Buchan's Jaikie Galt.

Walking from A to B for a day or for an afternoon is not that hard to do, given some planning with maps and bus or train timetables. Walks of this type, even in familiar territory, bring a new sense of adventure. Doing it as part of a holiday on foot in unfamiliar terrain is another thing. B is a new place. You have little or no idea of what it will be like. You have looked at the map and have worked out how to get there. But it remains to be seen how your impression of the land to be covered will convert to the reality on the ground. As you start out in the morning, that sensation of being on a journey, of travelling on foot, buzzes through you. You are exploring. An excitement as you take your first steps, adjust your rucksack, fall into your familiar rhythm. My father wrote in his diary of 'a heightened awareness of everything which combines an element – not of anxiety – but of slight uncertainty as to what the day will bring'. New landscapes unfold in front as you reach the top of a ridge or round a hill. At each new vision, your eyes scan forward, surveying the ground. They often settle quickly on the horizon: always to be crossed, whether today, tomorrow, or sometime in the days to come. You peer ahead, seeking out where that crossing might be, wondering how long it will take.

So it was with our walking out of Caen that May morning. Each pair of red and white paint marks of the path – on a house, on a telegraph pole, on a wall – beckoned us on. France was opening.

* * *

If you hurry east by car on the *autoroute* towards Rouen and Paris, as I had done over the years in the rush to get to Italy, you bypass all the country to the south of Caen. Meandering its way in huge loops, the Orne has carved through the end of the great plateau of granite and schist known as the Armorican Massif that runs east from Brittany. Steep wooded valleysides dotted with enormous cliffs overlook the river as it pushes its way towards the sea. A day's walk from the city brings you to this area known bizarrely as the Suisse Normande. The plateau on either side of the river runs up to not much more than a thousand feet. But the drama of the valleys does conjure up an alpine feel at times, so that the Swiss label does not seem quite as silly as it first appears. One moment you are in a tree-lined gorge, the river running alongside, with the feeling that civilisation is far away. Then you pop up onto the rolling plateau, full of farms, and the valleys below seem another world. The walking is a delicious mixture of riverside and woodland paths, farm tracks, field edges, and quiet country lanes. The disused railway line from Caen to Flers, with its nineteenth-century bridges and viaducts across the Orne, keeps returning as you drop back off the plateau. If you want a week of walking from A to B, close to a Channel ferry, you will struggle to find better than this.

And as anywhere in late spring, nature showed the Suisse Normande to us at its best. This was the month of *Floréal* in the new calendar introduced in the Revolution, the flowering month. Hedges of hawthorn – the 'May tree' – dripping, flat-topped white blossoms bowing down the branches. Huge beds of wild garlic beside woodland streams, pushing up dandelion heads of small white starry-pointed flowers above floppy, rabbit-ear leaves, the air filled with the plants' perfume. Orchids that I could not name. Arching stems of dog rose just starting to flower – pinky-white petals and delicate orange centres. Meadows full of buttercups and fields with yet more carpets of yellow, of oilseed rape in bloom. Walking into villages, we passed buildings covered in wisteria at its peak, dangling dozens of fat purple tresses. At one blue-shuttered cottage, rhododendrons paraded in full flower outside the door in pink and red.

As we passed through villages and little towns, built in local stone, three different hubs of communal life caught my attention. First, the bars, as we looked for coffee or occasionally sought shelter from a squall of rain, the weather having turned changeable soon after leaving Caen. Village youth like village youth anywhere, playing on the slot machines. Older men betting on the PMU, the *Pari Mutuel Urbain*, the long-standing state-controlled system of gambling on horse racing, now extended to other sports and to online poker. Second, the churches. I don't share my father's deep interest in church architecture – his diary in later years was full of detailed comments on the form of a clerestory or a triforium. But it was impossible not to note the frequent slate-roofed steeples, so different from the squared-off church towers of much of rural England. Original designs or nineteenth-century additions? (Father leaned towards the latter.) Third, the old village *lavoirs*, the communal wash houses, some dilapidated or crumbling but many carefully restored. A central pool, typically open, surrounded by sloping sides for beating the clothes and usually a roofed section behind, supported on wooden posts or iron pillars and covered with slates like the church steeples.

In the weeks that followed, my interest in the bars never flagged, although a desire for hot coffee started to turn into a thirst for something cold. Often, neither urge was satisfied. It is surprising how rarely in the course of a day's walk in France of fifteen to twenty miles you pass through a village at a time when you feel the need and find a bar both in existence and open. Not infrequently, I walked all day without coming across bar or shop – a reflection in part of France's great mass, a mainland two and a half times the size of Britain with about the same population. With one or two exceptions, my curiosity in the churches never rose that high. But if they were open I usually went in and looked around in an unschooled way, deciding what I thought of them. And I continued to notice just how many had the rounded Romanesque doorways that impressed me in Normandy and which would always turn your head in England. I carried on spotting the *lavoirs* with interest and started to look out for the remnants of those in smaller villages and hamlets. But it was several weeks before I thought more about why they are still to be seen and what they tell us about the past.

* * *

Finding our way was straightforward: we followed the red and white paint of the GR. My father would have wanted to stay with this particular set of marks until their end. For the path we were on reaches south from Normandy, winding down across France to the eastern Pyrenees where it finishes at the Spanish border. There, in a wide, upland valley called the Cerdagne, we had the holiday in my childhood that introduced me to this method of signing the way – in fact, I realised now, to flashes of paint of this very path. The Pyrenees had always held Father's affection rather than the Alps, which curiously he never visited. Hilaire Belloc's 1909 walking guide, simply titled *The Pyrenees*, was a treasured possession and the only source of information he had on his first walking holiday there, alone, in 1949. But I would be on the path with Andrew for just a week, before turning south-east towards Italy – and the Alps.

Those daubs of paint pull me forward. And the paths' marking on the map does the same. Each evening Andrew and I spread out an Institut Géographique National map on a scale of 1:100,000 – one centimetre to one kilometre – and reviewed our plan for the next day or two, the thick, dashed red line of the GR snaking its way prominently across the paper. I look at these red dashes and feel an ineluctable draw, so great that it becomes a siren call leading me to overestimate what can be done in a day.

These are fine maps with good, strong colours – the greens of the woods, the blues of the rivers and streams, the orangey-brown height contours supplemented by clever, subtle shading of the relief. And like the map of the whole country with all the GR paths on which I had roughed out a route, any one of these 1:100,000 maps immediately sets me thinking, the imagination running. Eyes always drawn to the passage of the clear, bold red dashes, which always seem so simple to follow. Suggestion threatens to outweigh information.

The 1:100,000 maps proved perfect for planning a week or so ahead. Andrew spotted that a span of one of our hands – the distance from the tip of the thumb to the tip of the little finger – was a long day's march, a rough and ready rule that served me well in the weeks to come, at least in lowland France, offering a resistance to the sirens trying to lure me further. But a map at this scale leaves quite a lot to be imagined for each day's walking and increases your reliance on the path's marking on the ground. Extra detail came through a cheap subscription for 1:25,000 maps for the whole country that I could download onto my phone.

A far cry from Jaikie Galt, whose 'sole map was a sketchy thing out of a Continental Bradshaw', a guide to mainland Europe's railways. Jaikie made no plans 'except that his face was always to the sunrise... dimly aware at any moment of his whereabouts'. And there is indeed a risk that a large-scale map preoccupies you with those whereabouts so that you are forever checking your position rather than just enjoying your surroundings. But the additional information both helps and informs. The French maps include field boundaries as well as many more tracks and paths, encouraging all sorts of departures from the GR. Andrew and I quickly started to experiment, usually with success. The post-war network of marked GRs is not a set of historic rights of way. Each one is more in the nature of a permissive path that has been negotiated with landowners by the Fédération Française de la Randonnée Pédestre, the national association of volunteers that develops and maintains the network. Not surprisingly, some owners refuse access. The result is that the paths sometimes loop in what seem strange detours that you as the walker, trying to get from A to B, may wish to cut off. Or the GR may follow a tarmac road for a while, which you want to leave as soon as possible. My French evening class teacher the previous winter had suggested that I never say I was *perdu*, 'lost', which sounds rather humiliating, but to refer more obliquely to being *égaré*, 'astray'. This was the explanation I was always ready to use when off the GR if I met a landowner. But I never met hostility the few times it happened. One farmer even shrugged off my apologies, saying the track across his land was there for the use of everyone.

And like any detailed map, the 1:25,000 series tells you much more about the countryside you are passing through. A lot is conveyed by the place names on the map. On our first day out from Caen, we passed *le Marais*, *le Pré*, *la Butte*, *la Carrière*, *la Grange au Sel*, *la Croix du Puits*, and several *moulins* and *bruyères*. The marsh, the meadow, the hillock, the quarry, the salt barn, the cross of the well, the mills and the moors (literally 'heather'). I began to realise that the suffix 'ère', common in farm names, often stands for 'the place of', although even after some research the meaning of a name could still escape me. Does Goupillières, which we skirted the next morning, mean 'the place of the pins', from *une goupille,* a pin? Or, perhaps more likely, it is 'the place of the foxes' from *un goupil,* an old word for a fox. A couple of weeks later, I was to stay at La Grenouillère. Not the bathing establishment on the Seine painted by Monet and Renoir, but one of many other sites in France called 'the place of the frogs', confirmed by the sound coming in through my window on the night airs of mass croaking from a nearby pond. Working out the meaning of place names adds to the sense that you are exploring the country, even if that exploration and your discoveries are only personal.

Other names providing interest or entertainment are on signs that you meet along the way. An upright lichen-covered slab of stone at the edge of a wood inscribed mysteriously '*N° 9 CC Pere*' with the date, 1818, three years after the Battle of Waterloo and the Bourbon restoration. A mark on the boundary of someone's property, perhaps? Other signs are more transparent. *Attention taureau,* for example – beware of the bull. Signs about hunting rights and fishing abound. *Chasse gardée* – private hunting. A firm instruction by a riverbank to keep only trout and to throw back any young salmon, *les tacons,* with information on how to distinguish between the two. High up in the crook of a beech tree, *pêche interdite tous les vendredis* – on Fridays you can eat fish but not catch them. Then there are the 'private – keep out' signs that you find in any country. One spoke of *danger – pièges,* traps, in a dark unspecified way. Man traps? Another made the risk very clear: *tir de mines,* explosions. Coming down a long track back into the Orne valley one morning, we found a café in a hamlet, the only one for miles around, with a sign saying that entry was forbidden to people with *les chaussures crottées,* muddy boots. A good slice of the potential clientele ruled out at a stroke. But it was shut so our only opportunity for coffee had evaporated anyway.

* * *

The hills of the Suisse Normande finally discharged us and still following the meanders of the Orne we walked into the little town of Écouché set in the flatlands beyond. Now here was a welcome sign for two weary travellers, the sign of the golden lion at the Hotel Le Lion d'Or, and we promptly checked in. Beer, baths, and food restored everything – hake terrine, duck, the customary cheese course, and poached pears.

Wandering across the road from the hotel before supper, I saw a little memorial garden and went in to have a look. A simple upright stone block was inscribed: 'À la mémoire des victimes du bombardement du 6 Juin 1944'. Around lunchtime on D-Day, two waves of Allied bombers attacked the railway line at Écouché, aiming to stop German reinforcements being brought up to the invasion beaches. An aerial photo taken soon afterwards shows the railway tracks intact but the southern part of the town alongside in ruins. I could just make out the building at the crossroads that was now the Lion d'Or. It looked badly damaged. The other side of the street, and down to the railway, was a mass of rubble. Forty-four people were killed.

Since leaving Caen, we had been focused firmly on the present. On the walking, the landscape, the joys of the countryside in spring, and the pleasures of the little hotels and *chambres d'hôtes* – the B&Bs – that put us up, for example the gracious couple on our first night out from the city who gave us the delicious chicken in cider followed by *teurgoule*, a Norman rice pudding with spices, dishes against which all others were then judged. (Our hosts did not usually provide supper and we had asked humbly whether we might have an omelette.) We had had little thought for the past – including for the Battle of Normandy that followed the Allied landings. But we had just walked through the western side of the area that in August 1944 had seen some of the most bitter fighting of all. The town of Falaise lies about eight miles east of the Orne. The battle for the 'Falaise Pocket' was an encircling of the Germans by British, Canadian and Polish forces to the north and the Americans and Free French to the west and south. There was an appalling loss of life, especially on the German side. Accounts of the aftermath on the battlefield are horrific; General Eisenhower wrote of 'scenes that could be described only by Dante. It was literally possible to walk for hundreds of yards at a time, stepping on nothing but dead and decaying flesh'. But the result was that the Allied armies were able finally to break out, over ten weeks after D-Day, and then sweep quickly east to Paris within days.

The civilian population of Normandy suffered greatly for their liberation. Estimates vary but some twenty thousand people are believed to have been killed. The huge destruction in Caen and Le Havre was mirrored elsewhere. Describing Falaise, a pre-war guidebook commented on 'the endless variety of pretty corners... its streets would give an artist constant employment for a month', while the 1947 *Guide Bleu* to Normandy simply states: '*Le centre de la ville n'existe plus.*' Villiers-Bocage, about the same distance to the west of the Orne, is listed as 'entirely destroyed'. The villages we had passed through along the river – Thury-Harcourt, Clécy, Pont d'Ouilly, Putanges – all endured the bombing of the Caen-Flers railway line and the fighting on the ground that followed. At Thury-Harcourt, for example, we had missed both what photos show to be the poignant brick and stone facade of the seventeenth-century chateau, all that remains after the building was burned by retreating German forces, and the Boulevard du 30 Juin 1944, which commemorates the earlier Allied bombing. On leaving Écouché the next morning, we passed another memorial – one of the Free French Sherman tanks that had taken part in the battle to liberate the village.

* * *

Our way from Écouché led south across what was now a wide, shallow valley created by the Orne and its tributaries. At this point, we were in the *département* that takes its name from the river as old road signs told us. Round iron posts at crossroads, the metal arms painted with a blue background and the place names in relief in white lettering joined by fletched arrows to the distances to be travelled to the nearest hundred metres. And each post topped with an outsized acorn like a giant boiled egg sitting in its cup, with '*Dépt de l'Orne*' proudly displayed beneath on a little plate in the same blue and white colours. I imagined the signs in the days when the roads were still untarred, showing the way to a pre-war motor car fitted with running boards or to a horse and trap – or to people like us, on foot.

Ahead lay a great wooded ridge, the sixty square miles of the Forêt d'Écouves, rising to some fourteen hundred feet and including Normandy's highest point. A significant watershed – once crossed, the rivers run to the Atlantic rather than the Channel. When we eventually reached the top I sensed we had moved at a stroke much deeper into France.

At the start of the forest, before the climb, we turned off the path on seeing a tiny, plain stone building in a clearing in the middle of the woods, surrounded by railings twined with roses. From a distance, it had nothing to indicate its use. But as we drew nearer we saw a small cross over the door. A chapel, the chapel of St Jean des Bois, dedicated to John the Baptist.

The building and its setting had a simple, forlorn beauty, the solitude of the spot almost overpowering. Inside the open doorway was a minute narrow bench on either side and then, behind a floor to ceiling grille, an altar with a painted statue of a boyish saint dressed in animal skins with a lamb at his feet – the Lamb of God as John had labelled Jesus. Plaques covered the walls, most with dates from the first half of the twentieth century, thanking the saint for his intercession: '*Reconnaissance à St Jean*', '*Merci St Jean pour une guérison* [a healing]', or simply just '*Merci*'. A handwritten note inside the grille gave the chapel's history: it was centuries old in origin, destroyed and rebuilt several times during the terrible Wars of Religion between Catholics and Huguenots in the second half of the sixteenth century as the French Reformation unfolded, and then reconstructed in the early nineteenth. A few yards away stood a small, roofed, open-sided hexagonal stone structure, about five feet wide and eight feet tall. It enclosed a pool, fed by a spring. A pipe emerged at one side, water gently running out. Water supposed to cure eczema, among other ills. The note inside the chapel said that a mass is held once a year on the saint's feast day, June 24. But the chapel's real continued use was shown by little votive offerings – flowers, a ribbon, a handkerchief, a seashell – and by the objects on the tops of the railings around the sides of the pool: an upside-down glass and two flannels of off-white towelling.

The climb from the chapel gave a steady pull on forestry tracks up through the woods. Stands of oak and beech and a bit of birch, together with Christmas tree-shaped Douglas fir and stately, rounded-top Scots pines. Huge stacks of tree trunks waited for removal at the side of the way in dappled sunlight. The open nature of this type of managed forest encourages you to wander off the path to see what you can find. A large notice from the Office National des Forêts reminded mushroom hunters that they were limited to one basket per person per day, that the mushrooms were not to be sold, and that no mushrooms were to be taken on Tuesdays or Thursdays.

Different types of wood have different sounds. The fast, high-pitched notes and trill of the tiny goldcrest in conifer forests. Here, among the oak and beech, we walked to the constant call of cuckoos and the haunting sound of the wood warbler. The wood warbler has two songs, so different that it is hard to believe that they come from the same bird. One is a plaintive, repeating 'pew, pew, pew'. But it is the other that we heard that morning. Gilbert White commented in *The Natural History of Selborne* on a bird that made 'a sibilous shivering noise in the tops of tall woods'. The shivering sound has been noted by others too – the First World War poet Edward Thomas described 'little waves of pearls dropped and scattered and shivered on a shore of pearls'. But the description that sums up the wood warbler best for me is the sound of a coin spinning on a plate or on a slab of marble, speeding up and falling in tone as the coin spins lower and lower.

* * *

We ate lunch sitting at the side of a track at the top of the ridge, still surrounded by trees. Lunch for me in the weeks ahead became largely a refuelling exercise, a staple of bread, cheese and tomato after some fruit and chocolate mid-morning perhaps. Or sometimes the French version of the sandwich, which a *boulangerie* will happily make up, often the classic *jambon-beurre* – half a baguette buttered and filled with ham. With regret, when shopping for bread, I averted my gaze from the rows of cream-filled *pâtisseries* and little round layered *macarons* of different colours that would not fit into a small, tightly packed rucksack. But by the time I stopped in the middle of the day, the desire for them had usually passed anyway. I had strong memories of lunches with Andrew when walking in the wilds of Knoydart in the west of Scotland. Days of tuna fish and digestive biscuits, the former his suggestion and the latter mine. For years afterwards I avoided tinned tuna. But now Andrew was more wide-ranging in his tastes than me and our lunchtime diet in this first week included also *pâté*, sardines, quiche, beetroot, carrot, yogurt and anything else that caught his eye.

Lunch with my father on our two walking holidays in the Pyrenees was typically bread and *saucisson*, both of us always keen to find the type that has thick slices of black peppercorns scattered through the meat. This was the diet recommended by Hilaire Belloc in his hundred-year-old guide to the Pyrenees. 'There is nothing else so compact and useful… it is wonderfully sustaining', Belloc wrote of *saucisson*, adding in characteristic style: 'You will soon hate it.' We stocked up every few days when we came to a village and I always carried the bread, strapped under the top of my rucksack, several loaves tightly wrapped in plastic bags to stop them going hard and pretty unattractive they were by day three. Back in England, Father had a firm view that walkers, like a caricature farm labourer, ate bread and cheese for lunch. Out for a day's walk in mid-Dorset in the 1980s with my brother and me, he walked up to the bar of a pub and asked confidently for 'Bread and cheese for three, please'. The barmaid replied, a little uncertainly: 'You mean a ploughman's?' 'No, just bread and cheese,' he said firmly with a smile, looking purposefully over his half-moon glasses. My brother and I tried to melt into the background. The interchange continued, Father carrying on insisting politely that all we wanted was bread and cheese in response to the statement 'Oh dear, we don't do that', saying that they could simply leave off the salad and the other bits and bobs of the ploughman's lunch. Finally, the publican was called. And eventually we got three large plates of bread and cheese, with far more of both than in a typical ploughman's and for a lower price. Father was quietly jubilant.

* * *

Late afternoon the next day, we emerged from the woods into another broad, shallow river valley. Fields of green wheat stretched out in front, the stalks now well formed and starting to throw up their heads of grain. And in the distance we saw a church steeple and other buildings of a large settlement. It meant that we had crossed Normandy. Alençon, with its thirty thousand people and our first decent-sized town since Caen, is right on the border of the modern-day regions of Normandie and Pays de la Loire. Here Andrew left me and caught a train to Paris and thence London. I would miss the all-day chat and the banter as we teased each other, sometimes with jokes stretching back for years. I would miss his help in the *chambres d'hôtes* as we struggled along in our rudimentary French over supper with our hosts. I would not miss his lurid yellow rucksack cover, pulled out at the first sign of rain, or his hiding of my hazel stick ('I bet that stick doesn't make it to Italy'). Big Andrew, powering ahead, always half a yard in front of me just as in our Scottish walking days.

The town seemed dead on our arrival, the streets deserted. All changed the following morning. Market day and the square near Alençon's cathedral was full of people perusing the stalls under the sycamore trees. Stalls selling cheese, one with huge rounds maybe two-foot across and six inches thick, others with a massive array of different varieties. Stalls with stunning displays of sparkling fruit and veg. Stalls selling yogurt, stalls selling mushrooms, stalls selling honey, stalls selling cider. The sights and smells helped banish a touch of loneliness after Andrew's train had left the station and I set out to enjoy a day off. To laze and wander, with no weight on the shoulders. And to be anonymous, no rucksack, boots or stick to signal 'walker'.

Alençon is the typical sort of provincial town ignored by many guidebooks so I might not have learned much had I tried to research my route in advance. I headed to the tourist office and picked up a leaflet and map. I skipped two things pushed prominently – the museum of lace, the town's principal former industry, and the childhood home of the hugely popular modern-day saint Thérèse of Lisieux. Lisieux is a town thirty miles east of Caen and Thérèse became a Carmelite nun there in 1888 aged fifteen. She died from tuberculosis nine years later after a simple life of devotion and was canonised in the 1920s. A huge church dedicated to her was built at Lisieux and is second only to Lourdes as a pilgrimage site in France with some two million visitors a year. (Construction started in 1929, the year in which Hilaire Belloc, a devout Roman Catholic, wrote in a letter that the existing shrine was 'almost as ugly as Lourdes', adding grumpily that 'a new and far more ugly basilica' was coming.) A few months after my day in Alençon both Thérèse's parents were canonised as well. And in the same year an official diocesan enquiry opened into promoting her sister Léonie to the sainthood too.

I had never heard of Thérèse. Our family were regular churchgoers during my childhood; but we were Anglicans for whom the saints have only a minor role, bar giving their names to many parish churches. No praying to saints for intercession, as at the chapel of St Jean des Bois in the Forêt d'Écouves – the Reformation had swept away all that. And the Church of England has no process for canonisation, so that the only saints formally recognised are those from before the split with Rome. As a teenager I had gone to a school founded by Methodists, who give the saints even less space. Nor as an adult had I picked up any awareness of Thérèse. I had known that I would find many examples of French history that were new to me, but this particular type of cultural ignorance caught me by surprise.

The status of the saints puzzled Robert Louis Stevenson during his journey by canoe in the north of the country in 1876 reported in his first book, *An Inland Voyage*. In Creil, not far from Paris, Stevenson – brought up a Presbyterian – noted the veneration of St Joseph, saying that 'the good man plays a very small part in my religion at home'. Votive tablets thanking the saint, like those to John the Baptist that Andrew and I had seen in the chapel in the woods, he labelled as being 'foolishness to us Protestants'. But he went on to wonder whether his upbringing meant he had simply missed the point and that, like me, he was just unable to understand 'some higher and more religious spirit than I dream'.

It quickly became clear that Alençon had much else to see on what was a bright, sunny May day. The town has an impressive mix of architectural styles and a compact, well-preserved centre with some fine public buildings. I stared long at the sunlit, glowing, flat red brick facade of an early-seventeenth-century chateau, the Hôtel de Guise, now the *préfecture* – the seat of the prefect, the national government's representative in the *département*. (Guise, Guise… where had I met that name before? Of course! Mary of Guise, mother of Mary, Queen of Scots, and forever fixed in my mind by Fanny Ardant in the 1998 film *Elizabeth*.) Big, tall windows with blocks of granite picking out the building's corners. Chimneys mixing brick and stone punctuating pleasingly the steeply pitched grey slate roof. The sweeping, curved facade of the stone-built *hôtel de ville*, the town hall finished just before the Revolution, the curve pulling the eye around. The courtyard within the large, simple circular stone building of the 1801 corn exchange, the Halle au Blé, topped by a vast, airy cupola of glass and metal. Seen from afar, rising above the rest of the building, the cupola looks modern but it is Second Empire, added in 1865. I appreciated the ornate post office, built a hundred years after the corn exchange, with '*Poste-Télégraphes-Téléphones*' inscribed in large letters in the stone above the main entrance together with the intertwined initials 'R F', *République Française*. Civic pride, missing from the place with the same function in my much larger home town in England, a counter at the back of a WH Smith.

And I liked the design of the memorial to General Leclerc, near the classical Pont Neuf over the River Sarthe, after which the *département* to the south is named. It was across this bridge that Leclerc's armoured division of Free French forced their way into Alençon in August 1944 before racing up through the Forêt d'Écouves to help close the Falaise Pocket. Leclerc went on to lead the liberation of Paris and then Strasbourg and later to fight in France's Indo-China war in Vietnam, before dying in 1947 at the age of forty-five in an air crash in Algeria. A bronze statue stands out front of Leclerc, wearing his kepi and leaning on the trademark walking stick that he had used since a riding accident in the 1930s. A huge cross of Lorraine with its twin bars, the symbol of the Free French, towers behind him, defined by the shape of the edges of two massive blocks of stone set a foot or so apart and angled like the pages of a book, inscribed with the names and dates of his principal battles. But for his death, some argue that Leclerc would have gone on to play a major role in post-war France. De Gaulle told his son-in-law that he had given up smoking when Leclerc died in case France now needed him instead.

2

Walking alone

'*Comment s'appellent celles-là?*' – What are those called? – I asked, as I left Alençon on a track along the riverbank, pointing to the stinging nettles that the old lady was picking.

'*Les orties,*' she replied. '*Pour le potage.*' For soup.

That made sense: nettles are *ortiche* in Italian. I should have then tried to tell her that we too used stinging nettles at home in a pasta sauce, with garlic and pancetta. But I couldn't remember the French for garlic. All I did was to smile and nod and thank her and walk on. Seconds later I was kicking myself. An opportunity lost. I would have to try harder now that I was walking alone.

* * *

Walking with an old friend for a few days is something special. Long discussions on subjects of common interest. The laughter, the pleasure from sharing new sights and little discoveries, and the confidences that come from spending time together day after day – the occasional glimpse into parts of each other's life that before had lain hidden.

But to really absorb the land you are passing through, you need to walk by yourself. As Stevenson put it in his essay 'Walking Tours':

> A walking tour should be gone upon alone, because freedom is of the essence; because you should be able to stop and go on, and follow this way or that, as the freak takes you; and because you must have your own pace... And then you must be open to all impressions and let your thoughts take colour from what you see. You should be as a pipe for any wind to play upon.

The excitement of the daily start is heightened – you are exploring on your own. Any problems will need to be confronted without the benefit of discussion. There is an added sense of achievement at the end of the day. You notice more: sights, smells, sounds. You are more likely to talk with anyone you meet, notwithstanding my failure to continue the conversation on that first morning. And a great glow of happiness comes from the sense of complete liberty, of doing just what you want – the whole time. In the days following my departure from Alençon, I found myself wallowing in that freedom 'to stop and go on'. At times, I just dawdled, pottering along at the gentlest of paces, lingering to look at this and that on a whim. At others, I stepped out briskly, eating up the miles. Few companions could have put up with such spasmodic progress. Nor would they ever have been asked to, for I behaved the way I did exactly because I was alone, 'a pipe for any wind to play on'.

My father often walked alone. He was by himself for his introduction to France in the Massif Central in 1939 and for his first trip to the Pyrenees ten years later. He wrote in his diary that when a neighbour asked him what he thought about when walking, the answer was 'nothing'. He then elaborated on his meaning in a manner similar to Stevenson – that he was open all the time to what the landscape and countryside gave him to see, to hear and to feel, and that his mind typically dwelt on what he was offered. He wrote of thinking of 'the lie of the land, the shapes of the trees, the flowers, rocks, and the horizon'. On sounds it was the birds of course, the insects, and 'the wind in the grass'. And then he noted the enjoyment of 'the feel of the ground underfoot and the difference between the surface of a sphagnum bog and a dry peat hag and deep heather and a stony path and clean, hard limestone rock'. The philosopher Frédéric Gros writes in the same vein about the different sensations experienced by the solitary walker: 'To be buried in Nature is perpetually distracting. Everything talks to you, greets you, demands your attention… It's impossible to be alone when walking… Who could feel alone when he possesses the world?'

Before leaving England, I imagined that from time to time I would have to find something to think about. I would need to occupy my mind by going over French vocabulary or by trying to learn a poem or song by heart. I am no Patrick Leigh Fermor, able to recite or sing from a vast store of material retained from schooldays as he progressed across inter-war Europe. The odd bit of Shakespeare and I'm done. With my smartphone, I reasoned, I would be able to download anything to amuse me, or I could listen to the radio or to music. But tedium was not a problem. Fatigue, yes. Stress, occasionally. Boredom, no. Nature did forever distract me, along with a host of other things stimulating thought: the agriculture, farm buildings, cords of firewood, the shapes of bridges, evidence of local history, and anyone I met along the way although these encounters proved to be surprisingly few and far between. However, it is fair to say that a good amount of time when walking alone is also spent thinking about the routine questions that surround your daily life – what the weather looks like doing, whether you have missed that fork in the footpath shown on the map, how much water is left in your bottle, whether the village ahead is likely to have a shop, how far it still is to your bed for the night, and why that strap on your rucksack is hurting your shoulder yet again. And because you have nobody to divert you from these questions, they probably take up more time than they would do otherwise.

And of course with a phone, you are not alone in the same sense as lone travellers in the past. Ping! A message arrives. Or even a phone call. You are bumbling along a track, minding your own business, thinking about 'nothing', and suddenly that other world is back again, that world you left behind. I only rarely found this an intrusion, and there was always the option of turning the phone off. And sometimes you have a thought that would be fun to share straightaway with family or friend – and you can.

* * *

My aim now was to reach the Loire, a good week or more away. The weather was set fair and I was as eager as I had been on the quay at Ouistreham. This felt like a fresh start – I had never walked alone like this before, day after day. A slight apprehension only added to the thrill. Nor did I have much idea of where I was heading, other than I was going to follow a line of red dashes on the map until they led me to Blois, on the river.

Setting off, south-east out of Alençon into the *département* of Sarthe, the first thing the dashes brought was another big forested ridge to cross – the Forêt de Perseigne. Lots of evidence of recent logging, whether cleared sections of forest or stacks of felled trees again, oak and pine, the trunks stripped of branches and piled up one on top of another end-on to the track like a giant ordered pile of spillikins towering above me as I passed, the air fragrant with sap. I came across the builder, a huge orange caterpillar tractor, the driver nimbly picking up the trunks with a massive claw on the end of a hydraulic arm and swinging them around to place delicately on the growing mound. The map showed the track I was following to have a massive dog-leg, which I cut off by plunging directly into the woods, here with only little undergrowth beneath the canopy, occasionally checking direction of progress on a small compass that sat ready in my pocket, used most often in the weeks to come when hesitating at a junction of paths or just to orientate the map to check out views. Deep among the trees, compass in hand, I felt a little silly – this was hardly *terra incognita* – but ridiculously happy, my failure to pursue the conversation by the river in Alençon long forgotten.

I stopped in a large clearing at the top to eat some lunch and pulled out of my rucksack for the first time my father's little volume of the Maudes' translation of *War and Peace*. He had written his name on the flyleaf with the date, March 1943; he had been in the navy for a year and had recently survived his first active service as a ship's surgeon, in a minesweeper on an Arctic convoy to Archangel to supply the Russians. The convoy gave him new birds recorded in his diary including 'great skua, Cape Wrath', 'little tern, Iceland', 'ptarmigan, Barents Sea' and on finally arriving after nearly three weeks, 'glaucous gull, Dvina river', together with descriptions and little drawings of several others he couldn't identify. No mention of the attacks by plane and U-boat that sank thirteen of the forty merchantmen. When he bought the book, the battle for Stalingrad had just ended, marking the failure of the German invasion of Russia and a turning point in the war. Perhaps his timing was deliberate. Or perhaps it was merely that like me he had felt ready in his twenties to try Tolstoy's epic.

I was quickly absorbed in the opening account of Anna Pávlovna Scherer's *soirée*, with its introduction to Pierre and Prince Andrew Bolkónski (Andrei, in my Edmonds translation) and their differing degrees of engagement in St Petersburg society conversation. Tolstoy's description of Prince Vasíli, Pierre's future father-in-law, filled me with envy: 'He spoke in that refined French in which our grandfathers not only spoke but thought.'

This became the lunchtime pattern when walking alone – find a good spot to stop, preferably one with a view, and read, the short self-contained chapters of *War and Peace* making it easy to do as much or as little as I wanted. I was usually too tired in the evenings and although reading at lunchtime made for a longer day, it added to an astonishing feeling of freedom and of indulgence. To sit in the open air and read, occasionally looking up to take in the landscape around – it seemed such an extravagance. Eventually I closed the book, put it away, and ambled down the other side of the ridge through the woods on a winding, open, sandy forest road, thickets of broom in yellow flower on the sunny side, fresh young green bracken ferns curling up on the other.

* * *

Walking alone, you can take as long as you like to watch a bird, examine a flower, or chase a butterfly. I had not brought binoculars with me on grounds of the extra bulk and weight. My first pair had been hand-me-downs from my father, lost somewhere on the slopes of Sgùrr na Ciche when walking with Andrew in Knoydart. When I told him of the loss, Father simply said 'bad luck' gently and smiled sympathetically, only increasing my feeling of guilt; the 'glasses', as he always called them, had in turn been handed down to him by my grandfather whose name was stamped on their metal casing. A photo on the landing in our house reminds me daily of the loss, Father as a teenager with the glasses slung around his neck. So, lacking binoculars, I did not linger much to look at birds – they distracted me mainly through their sounds. I am hopeless at wild flowers; both my parents were very knowledgeable but I had learned little from them, for which we probably shared the blame – they too reserved in their parenting and I too lacking in curiosity. This would have been a good opportunity to rectify matters. But what I knew already was so slight that my walking would have dwindled to nothing – I would have been stopping every minute.

Butterflies, however, were ideal. They pop up less often than flowers and you can get much closer to them than birds. I had been drawn to butterflies from childhood without ever studying them seriously. Something has always appealed to me in their varied colours, in the patterns in their wings – subtle or intricate – and in their ephemeral, fluttering forms: 'aërial flowers', as my grandfather's 1906 field guide described butterflies (the grandfather of the binoculars), '"blossoms" that arise from them [plants], although they are not of them'. And butterflies provide the thrill of the hunt as you try to stalk your prey to capture a photo or race after it wildly. I had never tried to push beyond a basic knowledge of obvious, common types but now I would.

Quite a few butterflies have southern England as the northern limit of their range and are much more common in France – you have a good chance to see what may be rarities back home. And France has far more different species of butterfly, around two hundred and forty compared to less than sixty in Britain, so it's easy to see something new. But coming down from the Forêt de Perseigne, I saw only butterflies that can often be found near my home in England. One was from the small group that manages to hibernate over the winter and that as a result is among the first to be seen in spring – a greeny-yellow Brimstone. It clung motionless to a stem of grass, wings closed in camouflaged outline imitating a leaf. Then a pair of Speckled Woods, the upperside of the wings dark brown with creamy white spots, a classic butterfly of the mixed sun and shade in woodland rides. Two males chasing each other round and round in tight little circles, battling for territory. Emerging from the forest onto country lanes, I spotted a Painted Lady on bare ground basking in the sun, its orange-brown wings with black and white patched tips stretched wide open soaking in the warmth.

These three butterflies, all of a decent size, I knew already. But then I saw a tiddler of the sort that I had never bothered with before and decided to give chase. It kept skipping ahead near to the ground but eventually settled long enough for me to get in close and take a photo. I worked out what it was with an app on my phone, my encyclopaedia as well as map and camera. Orange top half to the underside of the wings – the upperside is only seen in flight – containing a single black spot with a white centre. A Small Heath, never again to be ignored in my mind as just the clichéd little brown job.

I discovered that my phone app had the French names for butterflies as well as the English ones. The name of a butterfly, a flower or a bird in another language gives a different perspective, often suggesting an aspect that you had not thought of before or helping fix your find in your memory. A Brimstone is a *citron* in French, a reminder of its colour. The prosaic Speckled Wood, I read, is a *tircis* from the name of a shepherd in a seventeenth-century poem by France's famed writer of fables Jean de La Fontaine, although why is unclear. A Painted Lady is a *belle-dame*, very similar to the English but perhaps more polite. And a Small Heath is a *fadet commun*, the first word an old Occitan term for an elf or a pixie and the second confirming that I had not made a startling find.

* * *

I wandered on through hamlets and open farmland, with wide views back to the forest and forward to the country to the south. The land appeared as a pastoral idyll in the westering sun. Lush green fields filled with buttercups; knots of ash and oak bursting with vigour; swallows skimming low, hawking for insects; the almost constant churring of turtle doves; and a bright blue sky above. The revolutionary month of *Floréal* had given way now in late May to *Prairial*, the month of the meadow. Afternoon turned to evening. I had not found a bed for the night when looking ahead from Alençon, and I had set off in the morning knowing that in all probability I would be sleeping out. It had added to the pleasure of the day, removing any need to press on to a planned destination and allowing me to idle along as I pleased, 'seeking to travel and not to arrive', easy of mind given a forecast of reasonable weather, some food in my rucksack, and the new sleeping bag that would be coming out for the first time.

But where to stop? Not for me Stevenson's forest glade, 'secure and private like a room', from the famous passage 'A Night Among the Pines' in *Travels with a Donkey*. I like to find somewhere in the open. Woods at night take on a mystery, even a disturbing secrecy. The trees surround you in a way that never felt threatening during the day. They start to close in. The adrenaline begins to flow. The sounds of animals moving through the undergrowth are magnified in your imagination. Could that be a wolf, a bear – or a madman? The scream of a fox becomes an unearthly noise from a horror film. We are ingrained from childhood stories to be suspicious of woods in the dark – Kenneth Grahame's Wild Wood or Tolkein's Mirkwood. Fear of woods at night: nyctohylophobia.

One of my few experiences of sleeping deep in woods, many years earlier, looked at one point as if it might go horribly wrong. I was hitch-hiking down the west coast of the USA, in Oregon, and got a ride from a taciturn owner of a pick-up truck. He later stopped again for a couple who like me were just heading south with no particular destination. After hours on the road in silence, broken only by him reporting sightings of police patrol cars on his CB radio, our driver said that he would take us to the place in the redwood forests of northern California where he had camped out for several months, 'getting my head together' after serving in Vietnam. By now night had fallen and he stopped at the side of a minor road in the pitch-dark, turned off the engine, and led us down a faint path into the forest. I suddenly wondered whether this was when we would all be shot. But after warning us to put any food we were carrying well away from where we slept, on account of the bears, he abruptly left us among the trees close to the bank of what sounded like a wide, open river. Waking in the sunlight of early morning, I saw for the first time the huge redwood trees soaring way, way above me, the furrows of the cinnamon-coloured bark running up to the skies. The river ran shallow and fast over a broad bed of stones and beyond the sparkling water and the opposite bank forested ridges reached far into the distance. The water had the sweetest taste of any I had ever drunk. It was a magical start to the day.

That evening in France, as the light began to leave the land, I stopped on an open, grassy track running along a low ridge, unbounded by fence or hedge. On the right was a field of maize, the young plants just a few inches high in their neat rows in a reddish soil. On the left was a more advanced crop of green wheat. The sky reached large from one horizon to another. This was the sort of place I like. A wide verge of tall grass separated the track from the maize. Perfect. I trod down enough to make my lair for the night, repeated my lunch of bread and cheese augmented by a tin of sardines left over from the week with Andrew and slid into the new sleeping bag. It felt fine. And the thin new insulation mat at least provided an illusion of added comfort.

To stretch out in the open as night falls brings a mix of sensations. Finally off your feet after the day's efforts, a wave of relaxation washes over you – along with a slight sense of exposure especially when you have no companion. Like the hare in its form, you are now as any other creature of the field in the hours of darkness with no burrow underground. Sleeping out on your own gives a sense of solitude like no other I know, not unpleasant but unusually deep and intense. You are alone and you feel it.

You are perfectly positioned for the display to come – no need to crane your neck to look at the stars. You might try to lie north-south, all the better to appreciate their passage across the night sky, drifting gently from east to west. The best time to be ready in your bag is when there are still the remains of the day. The brighter planets, if they have the right aspect, come out first with the best of all, Venus, hanging in the west after sunset. (At other times Venus will be in the east before sunrise.) Suddenly you notice that one or two of the brightest summer stars are now out overhead, such as Arcturus and Vega. More stars appear quickly. Then hundreds. You start to search for any constellation you know – I recognise few – such as the Plough or the 'W' shape of Cassiopeia, either of which will point you to Polaris, the Pole Star. The moon may or may not be visible – a full moon rises at sunset, a waxing moon earlier and a waning moon later. And slowly you drift off.

In practice, your night may not start like this. It might be raining, at which point you could well regret your decision not to bring a little tent, depending on how waterproof is your bivvy bag – the separate nylon outer cover for your sleeping bag. On this first night, there was no rain but the clouds came over before I went to bed. It was too hot and there was nothing to be seen up above, except a vortex of flies not far from my head. At least they were not of the biting type – midges, mosquitoes and their like are much the worst part of sleeping in the open. (I was eaten alive by black fly one night that summer hitch-hiking in North America.) Eventually I dropped off to sleep. Later, the wind picked up, the clouds rolled away, and when I awoke some time after midnight the heavens above me were ablaze. I stared up in sleepy marvelment. Suddenly, a shooting star streaked across the sky. When it's like this, sleeping out is a spectacular night show from the snug of your bed.

Waking during the night goes with sleeping in the open. You awaken several times and see that the stars have moved on, that the moon has risen or has set, that the sky has clouded over or that the clouds have now gone. You feel that the wind has changed, or that a heavy dew has started to soak the ground. If you are unlucky, you are woken by drops of rain on your face. You hear owls hoot, the barking of a far-off farm dog, the cough of a deer, the rustling of smaller animals in bushes nearby, and the first hint of the dawn chorus. On this night, as often happens, it got colder towards sunrise and I pulled the hood of my sleeping bag up over my head and wriggled further down inside. As I did so, the liquid song of a skylark started up nearby as the bird climbed overhead into the new day.

Sleeping out may affect your dreams. That night, I dreamed of cows trampling me and of my sleeping bag falling into a river, no doubt brought on by the small anxieties of a first night in the open for a long time. My father wrote of dreaming that he was being attacked by an eagle with great noisy flapping wings, only to awake and realise it was the sound of his bivvy bag flailing in the wind that had risen during the night. Another time, the bleating of a sheep was incorporated into his dream as the complaints of an exasperated colleague.

As Stevenson said: 'Night is a dead monotonous period under a roof; but in the open world it passes lightly.'

* * *

It took several days to cross Sarthe, heading always in the general direction of the Loire. It was my third *département*, after Orne, and the first, Calvados. Eventually, I would cross fourteen. And only Calvados and what would be the last one, Savoie, do not carry the name of a river. In all, sixty-one of the eighty-three original *départements*, created after the Revolution, were named after rivers. In his illuminating account of French historical geography since the seventeenth century, *The Discovery of France*, Graham Robb argues that this reflects the importance of rivers for communication at a time when many roads were appalling. But rivers must also attract government officials trying to think of names for new administrative areas – good geographic descriptors that favour no particular town or people. I tried to think of a new English county named after a river and came up straight away with Avon, where I had been in secondary school, an entity containing Bath and Bristol carved out of Gloucestershire and Somerset in the early 1970s and then abolished in the 1990s. The metropolitan counties created at the same time of Tyne and Wear, and Merseyside, live on, at least in name.

Sarthe is unspectacular, gentle country in the main. If you drive down from the Channel to south-west France towards Bordeaux, you pass through Sarthe on the *autoroute*, skirting its capital, Le Mans. The agricultural improver Arthur Young, whose *Travels in France* documented great swaths of the country in the run-up to the Revolution and during its early months, wrote of the area south of Alençon as 'good land, well enclosed, well built and tolerably cultivated… the whole country finely watered by rivers and streams'. The mixture of meadows, arable, woods, little valleys and low hills, dotted with small towns and villages, made for steady and agreeable progress.

I was now on a GR that was less well marked than the paths in Normandy. Early one evening, I came down to a river at a point where the landowner had made a good attempt to block off further progress. I threw my rucksack over a fence and squeezed under. A sign in English said 'crocodiles – no swimming' and as I tried to cross on stepping stones a herd of cows defended the opposite bank. The crocodiles threatened to reappear the next morning when I passed a sign to a farm called Le Croc. 'Fang Farm' seemed an appealing translation at the time – my phone told me that *un croc* is an animal tooth – conjuring up suitable neighbours for the Starkadders of Stella Gibbons's *Cold Comfort Farm*. However, I discovered later that 'croc' is also an old Anglo-Saxon word for a croft that has worked its way into French place names.

But usually the path was not a problem to follow, the red and white flashes of paint holding to their task even if they needed a little more finding than before. Several times I walked through deep holloways, centuries-old tracks worn away by feet, hooves and cart wheels and eroded by the passage of water. These *chemins creux* were up to ten or twelve feet deep in places, the hedges on the tops of the banks on either side sometimes meeting above to form inviting tunnels. One was almost blocked by huge mounds of earth excavated out of the banks. I wondered how and why a mechanical digger could have got in to do the work, before seeing the crescent-shaped holes of the entrances to badger setts. At the side of another path, this time in the open, I caught a fleeting glimpse of a much smaller digger – a mole disappearing down his hole as he heard me coming.

I crossed bridges over the *autoroute* to Le Mans and over a line of France's extensive network of high-speed trains, the TGVs, *trains à grande vitesse*. I was now becoming so used to spending my days on paths and bridleways or at worst minor roads, that I stopped to look down and even photograph what seemed things from another world, alien intrusions on the landscape. I slept in the open within distant earshot of the TGV line and drifted off listening to the late trains thundering up the track as if they were huge wild animals and then receding away into the night.

Walking alone, I took more notice of the frequent wayside crosses that dot the French countryside, made of stone, wood, or iron, starting to use them to establish exactly where I was – whether big or small, they all seemed to be marked on the 1:25,000 maps on my phone. (As a point of honour, I was not going to use the phone's GPS function.)

Most crosses have little or no indication as to their origins. These are varied – showing boundaries, blessing villages, protecting travellers, commemorating deaths from epidemics or marking graves. Huge water towers, *châteaux d'eau*, also became daily landmarks shown on the map, gleaming pillars of white concrete flaring out towards their tops like massive chanterelle mushrooms. Other regular sights – the little yellow postboxes attached to walls and the small yellow Renault post vans making rural collections and deliveries. Transport from an earlier age, old carts, started to catch my eye as I passed farmyards, some restored and brightly painted, others mouldering away in a corner among the weeds. I began to admire the simple decorative iron railings on many small bridges where minor roads crossed streams and rivers. The local architecture caught my interest more. Massive doorways to farms and barns framed with alternating broad bands of brick and blocks of limestone. Brick used alone, mixing red and yellow, around town-house windows. Lines of overlapping tiles on edge used as a decorative fascia beneath roof eaves.

Each town and village offered up things to see and think about. Mamers, for example, its priory church with a colossal, recessed, Gothic-arched porch, perhaps thirty-foot high, dwarfing double doors below; and in the square a poster advertising the annual trotting races at the town's little grass track on the big public holiday of *Pentecôte*, two days after I passed through, with a *déjeuner champêtre* – an open-air lunch. The immense medieval gateway to La Ferté Bernard – *ferté* means 'fortified' and I began to see the word cropping up in other place names too. Montmirail, from 'mons mirabilis', eight hundred feet up and from a distance like a Tuscan hilltop town, with its chateau dating from the fourteenth century, built, so an information board explained, to defend the Chartres-Le Mans trade route. Villages and hamlets galore named after saints I'd never heard of – St-Rigomer, St-Longis, St-Rémy, St-Cosme, St-Jouin, St-Ulphace, St-Oustrille, St-Bohaire… you could exhaust yourself just looking them all up. Died in their beds or met grizzly ends?

And my French slowly began to improve as I pushed myself to chat more in shops and bars or I just had to when eating with my hosts in B&Bs. I ate vigorously and talked haltingly for hours through an enormous supper with an elderly farming couple in the long dining room of their imposing farmhouse built on the remains of a castle from *la guerre de cent ans* they told me, the Hundred Years War, complete with *une oubliette*, an underground dungeon for the forgotten, and a vast series of dark cellars through which I was led that extended far beyond the footprint of the current building. I was the visitor and I was expected to talk. And my hosts acted as if my French were perfect, never batting an eyelid as I savaged and mauled my way through the evening. It left me exhausted but elated – the realisation that I could just, just about do it.

Plus, of course, nature continued to distract. I walked along the edge of a chestnut wood and saw a pair of red squirrels skipping across the track ahead. I nearly trod on an asp viper asleep on the path, its short, thick body striped in light and dark brown bands. Early one morning after a night of showers I passed by a field of young wheat, full of cobwebs dusted with droplets of rain lit up by the sun behind – thousand upon thousand of delicate little lace curtains sewn with diamonds. Even I could name the knee-high white campion often growing at the wayside and the banks of similar height oxeye daisies, John Clare's 'nodding oxeye [that] bends before the wind'. False acacia or black locust trees were in full blossom with great tresses of pea-like white flowers, the air heavy with their sweet scent. This tree is most often found in England in towns and cities, planted as an ornament in a suburban pavement. In the *département* of Sarthe it grows in the countryside in the way I was used to from life in Tuscany, springing up everywhere like an invasive weed through its root suckers and reaching fifty or sixty foot in height, the bark on the main trunk fissured like an ash. Later in the month, on a windy day, I came across a drift of acacia petals at the side of a road, several feet long and inches deep. A tree to love and hate. Run your hand around a fresh pliable stem of the year's new growth of translucent oval leaves, arranged in pairs, and feel its caress. Then try clearing young saplings, branch and trunk fending you off with brutal inch-long thorns.

More butterflies. I chased a small blue butterfly and finally got a photo when it settled on a white flowerhead of clover. Just a Common Blue, the French name this time only repeating that information: *azuré commun*. 'This is the most common blue butterfly in Europe', my phone app told me flatly. At least I now knew what it was and had started sorting out the large family of blues. And after another chase and photo a couple of days later I could distinguish it from the Holly Blue, the *azuré des nerpruns* or 'buckthorn blue', which has a much plainer underwing of silver-blue wash with tiny delicate black spots.

Birdsong. At its height in May, all the summer migrants back to join the resident singers. Wrens firing off in the bushes left and right as I passed, their tiny bodies pouring out a huge volume of sound. Thrushes still pounding out the phrases, insistently repeated. Blackbirds, as melodious as ever. Chiff-chaff, the bird that tells you its name. Blackcap, whitethroat, and a host of other warblers returned from Africa that more often than not I couldn't identify.

Walking up the side of a field of knee-high green wheat one morning, a loud tuneless 'whit, whit-whit' came from somewhere out in the middle, repeated quickly three or four times. Then again, and then another time. What was it? The question nagged me for a day or two before I had the answer. A quail, *une caille*, rare these days in Britain – my father's diary recorded each of his few encounters, including when a patient phoned him over breakfast to tell him where to hear one that morning – but more common in continental Europe. Quails do not fly unless they absolutely have to and they spend their time creeping around in long grass or crops, feeding on seeds and insects. Their call is sometimes described as the command 'wet my lips', or by the French as '*paye tes dettes*' – 'pay your debts'.

And perhaps the best that nature had to offer was another bird, also very hard to see. A bird that was everywhere around us during our time in Italy, singing away in dense undergrowth in spring and early summer, morning, noon and night. A bird that I had tried countless times to creep up on to get a good look, always failing – inevitably it would sense me, fall silent, and flit away. Nightingales are unlikely to have ever sung in Berkeley Square, in the centre of a city, but they were far, far more common in southern England than now (their range has never extended to the north): numbers have fallen by some ninety per cent since the 1960s. The dull-coloured nightingale, *le rossignol*, skulks deep in the bushes and thickets whence he sings (it's always a male trying to attract a mate), his allure only increased by being so difficult to spot – no singing from a prominent perch like a thrush for him. Removal of scrub and a decline in coppicing are the probable causes of the collapse in numbers with a contributory factor an increase in deer, which graze on their habitat. My father's diary for the 1970s and 1980s recorded his efforts to find them near our family home in north Dorset and after several late-May evenings of searching and listening he usually reported just a handful. One June, a tractor driver making silage told him that he used to be kept awake at night by the nightingales but that he had heard none that year.

How to capture the magic of the nightingale, Sappho's 'angel of spring'? Chaucer, Milton, Blake, Coleridge, Wordsworth, Keats, Shelley, Clare, Hardy... all had their go. The song has great variation but the key elements are a mixture of repeated soaring high notes and trills, pauses held for two or three seconds, and lower phrases or gurgles commonly reported as sounding like 'jug-jug-jug', the whole performance often lasting many minutes. There is both power and precision. The naturalist Richard Mabey writes of the mesmeric nature of the 'glass-clear' sound and of a rash of goosepimples on a first encounter. Heard in the still of night, it has an ethereal quality, not quite of this world. Father wrote of learning the song from famous live radio broadcasts by the BBC in the 1920s of a nightingale accompanied by a cello. I learned it from him our first spring in Italy. Nowadays, you can learn it easily from a website or from a bird app on a phone. Once heard, recognition in the wild will be instant.

That week in Sarthe, I heard the bird for a first time in a stand of blackthorn by the side of a track, bringing me to a halt. I heard two more the next day. And then the song became so frequent that I almost stopped noticing it, before realising a few weeks later that the nightingale was to be heard no more that summer, his singing season over.

* * *

Back in Normandy, the obvious memories and signs of war had been of 1944, of the Second World War. But on moving deeper into rural France, it is another conflict that keeps giving you reminders. Every village has its little war memorial and the vast bulk of names are from 1914-18. Designs vary, more so than back home I thought as I began to take closer note of what I was seeing, and later research confirmed this to be the case. The law of 1905 on separation of church and state forbade the use of religious symbols on monuments put up on secular ground and the crosses so familiar from British memorials are mostly absent or only included discreetly. (A symbol often seen, a cross with four flared arms of equal length incorporating a pair of swords, is a military decoration, the *croix de guerre*, an award for valour instituted in 1915.) Many French memorials are just simple obelisks but others incorporate sculptures of various types. The obelisk may be crowned by a defiant *coq gaulois*, the Gallic rooster. Some memorials have a grieving widow and child. But the most common designs with statues feature a helmeted soldier, the uniform sometimes painted in the blue-grey hue used by the French army during most of the war. Tricolour flags in holders flanking the memorial add further colour, the blue, the white and the red.

Looking more closely at the memorials, *les monuments aux morts*, you are struck by the sheer number of the dead. Even small villages often have twenty or thirty names from the First World War. One day, I passed in succession through the villages of Cormes (an obelisk), Courgenard (a painted soldier) and Montmirail (a broad slab). The map told me that the current populations of these communes – the village and surrounding countryside – were, to the nearest hundred: eight, five, and four hundred respectively. The numbers of names of First World War dead on each memorial were thirty-eight, twenty-two and twenty-three. In each case, these figures represent about ten per cent of the current male population of all ages, including the young and old well outside the relevant age for military service. The memorial obelisk in Vibraye, a larger commune of 2,600 people that I came to the next morning, had a hundred and twenty names from 1914-18. Viewed against the current population, the death toll was similar to that in the three smaller villages of the day before.

The figures seemed enormous relative to the number of people now living in each commune. But the current numbers of residents can be very different from those at the outbreak of war in 1914. On the one hand, France's population has grown a great deal since, by about sixty per cent. On the other, there has been a large movement of people away from country areas into the cities. I found the *mairie* in Vibraye and queued up at the enquiries desk behind people with questions about the refuse collection and the nursery school. When my turn came I asked what had been Vibraye's population in 1914, explaining as best as I could why I wanted to know. The helpful clerk on the desk looked a bit surprised but later that day emailed me the answer: the closest figure she could give me was from the 1911 census – 2,906. Not so different from today. Population growth and rural depopulation had roughly cancelled each other out although the latter had just won – Vibraye was a bit smaller now than a hundred years ago. I guessed that a third of the male population at the outbreak of war had been aged less than eighteen and another third aged over forty. If that were the case, the hundred and twenty men from Vibraye who died in the fighting would have represented about a quarter of all men in the commune between these two ages at the beginning of the war.

I was staggered. Surely this horrific level of loss was an exception? Perhaps Vibraye and the nearby villages had been particularly unlucky, their men all joining a regiment that suffered especially high casualties. That evening I looked into figures for France's total number of deaths among its military during the First World War. The estimate most widely cited is 1.3 million. Considerably higher than the 750,000 British deaths, while the pre-war total populations of France and Britain were similar. The French statistical office gives the male population aged eighteen to forty at the start of 1914 as 6.9 million. The number of French war-dead represents just under a fifth of this total, an enormous level of mortality. Vibraye had been somewhat unlucky – if my assumptions about the age structure of its population at the time were correct – but not exceptionally so. In fact, it turns out that rural areas throughout France suffered more casualties on average than the cities and large towns. Their young men were less likely to be in reserved occupations, exempt from military service, and when called up were more likely to serve in the infantry, who suffered the highest casualties.

Many memorials list the dead by the year in which they died. Thirty-two deaths are recorded for 1914 on one side of the memorial obelisk in Vibraye, just over a quarter of the total for the entire war across the five years in which there was fighting (the armistice came in November 1918). Again, statistics for the country as a whole show that this figure for Vibraye was not exceptional: 1914 saw the second highest number of French deaths of any of the war years, 301,000. But hostilities broke out that year only in August. The fighting started immediately with horrific loss of life. The Battle of the Frontiers that month in eastern France and southern Belgium saw the French take huge numbers of casualties in the open warfare that preceded the construction of fixed trench lines. As many as 27,000 Frenchmen were killed on a single day, August 22, more than even the horrendous figure of 19,000 British deaths on the first day of the Battle of the Somme in July 1916.

The painted figures of soldiers that I noted on the memorials are not in the uniform that the French infantry were wearing at the outbreak of the fighting. That uniform was essentially the same as in the Franco-Prussian war over forty years earlier: kepi, dark blue jacket – and red trousers, which are said to have helped pick out the soldiers as targets in 1914. However, according to Max Hastings's account of the war's beginning, *Catastrophe*, the main explanations for France's colossal fatalities in the early weeks of the war were a rigid hierarchy of command and outdated battlefield tactics in the face of modern weapons.

I saw a poster in Vibraye for an exhibition that had taken place a couple of months earlier. Faces stared out from a dim black and white photo of French soldiers in the trenches. The title underneath read '*La guerre, eux, ils en parlaient peu...*' – 'The war, them, they spoke little of it'. It was not so long ago. Many people of my generation could have talked with our grandfathers and great-uncles about their experiences of the horrors of that war; if they had been prepared to talk – and if we had had sufficient curiosity to ask.

* * *

On a long, warm afternoon, I walked over hills up above the River Braye, a week out from Alençon and making good progress. I was feeling on top of the world. That morning, on leaving the village of Mondoubleau, I had decided to change my planned route towards Blois and to loop around south-west and then east to rejoin it later. My B&B hosts of the night before confirmed what the map suggested: it would make for a more interesting couple of days. I had found a hotel in the village of Bessé-sur-Braye where I was going to stay the night, a stop that would be very welcome since by Andrew's ready reckoner – a hand's span on the 1:100,000 map – I had a long day's march in front of me. I could not get through to the hotel on the phone but no matter, mid-week in May there would be plenty of space. I finally dropped down into the valley of the Braye in lengthening shadows of the early evening and arrived at my night's lodgings, tired and hungry. A handwritten sign on the front door said that the owner had retired – the hotel was shut, and had been for months.

Well, there was nothing to be done about it. Pride in my happy-go-lucky existence had come before the fall and at least I had a sleeping bag. So it was back up the hill on a clear, still evening to sleep out at the side of the track. I chose a place next to a field of barley that was just starting to ripen, the crop now a greeny-yellow colour but with the long feathery heads of grain still soft to the touch as I ran my hand over them. I dozed off watching Venus and Jupiter low in the sky in a perfect straight line with a waxing moon, a few days off the full.

In the morning I was up and away early, hungrier than ever, to walk the three or four miles south across higher ground to the village of Trôo. I did not know it at the time, but for several years this was the summer home of the critic and poet Geoffrey Grigson. His book *Notes from an Odd Country*, centred on Trôo, is part elegy of rural life in this corner of France in the 1960s and part description of the valley of the Loir. The waters of *le Loir* eventually join those of *la Loire*, much the bigger river, still a few days off. The book is also an appreciation of the great Renaissance poet, Pierre de Ronsard, who lived nearby. I realised afterwards that I had unknowingly met Ronsard already, through W. B. Yeats's famous ode to Maud Gonne, 'When you are old and grey and full of sleep, and nodding by the fire…' Written by Yeats at the end of the nineteenth century, its first lines are a loose translation of one of Ronsard's sonnets written three hundred years earlier inspired by his own muse Hélène, '*Quand vous serez bien vieille…*' (Patrick Leigh Fermor of course knew this all along, referring casually to 'the Ronsard paraphrase' as among the Yeats that he could recite by heart – together with Ronsard's original.)

Nor did I know then that Trôo had been one of my parents' favourite places in France. They had kept coming back over the years, sometimes staying for the night when heading south, sometimes just stopping for coffee on the way back north to catch the ferry home from Cherbourg. Father wrote in his diary on their last visit in the 1980s that the bar 'is empty and for sale – how tempting to make an offer and perhaps even retain the licence… Of all the cottages we have coveted on our holidays, this is the most desirable.'

Trôo sits on the top and side of a south-facing chalk escarpment that has the Loir at its foot. The church is on the crest of the scarp with its twelfth-century tower capped by a little slate-covered pyramid, which, as Grigson put it, reflects the circumflex accent in the village's name. Beside the church, between two horse chestnut trees on the edge of the ridge, is a large rectangular prism constructed from blocks of stone and set on a plinth – a war memorial with its twenty-five names, arresting in its simplicity and quite unlike those I had seen before. It turns out it was designed by Antoine Bourdelle, a collaborator of Rodin and a friend of someone living in the village. (Copies of his bronze figure 'Hercules the Archer' are held by museums around the world.) To the left of the memorial is a great circular mound that almost matches the nave of the church in height. A path winding up around its side brought me to the top. The mound is all that remains of a Plantagenet castle, the Loir here the old border of the Angevin lands of the English kings.

Coming from the plateau to the north, as I did that morning, a huge view suddenly opens out over the river flats below, with their rows of poplars and grey willows and the Loir gliding by. The land then rises gently again to the remnants of the Forêt de Gâtines beyond, of which Ronsard had lamented the clearance ('Listen, woodman, rest your arm awhile'). Looking to the east, I saw down in the valley bottom a few miles away what seemed in the early-morning haze to be a huge, tall isolated church with a square tower that I could not identify on the map. Further on, in the same direction, high on a promontory above the other side of the river, I thought I could just make out what the map suggested was the ruins of the castle of Lavardin – held by the French when the motte that I was standing on was an English possession. Below me, a little way down the escarpment, was the site of the bar my parents coveted. On an earlier visit, Father wrote of its peeling and rusting iron tables and chairs on a terrace of dappled shade, 'looking south over France... a spot to sit in all day and drink coffee and beer and rosé from breakfast to supper time and then drop down to the lower town for dinner.'

All I wanted was breakfast. And all Trôo had to offer was a baguette machine. For a euro I was promised a baguette placed in the dispenser that morning. No shop, no *boulangerie* – there had been two in Grigson's day ('factory bread has not yet come to Trôo', he reported). The bar that had tempted my parents long closed. Is this the future of rural France? Trôo is not poor, like villages I would see further south in the Auvergne. It has restaurants and bed and breakfasts and second homes, some in troglodyte houses half-dug into the chalk hillside. But like many well-to-do villages in southern England, it seemed now to lack life.

I turned down the baguette. I still had a bit of bread and

chocolate and I realised that above all it was coffee that I craved. Instead I pushed on east up the river for several more miles, buoyed up by a first sight of rows of vines, a sign that I was indeed slowly moving south. The Loir is not only an old political border with the lands of the kings of France. It is a geographic one as well. Grigson wrote of this area as the northern border of the south, where the vines had begun in the 1960s too, 'replacing the cider orchards of sour lands a few miles north'. Global warming seems yet to have moved that boundary, the importance of geology and geography dominating still.

A brief sighting of a spectacular large pale yellow and black butterfly diverted me momentarily from thoughts of coffee. The Swallowtail can be seen in much of France. But it is exceptionally rare in Britain, found only in a normal year in the Norfolk Broads. Its English name is a reminder of the two small tails that trail out from the rear of its wings near twin red eye spots. But in France this is a *machaon*, drawing on part of the scientific name given in the eighteenth century by Linnaeus, and in this case providing interest rather than description: according to legend, Machaon fought on the Greek side in the Trojan War. And an example of how the classical mythology present in many butterflies' scientific names passes through to a good number of the French ones.

The Swallowtail I could recognise easily as they are common in Italy but the next day, in a meadow thick with flowers alongside a tributary of the Loir, I saw two butterflies in quick succession that I had to look up. I realised they were fritillaries, but what sort? Fritillaries are a sizeable group of mainly medium to large-sized butterflies and in the past I had made only half-hearted attempts to distinguish one type from another. The term 'fritillary' is applied rather arbitrarily to similar looking species with upperwings that are a chequered patchwork of golden orange and black or brown. This time the French name for some of them – there is no overall label for the group – describes the pattern well, *damier*, 'draughts board', also a word for any check pattern. I managed to get reasonable photos of both and soon worked out that they were again butterflies you would be delighted to spot in Britain, a Heath Fritillary and a Glanville Fritillary. A *damier athalie*, after Thalia, youngest of the three Graces, the daughters of Zeus. And, less graceful in name, a *damier du plantain*, from the Glanville caterpillar's favoured food source. The Heath is to be seen in just a few places in Devon, Essex and Kent; the Glanville, even rarer, only on the Isle of Wight.

Nearing the town of Montoire-sur-le-Loir, the huge isolated church I thought I had seen from Trôo turned out to be a cement works. But Montoire itself did not disappoint – 'that dearest and neatest of little towns… [that] exhibits such a quietness and a sweetness,' wrote an approving Grigson. A large oblong central square provided a bar that was open and a *boulangerie* next door. I sat outside having a very late and long breakfast, looking over the comings and goings of provincial town life. I decided to call it a day and look for a hotel. The square produced a rough-looking place that wanted payment in advance and instead I splashed out on a smart establishment in a side street, which produced a meal that evening that is magnificent in the memory although my diary records nothing of what I ate.

Sadly, I learned the next day that Montoire is best known in France as the place where in October 1940 the elderly Marshal Pétain, the First World War 'Lion of Verdun' and the leader of the new Vichy regime, met with Adolf Hitler and, infamously, shook his hand – *la poignée de main de Montoire*. Afterwards he declared on the radio that he had accepted the principle that France should now collaborate with Germany and he invited the French people to follow his lead.

* * *

An easy day over the hills took me from Montoire to Vendôme, the largest town on the Loir. As with Alençon, I had no idea of what to expect but thinking of the Place Vendôme in Paris and the town's position on a river made me hopeful. (It turns out the Parisian square was once occupied by the townhouse of the Duke of Vendôme.) That hope was not misplaced. The Loir bifurcates here and the neat and compact old centre of the town is built on a series of islands in between the two main channels with parks and back gardens giving onto the water. Vendôme suffered a major Allied bombing raid in June 1944 but a great deal of the heart of the town remained intact and there are many fine grey-roofed stone houses and a large Benedictine abbey church with enormous flying buttresses. The abbey was the proud possessor of a phial with a tear of Jesus, until it was trodden on in the Revolution. I especially liked the elegant, seventeenth-century building that now houses the *hôtel de ville*, with its inner brick and stone facade looking down over a courtyard planted with young palm trees, swifts screaming around the roofs. For many years it was a school, a sign told me, where Balzac was a pupil in the early nineteenth century.

I left Vendôme on a Sunday morning after buying bread at a *boulangerie* recommended by my landlady, its popularity underlined by a long queue snaking outside the door into the street. I crossed the Loir, climbed the steep river bluff with its ruined castle, and was soon out of town and heading south-east again. I found I was on a vast fertile plateau. Huge prairies of corn ran into the distance, the skyline broken only by the occasional water tower, church spire, or grain drier. I stopped and chatted with a man tending his garden in the village of Selommes. 'You've got some boring walking ahead of you today,' he warned.

The plateau I was crossing is the southern end of an enormous flat plain called the Beauce, which stretches far up past Chartres, some sixty miles north of Vendôme, and on beyond towards the Seine. My father had never found it boring. His diary entries showed that he loved the openness, the feeling of space, the landscape 'like the western ocean in a long swell with villages seen far away on the summit of a wave... here and there a poplar on the horizon like a sailing ship hull-down'. He dreamed of 'spending a few days in the complete quiet of this countryside, painting and soaking in the sun and the silence with the enormous sky overhead'. Geoffrey Grigson liked the Beauce too, appreciating its contrast with the intimacy of the valley of the Loir at Trôo. But he despaired sometimes of convincing family and friends of its attractions. The trump card, to be brought out when all else had failed, was to mention Émile Zola.

Zola's novel *La Terre* was published in 1887 and is set a generation earlier in the Second Empire of Napoleon III. The book is a brutally realistic account of internecine struggle in a peasant family in the Beauce and is set in the village of Romilly-sur-Aigre, re-named Rogne by Zola, just a day's walk to the north of where I was crossing the plateau at Selommes. Like my father, who I am sure never read *La Terre* given the nature of the novel, Zola described the Beauce as a sea: in spring it is 'a sea of cereals, rolling, deep, unbounded... one wave succeeding another'. I had not tried any Zola before and I read a translation when I returned to England. It's a gripping story, with superb portrayal of the various characters, of the Beauce landscape in its different seasons, and of the harsh realities of peasant life, with some good humour mixed in. But it did not surprise me to learn that the first English version, published only a year after the French original, resulted in the London publisher, Henry Vizetelly, being successfully prosecuted for obscenity. Tennyson is reported to have said: 'The name of Zola is synonymous with sewage.' Victorian prudery could not cope with Zola's description of rape, incest, and a great deal of casual sex, despite Vizetelly's bowdlerisation. The domestic violence is harrowing. One character is violated by her brother-in-law, just before she is killed by her sister. Another is a nymphomaniac. The richest family in the village lives off the proceeds of their brothel in Chartres. On finishing the book, I sympathised with the view I heard in a radio programme on Zola that Dickens and Hardy were 'by comparison, softies'.

The landscape of the Beauce that you see today differs from the one described by Zola. For a start, it is largely empty. No longer are there men and women everywhere working in the fields, their numbers swelling at key times during the year, such as haymaking or harvest, until people 'stretched out in long black lines, like trails of ants, right up to the skyline'. In 1870, the end of the period in which *La Terre* is set, a half of the working population of France was still on the land. Now in the Beauce, you see just the occasional tractor driver at the wheel of a two hundred horsepower machine.

And those tractors are working fields that, in one sense, are now vastly bigger than before. In Zola's time, they were often tiny, albeit only divided one from another by just an open furrow or a narrow strip of uncultivated soil. These little parcels of land were farmed as an open field system of the sort that enclosure had largely done away with by then in England. The family battle in *La Terre* is about land. The elderly head of the family, Old Fouan, divides up his nineteen acres between his three children. Primogeniture – the firstborn inheriting all – was suppressed by legislation that followed the Revolution. Napoleon's Civil Code of 1804, which still underlies the law governing bequests in France today, confirmed the new system of partible inheritance, a reform intended to promote the new state's principle of *égalité*. In the north of the country, division of land in this way had often been the custom among peasant families already. When giving away or bequeathing property, a person with three children, like Fouan, was obliged by the code to divide at least three-quarters of it equally between them. The laws were labelled by the nineteenth-century political thinker Alexis de Tocqueville as a 'land-mincing machine'. In *La Terre*, each piece of Fouan's land, much of it in little parcels that are already not contiguous with one another, is split into three. The surveyor charged with the job rails against the excessively small holdings that this produces: 'When you had plots of land no bigger than a pocket handkerchief, didn't it make movement and transport ruinously expensive? Was it proper farming when you had little garden-sized plots where you couldn't use the right rotation or machines?' But Fouan insists – this is how it has always been done. The terrible climax of the book is partly provoked by the division into two of a field that had been owned by Fouan's brother, next to land now owned by one of Fouan's sons. Through marriage to his cousin, the son gets half of this field – but not the half bordering his existing land, a situation that consumes him with rage.

By the late nineteenth century, the division of holdings as they passed from one generation to another had produced a highly fragmented pattern of land ownership. A survey of cadastral records in 1891 showed that the average size of an individual parcel of land in France was just under one acre. One of Fouan's fields is less than half this but it is still divided into three. As his surveyor noted, farmers were forever moving themselves and any machinery they owned from one little piece of land to another. The smallest fields were also awkward to work, whether with draught animals or later with tractors – a furrow was hardly started before it became time to turn the plough. It was only in the 1950s that the French government at last pushed through a determined policy of regrouping land holdings with the aim of increasing agricultural productivity, contributing to the economic growth of *les trente glorieuses*. Land started to be redistributed compulsorily among owners by local commissions. The policy is called *remembrement* – when I first read the word I was slow to link it with the English word for what it is designed to reverse, 'dismemberment'. By 2007, nearly eighteen million hectares of land had been subject to *remembrement*, about a third of all France and well over half of all farmland. The regrouping has been concentrated in the northern half of the country. The huge fields of the Beauce that I now saw are in part the result.

Two short days' march across the corner of the Beauce, through the sea of young wheat, brought me finally to the Loire.

3

Town and forest

The river was an inland sea. A west wind blew briskly upstream whipping the surface into waves, their crests breaking white. Terns tumbled in the breeze downstream of a many-arched bridge; hovering, forked tails fanned out, before plunging down with a splash after their prey – what were these 'sea swallows' doing here so far inland? Black-headed gulls cruised back and forth, buffeted by the gusts. A bright afternoon sun danced on the water, flashing light at all angles. I stood staring, dazzled. Was this really the languid, gentle Loire?

The town of Blois. It's still over two hundred miles to the river's mouth at St-Nazaire on the Atlantic coast. But over four hundred miles from its source, high in the mountains of the Massif Central. The Loire is said to be Europe's greatest untamed river, free of dams in all but its headwaters. My memory of a first encounter, driving south with my parents, is of a tranquil scene; the day hot and the river full of shallows, bubbling its way slowly past little sandy islands. It had a seductive air and was unlike any river I'd ever seen. But that tranquillity is deceptive. The Loire and its tributaries drain a vast area of France – over a fifth of the country – and the river is capable of huge surges. Here at Blois it is crossed by the eleven spans of the early-eighteenth-century Pont Jacques-Gabriel, three hundred yards long, built to replace a medieval bridge that had been swept away. The upstream sides of the bridge's piers collect great stacks of branches washed down in winter floods.

The Loire, the Loire! I had raced through the streets of Blois, eager to see the river at last. Arriving at the Loire that afternoon, on the first day of June, brought elation. These lower reaches of the river were among the few features already on my mental map when I set out from the Channel and getting to the Loire was my first big goal. If I managed that, I thought, all would be well. And the Loire gave a conduit into the rest of France. Although I would leave the river a couple of days later, I would return after a week and then follow, leave and return, and again, follow, leave and return. Eight of the fourteen *départements* I crossed are named after the Loire or one of its tributaries. Easily France's longest river, it would be the end of the month before I left the Loire behind me for good.

* * *

Blois stands on the right bank of the Loire, here the northern side. The old centre is built in an amphitheatre on the edge of the Beauce plateau, looking out over the river. As it grew, the town spread back across the plateau, away from the water rather than across on the other side. Technically, you may still be in Blois at the other end of the Pont Jacques-Gabriel but you feel as though you've already left. You are on the river flats, in what used to be the fishing village of Vienne, opposite the town. This is where I stayed, in a quiet street close to the bridge. I was taking two days off from walking. A luxury.

Looking back north across the river, the skyline downstream is dominated by the twin towers of the church of St Nicholas, upstream by the cathedral, and between them, near the bridge, by the chateau. The chateau is firmly on the list of the Loire's best. 'Americans pour through in summer flood', Hilaire Belloc wrote of Blois after a visit in 1923. Still true, although the flood is of many different nationalities now. I sat having lunch on my first day in Blois at an open-air café on a terrace overlooking the river with the entrance to the chateau on my right, visitors flowing in and out – *omelette aux fines herbes* washed down by beer. Suddenly, the tall windows opened on the first and second floors of the nineteenth-century building on my left and huge plastic dragon heads emerged and gyrated this way and that with deafening roars. It happens every half hour. This is the Maison de la Magie, a museum of magic. If your children put up with being dragged around the chateau, this can be their reward.

Henry James, one of Belloc's American flood from an earlier time, visited the chateau in 1882, reporting his reactions in *A Little Tour in France*, an account of a journey intended to show that there was much more to the country for the visitor than just Paris. 'It is too rich to describe – I can only touch it here and there', he said of the chateau at Blois before giving a lengthy description. There is indeed much that can be said. The different sides around a central courtyard reflect the interest and investment of several French kings, for whom Blois was their principal residence outside the capital. I liked the exterior very much – the late-Gothic red brick and stone of the Louis XII wing built at the end of the fifteenth century and the out-and-out Renaissance of the white limestone François I wing, built only a couple of decades later but seeming of a different age, marking the introduction to the Loire valley of the new style from Italy. A famous feature of the François wing is the large external spiral staircase, described by Henry James as 'a kind of chiselled cylinder'.

The inside is a different matter. First, it helps to have a good appreciation of French history. Lacking this, as I did, you may fail to be moved immediately by something that features prominently. 'Every spot connected with the murder of the Duke of Guise is pointed out by a small, shrill boy, who takes you from room to room', wrote Henry James. The boy has long gone and in his place is a video on a continuous loop showing the fifteen-minute silent film from 1908, *La Mort du Duc de Guise*.

I mugged up on the Guises on my phone. Henri, Duke of Guise, was cousin to Mary, Queen of Scots – his father was the brother of Mary of Guise (or Fanny Ardant in my mind); the same Guises who left their name on the chateau I had admired so much in Alençon, key players in the politics of the French Reformation. Duke Henri became leader of the Catholic faction in the Wars of Religion and probably had a hand as a young man in planning the St Bartholomew's Day massacre of the Huguenots. The duke began to usurp power from the king, Henri III, forcing him to flee Paris. In December 1588, during a meeting at Blois of the Estates General, the consultative assembly of the *ancien régime*, the King called the duke to his private apartments in the chateau. And there he had him murdered. The importance of this event is shown by the effort that went into the 1908 film. The director and principal actors were well known from the stage. Saint-Saëns, by then in his seventies, wrote the accompanying music, the first time a film score had been contributed by an established composer.

The film portrays the Duke of Guise as a tall, open-faced man dressed in white in the height of fashion, while King Henri looks shifty and is darkly clothed in more everyday garb. Henri crouches melodramatically as he instructs his bodyguards on his wishes, hands out daggers, and then retires to watch from behind the curtains of his bed. The bodyguards bow and scrape to the duke and then rush him when his back is turned. For good measure, Henri also had the duke's brother, a cardinal, killed the next day. The murders did him little good. Public opinion was outraged and in the summer of the following year Henri was assassinated by a Dominican friar, to be succeeded by his distant cousin Henri IV, the first Bourbon king.

Second, the interior of the chateau all seems terribly oppressive. My diary records: 'Heavy, dark, too much paint, drapes, etc. – skip quickly through everything and pleased to be out.' I felt a bit guilty. How could I have dismissed it all so readily? Other visitors were happily photographing the lot. Later I found that I was not alone in my reactions. Henry James described the restoration undertaken in the middle of the nineteenth century as 'a terrible process', while recognising the necessity of having done something after the chateau had been used as barracks since the Revolution. 'There is now scarcely a square inch of the interior that has the color of the past upon it,' he wrote. 'The fireplaces and the ceilings are magnificent; they look like expensive "sets" at the grand opera.' Geoffrey Grigson, visiting for the day from Trôo, simply reported 'boredom in room after room'. I felt vindicated.

Back outside, from the terraces in front of the chateau, you look down over the river to woods beyond my B&B

in Vienne that stretch as far as the eye can see. Below you, in a park a little upriver from the bridge, is an equestrian statue of Joan of Arc, who rode from Blois in 1429 to raise the English siege of Orléans, forty miles to the north-east. The statue is a copy of one by the American sculptress Anna Hyatt Huntington, given to the city in 1921, not long before Hilaire Belloc's visit. Joan stands in her stirrups, sword raised high. 'The figure is good, the horse admirable, the situation superb,' wrote Belloc. I checked and discovered that the original is on Riverside Drive in upper Manhattan. Was Joan therefore looking out over the Hudson to the Palisades on the other side, the wooded cliffs that face the city across the water? Despite the obvious difference between little Blois and big New York, there seemed something similar about the view, down across a river to woods beyond even if the Loire lacks the bluffs that rise up from the Hudson. I emailed my friend Jon in New York, who had brought over my thin camping mat. 'Joan is in a wooded area,' he replied, 'so I don't think she sees much of the Hudson, except in winter. When she does, she gets a grand view of North Bergen, NJ, one of the more developed and ugly parts of the Palisades.' Ah well.

* * *

Arrive by train in a large town and you typically step out into the centre after seeing little of the outskirts – maybe just the backs of buildings, railway cuttings and tunnels. The same is often true when driving in on a main road. An urban dual carriageway may bring you quickly through the suburbs. But when you walk in, you see much more. Slowly. You see the development of a town, backwards in time, from the outside in.

The lopsided layout of Blois meant that I had had to get through nearly three miles of built-up area before arriving at the Loire. After leaving the fields of the Beauce, I was suddenly among tired-looking blocks of flats that had been built on the plateau as the town spread out northwards. Many people on the streets were from North Africa and Turkey, their origins reflected in the characters of shops and bars. This was the Blois ZUP, *zone à urbaniser en priorité*. Built in the 1960s, the ZUPs were intended as an answer to France's housing shortage. Blois has a large ZUP, the home to over a third of the town's population of about fifty thousand.

The people of the Blois ZUP are, literally, on the wrong side of the tracks. They are to the north of the railway line. The centre with its chateau and tourists are to the south. It is tempting to see them as two quite different towns. An internet search on 'Blois' quickly gets you to the chateau and the Pont Jacques-Gabriel. The town's official website invites you to 'Spread the word, Blois is a good place to live!' declaring: 'Blois cultivates gentleness and quality of life, economic dynamism.' My search on 'Blois ZUP' produced, among other things, a rap video with images of guns and drugs and several news reports of unrest a few months before my visit – of a young man who lost an eye from a shot from a 'flash-ball', a non-lethal handgun used by French police, fired during what were labelled as *émeutes*, 'riots', and of twenty cars burned out a couple of weeks later. In the run-up to regional elections in the months after I left Blois, Marine Le Pen's *Front National* website provocatively reported on further burnings of cars under the headline '*Weekend ordinaire à la ZUP de Blois*'. My guess is that a normal weekend for most people in the Blois ZUP involves just getting on with their lives, as in the rest of the town to the south of the railway line. I walked through the ZUP on a quiet Sunday. It is too easy to exaggerate the differences.

Nevertheless, there is certainly a big gulf in living standards between the two parts of town. A ZUP has become an obvious candidate to be a ZUS, a *zone urbaine sensible* (recently renamed as a *quartier prioritaire*), a classification introduced in the mid-1990s as part of what is known as *la politique de la ville*, a series of actions by the French state to reduce urban inequality; a ZUS is an area 'in difficulty... [of] degraded housing and an accentuated imbalance between housing and employment': an area of high unemployment and in need of renewal. These zones lack the 'economic dynamism' claimed by the Blois website. Two thirds of the residents of the Blois ZUP are also in a ZUS. Official statistics show average income in the Blois ZUS to be only half of that in the rest of town.

This book is about a journey through rural France. It is not about Paris and other large cities with their problems of the *banlieues* that often dominate the news. But in Blois, one of the few towns of any size that I passed through, I felt the light brush of a reminder of that other France.

* * *

I spent my first day off in Blois to the south of the railway line, wandering the centre with a map from the tourist office, the sun shining and the wind still blowing hard. Now I was not *un marcheur*, a walker, but something at times approaching *un flâneur*, the city stroller of nineteenth-century French literature described by Baudelaire and others. Frédéric Gros is clear in his view of a real *flâneur* as being an active observer, despite a gentle pace: 'the flâneur's body moves slowly, but his eyes dart about and his mind is gripped by a thousand things at once.' However, I was often merely *un badaud*, another urban figure of writers of the time, a bystander or onlooker, one of the masses, with an idle curiosity but gripped by little and rather vacantly taking in my surroundings. (And I was certainly dressed more like a *badaud* than a dandified *flâneur*.) What pleasure to saunter here and there aimlessly, stopping for cups of coffee, glasses of beer. Sitting in the sun out of the wind. Writing postcards. Reading. It felt almost decadent. I lounged on the terrace of a small café at the top of the Denis Papin steps, an enormous, monumental staircase built in the late nineteenth century that extends the road of the same name running north from Pont Jacques-Gabriel, a road created to lay open the old centre like a Haussmann boulevard in Paris, the stairs rising in a straight line towards the upper town.

I looked down the long set of steps, down over the bridge, across to Vienne and to the forest beyond that would soon envelop me – and pinched myself. Life seemed gloriously unreal. More than two hundred miles of walking behind me with all that it had given and I still had most of France in front yet to discover. Time seemed infinite, stretching forward in that way I remember in my teens my whole future reaching out. When a year was an enormous length of time and there were so many of them to come and who knew what they would bring. Now I just thought of the next day or two with weeks and weeks still ahead before I reached Italy. I ambled contentedly around the streets in the upper town, looking down over the pale white stone-built houses, the steeply-pitched grey slate roofs, the tall red brick chimney stacks, forever seeing the river below and my way ahead across the woods that unrolled south and east.

This way was going to lead me further into the *département* of Loir-et-Cher, in which I had been since the long day ending beneath the stars after the disappointment of the shut-up hotel. I have written earlier of the *départements*, but I never really cracked them when walking through France – not infrequently I had little idea of which one I was in unless a road sign gave this detail or maybe a board outside a building site listing sources of permissions or finance. Still less the *régions*, with one or two exceptions. Metropolitan France – France not counting its overseas territory – has regions as a layer of elected government that date only from the early 1980s, twenty-two in number then but reduced to thirteen in 2016. Some bear the names of the old provinces, abolished after the Revolution when the *départements* were created, for example Normandy, Brittany and Corsica. Here, identification with one's region can be strong. But who can identify with a region called 'Centre', where I now was in Blois, even with the concession after more than thirty years of a name revised shortly before my visit to 'Centre – Val de Loire'. This region takes in most of the old provinces of Touraine, Orléanais, which included Blois, and Berry, which I would soon clip the edge of, names along with those of other provinces still in common use today even if they have officially disappeared from the map – names redolent with history such as Picardy in the north, Anjou further down the Loire, Bourbonnais and Nivernais in the middle of the country, and Gascony in the south. 'We are from Berry,' I was told by a couple I met a few weeks later, and a poster advertising a street festival when I passed through the former province featured the 'Orchestre du Berrykistan' as one of the acts, with *Le Berry Républicain* the local newspaper.

On the next day I meant to take the train a few miles down the valley to look at nearby Amboise, a smaller town with another notable chateau. Another day of lounging and loafing. Instead, on impulse, I borrowed a battered old mountain bike from my B&B hosts and headed upriver on the cycle path on the left bank, the ever-present west wind barrelling along behind me, in the direction of another of François I's creations and the largest of all the Loire chateaux: vast, flamboyant Chambord. As I got close, my enthusiasm to see Chambord waned – the scale seemed all wrong for my state of mind. 'An enormous fantastic mass' as Henry James put it. 'Black-hatted pomp' according to Grigson. Perhaps, I thought, I should just make do with memories of an earlier visit when a student – the holiday that switched from bike to car when Andrew pulled out. As if in sympathy, the bolt holding the bike's saddle sheared off. Now I was stuck! But a kindly old man who was fixing his gate found and fitted a substitute. And I gave up, crossed the river on the bridge at Muides-sur-Loire, and cycled back to Blois on the right bank – into the wind. I had pedalled the best part of thirty miles and was worn out, muscles hardened by walking not the right ones for the job. I ate supper ruefully in a back street in the upper town, sitting outside on a warm evening.

I walked back in the gloaming over Pont Jacques-Gabriel to my lodgings. The wind had dropped. White-flowered clumps of water crowfoot weed waved slowly in the current. The northern arches bring the bridge quietly to an apex in mid-stream, marked by an obelisk, before the southern arches let it gently down again to the other side. I turned along the embankment and headed for bed in what felt temporarily like home. The moon, a day after the full, had risen in the east and hung above the ornate street lamps that line the bridge, the river at last languorous.

* * *

Look at a map of land use in France and you will see a large green area to the south of Orléans, enclosed by the great bend in the Loire as the river finally turns after running north from the Massif Central and heads south-west towards the Atlantic. This is the Sologne, an ages-old name for a vast, flat area of forest that I would now cross to cut off the river's loop. It is over sixty miles in a straight line east from Blois to Gien to reach the Loire again. But my way was going to zigzag from village to village. It would be nearer a hundred miles of walking before coming to the river once more.

On a clear blue morning, I was joined at the southern end of Pont Jacques-Gabriel by my companion for the week, Jay. We had not known each other that long and the crossing of the Sologne would be an opportunity to deepen the friendship. Jay had on an old pair of trainers, with some sandals in reserve that saw more and more use as the days passed. He carried a small rucksack borrowed from his son that seemed to contain very little. Belloc would have approved. Despite my careful lightweight packing, I felt over-equipped by comparison. Jay's preparation was a reminder that walking is something to just get out there and do. An everyday activity.

In *A Walk in the Woods*, an account of hiking on the Appalachian Trail in the eastern USA, Bill Bryson describes the monotony of walking day after day among trees: 'Every bend in the path presents a prospect indistinguishable from every other, every glimpse into the trees the same tangled mass... trees surround you, loom over you, press in on you from all sides.' At least when Bryson did get views out from the woods, they were of panoramas down from the crests and ridges of the mountains he was walking over. But the flat terrain of the Sologne meant that when the trees parted Jay and I were not going to get anything resembling a distant vista. When planning my route across France, a crossing of the Sologne kept appearing as the obvious route to take. I would just have to accept a flat week in the woods.

However, it never struck me as a dull prospect. It seemed unlikely that the forest would all be the same. There would surely be different kinds of trees, different types of wood, with the variation in sights and sounds that these would bring. The 1:100,000 map showed several small rivers and a multitude of little lakes, which looked intriguing, plus many more bits of open ground than a map of all France implies. And the villages would surely offer something more than just food and lodging.

The one thing I did already know about the Sologne is that it was the setting for the mysterious demesne in Alain-Fournier's 1913 coming-of-age novel, *Le Grand Meaulnes*. It is in the Sologne where the teenage Meaulnes meets and falls in love with the beautiful Yvonne de Galais at a costume party in a small chateau that he stumbles on having seen 'the spire of a turret above a large grove of fir trees'. Meaulnes cannot find the place again – and his life is changed forever. I read a translation in my twenties and was beguiled by both the story and the descriptions of the countryside. The poignancy in the plot is matched by the book being Alain-Fournier's only novel – he joined the army at the outbreak of war in August 1914 and was killed shortly afterwards in the dreadful first few weeks of fighting when French losses were so high.

No, I was looking forward to the Sologne. It promised a week that would be very different to the rest of my walk through France. Had I read it, my father's description would only have increased my enthusiasm: 'all sorts of trees, heather, occasional farms... small lakes with reeds and lilies and coots and waterhens, blue and red damsel flies, turtle doves, kingfisher... an area to idle and drowse in.'

Father had written his verdict without having done much walking in the area. My first day with Jay proved hard work. We started late. There was too much open country on a searing hot, still afternoon that arrived out of nowhere. We had not quite enough water. Walking became an effort. We staggered into the village of Bracieux in the early evening after fighting off mosquitoes in the woods, ate at a table under the roof of the old covered market in the square, and rolled into our beds in an *auberge* over the road.

* * *

Geology, geography and history combine to explain what you see today in the landscape of the Sologne. The region has poor, thin, sandy soils on which the original forests of oak, hornbeam and birch thrived – the chateau where Meaulnes first meets Yvonne de Galais is 'Les Sablonnières', the sandpits – coupled with silty deposits of clay in the numerous little hollows and depressions that dot the flat terrain. Three principal rivers thread their way slowly in a westerly direction through the woods before eventually feeding the Loire or its tributary, the Cher. Various other little rivers and streams join them. The lakes, *les étangs*, of which there are over three thousand, are almost without exception man-made. The Middle Ages saw much clearing by monasteries of the forest that had covered the Sologne and damming of the clay-lined hollows to make the lakes and hence create an important fishing industry.

The forest clearing continued through to the Revolution and was excessive. By the early nineteenth century, four fifths of the trees were gone. Trees had been vital to take up the groundwater. Marsh and bog spread in their absence. Much of the rest of the land became heath. Farming and living standards declined and the Sologne became notorious for its poverty and ill-health. Infant mortality rates were among the highest in the country with as many as one in three or even one in two children dying before their first birthday in some parishes. Arthur Young, visiting in May 1787 on the first of his three great journeys around France, wrote in his journal of 'the miserable province of Sologne' on the day he arrived and on the next: 'The same wretched country continues… the fields are scenes of pitiable management, as the houses are of misery.' The Sologne stayed that way for at least another half-century. '*L'air est un miasma*,' commented the journalist and socialist politician Félix Pyat in 1841, recommending with irony the Sologne as a 'French Siberia' whither to banish dissidents rather than the government looking for places to send them overseas. When called up to serve in the army, a half of young male Solognots – the people of the Sologne – were rejected on medical grounds.

Reforestation and a turnaround in living standards came in the nineteenth century, especially during the Second Empire of Napoleon III, the nearly two decades of rule by Bonaparte's nephew after the final departure of the Bourbon kings in 1848 and the brief Second Republic. This period saw substantial economic growth with colonisation – a word used at the time – of the provinces by the Parisian rich alongside a nationwide programme of road, rail and canal building. The marshes and swamps of the Sologne were drained and the fishing industry was revitalised; one estimate has the lakes at this time producing eight hundred tonnes of carp and roach a year, a tenth of the national total. Napoleon himself bought a big estate in the heart of the Sologne at Lamotte-Beuvron where he planted ten thousand hectares of Scots pine (prior to the nineteenth century the Sologne had been free of conifers). Land was bought up to form other large private estates, some with new, small chateaux. Yet more trees, both pine and deciduous, were planted by their owners: the Sologne is notable for the high concentration of forest in private hands, some eighty-five per cent, a figure not matched elsewhere except in the Landes, south of Bordeaux, another focus of the colonisation and forestation (*landes* are 'moors' or 'heaths', now lost to trees). The tree-planting and chateau-building went hand in hand with the creation of great hunting reserves and *la chasse* remains a prominent feature of the Sologne today: as Jay and I left Blois, we saw a poster for a large game fair in Lamotte-Beuvron. Living standards rose. By the end of the century, Solognots were no more likely to be rejected from the army than recruits from elsewhere. And the population had increased by fifty per cent, outstripping the growth for the country as a whole.

* * *

By our second day, we were into our stride and the Sologne was working its charms. The temperature had dropped a little, we were in the shade most of the day, and the mosquitoes that had plagued us just short of Bracieux were absent.

Walking through the woods of the Sologne can be summarised by that hackneyed word 'delightful'. Despite the widespread planting of pines from the mid-nineteenth century, most of the woods are deciduous – you are not walking among monotonous conifers all day. Oak, birch, and chestnut make up nearly two thirds of the forest and there is also plenty of hornbeam, lime, beech, hazel and alder. The going is easy: flat. The flatness becomes so familiar and natural that you are surprised and a bit put out when you have to climb any minor rise. The paths and tracks are sandy and inviting – they pull you forward, winding their way through the forest and the short open stretches in between. It is easy to clock off the miles. And you have to if you are looking to sleep in a bed: villages are relatively few and far between and the hamlets and farmhouses that might offer bed and breakfast in other rural areas are thin on the ground.

Jay and I bowled along, deep in conversation most of the time. Suddenly on that second day, around noon, out of the corner of my eye I saw a medium to large-sized butterfly gliding steadily along at the side of the track. A dark brown upper side to the wings, verging on black, with a single, thick white stripe on each. No flapper this: 'Almost all writers on our butterflies have commented on the graceful flight,' reads my grandfather's old field guide, 'as it skims aloft and alow through the woodland glades.' It was a White Admiral. They occur in England but are far from widespread and I had never seen one. I had hoped to find them in the Sologne as they are butterflies of deciduous woodland rides. Their French name, *le petit sylvain*, reflects this, which seemed clear at the time when I looked it up. But it turns out that the link is perhaps more obvious to an English speaker: *Sylvain* was indeed our 'sylvan' in late medieval French but is now just a boy's name (the modern adjective is instead *sylvestre*).

The upperwing of the White Admiral is striking for the simplicity in its colour and markings. But the real glory is below: the underwing. A mix of patches of white and orange and brown with dark spots, seen in half sun and half shade it holds you transfixed. Jay waited patiently while I managed to get a couple of photos of both sides as the insect settled on a leaf and lazily opened and shut its wings before rising again and drifting off into the trees.

A few hours later we came down a track that wound through a wood of oak and chestnut and then arrived at a small lake, *l'étang du Temple*. Silence reigned, the trees thick around seeming to block out the rest of the world. The still water reflected perfectly the blue sky and a few puffy clouds – '*Les étangs de Sologne sont de pâles miroirs*' wrote Victor Hugo in a poem on escaping to the area from Paris. My father recorded a similar stop: 'a pause at an *étang*, absolutely peaceful – not a sound – the quietest minutes of the whole holiday.' A grassy bank between bushes ended at the water. We stripped off and went straight in. Striking out towards the middle, changing layers of water warmed and cooled us in succession. Feet felt the sand and clay on the bottom, squidging up through toes. We lazed on the bank afterwards, chatting idly, luxuriating in the sun and in the glow of the swim.

At last, we forced ourselves to our feet and wandered on happily a few more miles through the woods to our destination for the day, La Ferté-St-Cyr, which sits on the Cosson, the most northerly of the three principal rivers of the Sologne. We ate in a pizzeria, surprisingly well. The pizza may yet not have completely conquered France but it seems close to doing so. I had become used to seeing signs for *pizza à emporter*, takeaway pizza, with at least one pizzeria in every little town. This took me aback as I had no memory of pizza from past visits to France, or maybe I was just now more sensitised to pizza after the years in Italy. One report cites the French as eating 750 million pizzas a year and claims that France is the second largest market for pizza in the world after the USA. But dessert was very local in origin: *tarte tatin*, the caramelised apple tart first made in nearby Lamotte-Beuvron.

The following days merge together in my memory and my diary is little help. We zigzagged our way east from village to village, in and out of the woods, past more little lakes, neat little nineteenth-century chateaux, and signs declaring '*proprieté privée*', '*défense d'entrer*', '*chasse privée*', and, to really underline the message on collecting mushrooms, '*ramassage de champignons INTERDIT*'. Down across the Beuvron river – named after an old word for a beaver, *un bièvre*, and the middle river of the Sologne's three largest – to St-Viâtre, with its crooked slate-covered church spire. Back across the Beuvron up to Chaon. Down again to Argent-sur-Sauldre, on the third of three main rivers, the Sauldre. In contrast to the limestone of Blois, the villages of the Sologne are built mainly in brick, older houses often with exposed timber frames. The houses of Chaon, for example, standing clear in early-morning sunlight, set around a village green with two lines of pollarded lime trees. A family of second-homers, presumably from Paris, were getting into their packed car to leave after the weekend, saying their goodbyes to their elderly neighbour and telling her when they would be back. It was impossible to imagine *la misère* of the early nineteenth century that Chaon must have shared with the rest of the Sologne. But like villages elsewhere in rural France, shops and services in today's smart Chaon are threatened. The old white-shuttered, brick-built Auberge du Sanglier, the wild boar inn, is no more, its name just visible beneath a layer of paint. We bought bread from the mayor's cheerful secretary in the *mairie*, which was acting as *un dépôt de pain*, dispensing a daily delivery from elsewhere pending the opening of a new *boulangerie* – the previous one having lasted only a few months.

Not far short of Chaon, in the middle of the woods, we were brought up short by a long stretch of still water. It bent mysteriously away around a corner between the trees, a green band about twenty-five feet wide. A canal. It seemed such an unlikely place to find one. And this canal turned out to be unique in France: it has no connection to any other canal or to a navigable river. The Canal de la Sauldre runs west for thirty miles from Blancfort, just outside the Sologne beyond Argent-sur-Sauldre, to finish in its centre at the home of the *tarte tatin*, Lamotte-Beuvron. Despite the lack of connections to the French waterways, the canal's creation was part of the effort in the middle of the nineteenth century to reinvigorate the Sologne. Early plans to connect the canal at either end to other navigations were quickly dropped but construction still went ahead as its main purposes were to bring water for irrigation into the Sologne and, even more important, to transport marl – agricultural lime – to the region to improve the acidic soils. In 1887, for example, over 40,000 tonnes of marl were carried in on the canal. There are twenty or so locks, despite the flatness of the landscape, and numerous little bridges, often only carrying a private estate track.

The next day we walked along the canal's sandy towpath for several miles, stopping to read the greening bronze plaques on the lock-keepers' cottages that give the distances each way to the next lock and admiring the tracery of the iron railings on the sides of each bridge, which reminded me of those on the country road bridges back in the Sarthe. The transport of marl ended in the 1920s and all commercial navigation ceased in 1941. There is no use by pleasure boats as the locks no longer function. But the canal remains in the woods, its towpaths kept clear and its bridges intact, a quiet reminder of the past, its waters now cruised only by wildfowl.

* * *

Just outside Chaon, a gaunt, reddish-brown tree some twenty feet high, bare of leaves, stands beside a low modern building with a single pitch roof. The branches carry large, strange-looking fruit. As you draw closer, you see that the brown is rust and that the tree is a sculpture made of metal. The fruit are contraptions that involve springs, steel hoops, and teeth. You realise they are traps, although whether for animals or humans is unclear. You are at the Maison du Braconnage, a museum of poaching. *Braconner*, to poach, *un braconnier*, a poacher.

Where there is hunting and fishing, there is poaching. The restrictions of the *ancien régime* gone, the Revolution saw a brief free-for-all for anyone who wanted to hunt or fish. Six weeks after the storming of the Bastille in July 1789, Arthur Young, now in Provence two years after his visit to the Sologne, noted: 'For a few days past, I have been pestered with all the mob of the country shooting; one would think that every rusty gun is at work.' But new laws quickly gave landowners property rights that included the game and the fish. Poaching was punished with fines and prison. Hunting laws, including the penalties for poaching, were then toughened in the 1840s, shortly before the new *bourgeoisie* started investing in the Sologne to create their estates. As the second half of the nineteenth century wore on, the enforcement of the rights to game and the penalising of poaching became even stronger than before the Revolution.

Chaon's museum, which claims to be unique in its focus, reflects the importance of both legal hunting and illegal poaching in the Sologne's economic history. The exhibits include the different traps and ploys used by Solognot poachers, seeking to supplement their family's food or to sell game and fish to local hotels or even to Paris after the opening of the railway to Lamotte-Beuvron and beyond. The fifty-yard-long net for catching rabbits. The pole carrying a smouldering sulphur wick to be raised under a branch where a roosting pheasant would half-suffocate, lose its balance and fall to the ground. (My New York friend Jon confessed to having tried this as a teenager in rural Illinois, without success.) The wooden clogs with reverse-pattern soles, the heel at the front, so that anyone trying to track the poacher would search in the wrong direction. All manner of metal traps, as on the sculpture tree outside. A man trap in the form of a gun that would go off when triggered by the unwary.

But poaching in the Sologne is best known to the rest of France through a novel I learned of in the museum. *Raboliot*, by Maurice Genevoix, was published in 1925. Like Alain-Fournier, Genevoix fought in the French infantry as a junior officer at the outset of the First World War. He survived the fierce clashes of August and September 1914 – on the day Alain-Fournier died near the River Meuse south of Verdun, Genevoix's diary shows he was fighting hand-to-hand in the woods just a couple of miles away to the north – and he then went on to write several well-received accounts of his wartime experiences. With *Raboliot* he achieved major success. The book won the Prix Goncourt, France's top literary prize, and by 1985 it had sold over half a million copies. It has been made into a film several times. But no English translation has been published. Poor French speakers like me cannot easily read a beautiful evocation of the Sologne as well as a powerful story of the battle between poacher and the agents of the law.

'Raboliot', meaning 'wild rabbit', is the nickname of the hero of the novel, much of which is set between the Beuvron and Sauldre rivers in an area that Jay and I walked through. Raboliot is an habitual poacher and he starts to clash with a new gendarme, Bourrel, who is intent on applying the law and bringing Raboliot to book. Bourrel is aided by the 'guards of St Hubert', essentially a private security service formed to help landowners protect their game. (St Hubert is the patron saint of hunting.) The conflict escalates and after several months on the run, living rough in the woods, Raboliot returns for a final showdown with Bourrel. When I got back to England, I bought a copy of the DVD of the 2007 film of the novel, also entitled simply 'Raboliot'. There were no English subtitles and I struggled with the dialogue. But the scenes of the watery, wooded landscape of the Sologne took me straight back. And even I could understand that the ending had been changed. Bourrel shoots Raboliot dead, while in the book Raboliot surrenders to the law – after killing Bourrel with a poker.

That year, 1925, also saw the publication of another best-selling poaching novel with an eponymous hero. Imagine that the Count of Remilleret, the landowner in whose woods and lakes Raboliot hunts, and two of his neighbours all receive letters from someone who seems to be from the Parisian upper classes. The writer says that he will shoot a stag or catch a fish on their land between particular dates, challenging the owner to stop him. This – with landowners in the Scottish Highlands and letters sent from London – is another book from my teenage favourite, John Buchan, *John Macnab*. The challenger, John Macnab, is a cover name for three old school friends, a lawyer, a banker, and a Cabinet minister. They decide on their poaching dare simply because they are bored. 'We're on strike,' says one of them, 'against our privileges.' The book ends with the friends' host in Scotland, from whose house they make their forays, marrying the daughter of one of the landowners from whom they poach. The story could not be more different from *Raboliot*. But the two books share more in common than a story of poaching, eponymous heroes, year of publication, and commercial success – they each have loving descriptions of the landscape in which they are set and a portrayal of the thrill of a clandestine hunt.

* * *

Then we were out of the woods and back to the Loire. A long, early-eighteenth-century bridge rising gently to an apex with a dozen or so arches. Terns criss-crossing the river, staring down for unwary fish. A chateau and church dominating, set on higher ground on the right bank. A view back down from the town, over the slate roofs and brick chimneys, across the river to a line of houses and forest stretching out beyond. Not Blois again, but Gien. And much smaller – Gien is a town of only fifteen thousand, about a third of the size of Blois. It has no ZUP or ZUS.

We checked into a hotel among the small collection of houses on the left bank and wandered across the bridge into town to eat. A poster caught my eye. The anniversary of Gien's bombing in June 1944 was to be commemorated the following week. Another French town that suffered heavily during the Allies' D-Day landings? The poster showed a black and white photo of a street of destroyed houses taken from below the chateau, the road entirely filled by rubble. The tall, steep-pitched roof of the chateau above, just a skeleton of trusses against the sky behind. But no, I had misread. June 1940, not 1944.

My knowledge of the Fall of France in 1940 was both weak and anglocentric. I knew of the German invasion through Belgium in May following the months of stand-off in the Phoney War, known in France as *la drôle de guerre* – 'drôle' here meaning 'strange' or 'odd' rather than 'amusing', in the same way as 'funny' has two meanings in English. And of course I knew of the British expeditionary force's evacuation at Dunkirk, just inside France, in the last days of May and the first of June. But I realised I knew nothing of what had happened to France afterwards until the Vichy regime was formed by Marshal Pétain.

This intervening period, between Dunkirk and Pétain's replacement of Reynaud as Prime Minister and his immediate seeking of an armistice with Germany, lasted less than three weeks. It was a terrible time for the French. The German army swept down towards Paris – for the third time in seventy years. Paris had been captured after a siege of several months in the Franco-Prussian war of 1870-71, which both ended the Second Empire and led to a unified Germany becoming the dominant continental power. (Fired up by Zola's *La Terre*, I then read the sequel, *La Débâcle*, which taught me most of what I now know about that conflict.) The Germans came very close to a repeat in the opening weeks of the First World War before being pushed back. In their fear in 1940, stoked by memories and folklore of the earlier invasions, the inhabitants of northern France left their homes in their millions: over six million in the official estimate, adding to two million Belgians and Dutch already in flight on the French roads. They all headed south, often on foot, in what became known as *l'Exode*, 'the Exodus'. Paris, entered by German troops on June 14, had been abandoned by perhaps three quarters of Parisians. The chaos is the subject of the first book in Irène Némirovsky's unfinished novel about the occupation, *Suite Française*, that she wrote over the next two years and which I read on my return home. There is a poignancy matching that when reading *Le Grand Meaulnes* in the knowledge that Alain-Fournier was killed in 1914. Némirovsky was Jewish. She was deported to Auschwitz following the mass arrests of foreign-born Jews in France in July 1942 and died a month later, her manuscript lying unknown until eventual publication in 2004 to critical acclaim.

The Loire was seen by the French government as a key line of defence and hence by the fleeing population as a vital river to cross. Gien, just a hundred miles from Paris and with a bridge over the river, became inundated. 'Hell is on the roads and at the entrances to the bridges on the Loire' wrote one observer in his diary. To prevent the retreat of the French army, the Germans bombed Gien on June 15 attempting to destroy the bridge. (One of Némirovsky's characters is approaching Gien when 'a black spot appeared in the sky'.)

A photo in the anniversary exhibition, taken from near the chateau, showed the centre of the town below in ruins – over four hundred buildings were destroyed – and the bridge intact. Two days later the Germans arrived and French forces retired across the bridge before blowing up a section of it themselves, together with the railway bridge a mile downstream. Some French troops remained in the town, their retreat now cut off, and fought on until they were overwhelmed. Other photos showed the awful outcome of the fighting – the physical destruction, the dead.

It was not the first time in living memory that Gien had seen such scenes, although the mass destruction from aerial bombardment was new. A section of the bridge was blown up by the French army as it retreated in 1870 and Prussian troops then occupied the town for several months. In his account of travelling down the Loire valley in 1913, the writer and journalist Douglas Goldring wrote of being shown Prussian bullet holes in the facade of a house on the left bank of the river near where Jay and I stayed. Nor would it be the last time. The Allies bombed the railway lines and bridge in June and July 1944 and the bridge was again cut in August, this time by the Germans as they retreated eastwards.

For us, Gien gave a day of idleness before Jay left by train the next morning. Another day in a town by the Loire, doing little, chatting about the week and about Gien, drinking coffee, eating ice cream. The day began at a café, looking out over the river from under the pollarded plane trees that line the old quay just downriver from the bridge. The trees are prominent in old photos and postcards of Gien, back to the nineteenth century, but they have grown so much that their foliage now merges and from the other side of the river they seem to form a huge hedge, suspended in mid-air. An obvious next stop was the chateau, built in red brick with light-coloured stone window surrounds, one of the Loire chateaux that pre-date any Renaissance influence. But the tourist office reported that it was closed for restoration – for at least six years. A visit to the ceramics factory and museum was offered. Faïence, tin-glazed pottery, for which Gien and other Loire towns are known, was introduced into France from Faenza, a town I knew just over the other side of the Apennines from home in Italy. But the connection was not enough to raise our enthusiasm.

We instead rambled around town, struggling to follow a self-guided tour of Gien's sights from a map in a tourist office leaflet – it had been easier to find our way in the Sologne woods. Other than an *auberge* where Joan of Arc is alleged to have stayed, the only thing we were sure we had correctly arrived at was the main church, dedicated to Joan. All but the bell tower was destroyed in June 1940. The church had been constructed of stone but it was re-built in brick. The plan and style are traditional but work well and the interior is pleasing in its warm, rosy red colour and in the lines of the vaulted ceiling of the nave and the round columns supporting the roof. The tall, stained-glass windows are striking: a modern design with panels of red, yellow, grey-blue and white that complements the conventional architecture.

I found out later that I had overlooked or missed entirely some other fine, post-war stained glass in Blois, both in the cathedral and in the twin-towered church of St Nicholas, the windows there designed in part by the same person, Max Ingrand, as those in Gien. Like Gien, Blois was bombed in both 1940 by the Germans and 1944 by the Allies. The bombing of France in the Second World War resulted in some 60,000 civilian deaths, the vast majority caused by Allied raids, a similar figure to the number killed in Britain by German bombing and V1 and V2 rocket attacks. And the destruction was enormous – the total tonnage of bombs dropped by the Allies on France was almost seven times that dropped on Britain. Many French churches lost their windows even when their structures remained intact, as happened at Blois, providing opportunities for imaginative renewal of stained glass.

* * *

We parted at the bridge the next morning, Jay crossing the river to walk into town and the train station, I turning right to head south-east, upstream, on the left bank, beneath another line of plane trees and above a huge expanse of sand stretching down to the water. After a couple of minutes, I turned to spot Jay, a lone figure just visible towards the end of the bridge in a battered panama hat. I then hitched up my rucksack and stepped out briskly into the sunny morning.

4

Heading upstream

Gien had alerted me to the events of June 1940. Briare too, my morning's goal upriver, saw the desperate multitudes of the Exodus. But a very different scene in the Fall of France that month was also played out nearby, to be followed shortly by an extraordinary offer from the British government.

On June 11, four days before the bombing of Gien, Winston Churchill, Prime Minister since mid-May, flew to the little aerodrome at Briare with his newly appointed Secretary of State for War, Anthony Eden. The French government had left Paris in the face of the German advance and a small chateau near Briare was the stage for the penultimate meeting of the Anglo-French Supreme War Council, set up at the outbreak of hostilities to oversee joint military strategy. The British delegation met with Reynaud, the French Prime Minister; General Weygand, the head of the armed forces; Marshal Pétain, aged eighty-four and now Reynaud's deputy; and General de Gaulle, who had just been brought into the government as a junior minister after commanding a division of tanks in the fighting of the previous month.

Churchill's aim was to convince the French to keep fighting. Perhaps from a defensive redoubt in Brittany that could be supplied by sea from Britain; or with a government in exile in London, like the Belgians and the Dutch, or based in France's North African colonies. Reynaud was keen and was supported by de Gaulle. But Weygand and Pétain had no appetite to continue. Weygand said that the French army had no reserves and that a German victory was inevitable. Pétain was concerned to end the destruction of French towns. The meeting was inconclusive and a pessimistic Churchill and Eden flew back to Britain the next day. Documentary film shows Eden, years later, recounting that Reynaud had said that morning of the defeatist Pétain, 'he looks cheerful, there must be bad news'. Churchill returned to France a day later for the last meeting of the council, on June 13, again on the Loire but this time to the west at Tours, downstream from Blois. The outcome was the same.

The last effort to persuade the French government to continue the war was on June 16, when a proposal, approved by the British War Cabinet, was put to Reynaud and his government, now in Bordeaux. It was relayed on the phone by an enthusiastic de Gaulle, who had flown to London that morning:

> The Governments of the United Kingdom and the French Republic make this declaration of indissoluble union... France and Great Britain shall no longer be two nations, but one Franco-British Union... Every citizen of France will enjoy immediately citizenship of Great Britain, every British subject will become a citizen of France.

Reynaud shared de Gaulle's enthusiasm but could not convince enough of his colleagues, especially the voices that counted. Pétain believed that Britain would soon succumb to German attack anyway and described the offer as 'fusion with a corpse'. Others were suspicious of Britain's intentions. Reynaud resigned, Pétain was appointed Prime Minister and immediately on June 17 he announced to the nation on the radio his intention to seek an armistice with Germany – an agreement to cease hostilities that would withdraw France from the war and allow French government to continue in situ. Meanwhile, the next day de Gaulle made his famous radio appeal from London to the French to fight on. The armistice was signed on June 22 and came into effect three days later. France had fallen. One and a half million French troops were taken to Germany as prisoners, nearly a million remaining there until 1945. Under the terms of the armistice, Germany occupied northern and western France including all the Atlantic coast. The French government remained in charge of less than half the country, the *zone libre*, the 'free zone' in the south, governed from the spa town of Vichy just to the north of the Massif Central. The French parliament granted Pétain sweeping powers and four months later he met Hitler with that infamous handshake at the little town of Montoire, near Vendôme, where I had stopped on my way from Normandy to the Loire.

The offer of political union was made in the crisis of an unfolding disaster. And it was motivated not by a long-term goal but by short-term aims: to keep the French in the war and draw on the substantial resources of the Republic that existed outside metropolitan France, including the colonial empire. (Having failed to gain the support of the large French navy, the British quickly attacked the fleet at its base in Algeria to stop it falling into German hands.) De Gaulle's enthusiasm for the offer, motivated by his conviction that France should fight on, contrasts with his antipathy for the British government for the rest of the war and his post-war attitude towards Britain's entry into the Common Market.

The circumstances in which the offer was made are thankfully consigned to history, with war between Germany, France and Britain now unthinkable. But the sentiment expressed might surprise in the context of the debate around the 2016 referendum on Britain's continued membership of the European Union – the key post-war institution that brought together the former combatants.

* * *

It was a hot morning, walking to Briare. I got used to being alone again, to just absorbing my surroundings and seeing what the day would bring, to thinking of 'nothing'. The path soon left the riverbank and climbed to higher ground. I passed through fields of near-ripe barley, dotted with the scarlet red and searing blue of poppies and cornflowers, the whiskers on the ears of grain now on the turn to needles sharp to the touch. And the stage when a gust of wind rippling across the field parts the crop and the stalks below still show green. From time to time, the shade of holloways and patches of woodland offered relief as the path snaked this way and that. And, for once, I chanced on a village bar at just the right mid-morning hour and gulped down a long, cool drink in the dark interior.

Turning the corner of a lane a few miles on, a panorama opened out to reveal what Briare is best known for today. A large canal swept around in a wide curve below me – and then miraculously sailed over the Loire. Looking more closely, I could just see the ornate entrance to what turned out to be an enormous aqueduct. This is the *pont-canal* of Briare, the 'canal bridge'. At over seven hundred yards, until recently it was the longest of its kind anywhere in the world. It connects the canal that was below me on the left bank of the river coming up from the south with another that starts far over on the other side of the Loire. I sat eating lunch on a bank in the shadow of a hedge, marvelling as a big cabin cruiser puttered down the canal beneath me, slowly rounded the bend, and then disappeared out of sight over the *pont-canal*.

My journey had started with a canal, the Canal de Caen à la Mer, and then there had been the isolated Canal de la Sauldre in the Sologne. But this was my first real encounter with the highly developed network of French inland waterways. The canal on the other side, the Canal de Briare, was a giant step forward in that development. It was initiated on the order of the first of the Bourbon kings, Henri IV – the successor to the Henri responsible for the murder back in Blois of the Duc de Guise – and was completed in 1642. It runs from Briare for over thirty miles to the north-east, connecting the Loire with the Loing, a tributary of the Seine. By climbing over a watershed to link two river valleys, the canal was a great technical achievement – the first so-called summit-level canal in Europe that uses conventional 'pound' locks. It predated the first such canals in Britain by well over a hundred years. The canal's economic importance in connecting the Loire and the Seine was that it allowed the needs of a growing Paris to be supplied much more easily than by the roads of that time. The produce and materials of the south could now be moved more efficiently to the capital – grain and wine, coal and charcoal for heating, wood and stone for building. Then at the end of the eighteenth century, just after the Revolution, the Canal du Centre was opened. This linked the Loire at Digoin, far away upriver, over to Châlon on the Saône, the huge tributary of the southerly flowing Rhône, thus creating an inland route by water between the Mediterranean and the Channel.

But to bring goods downriver to Briare and ship them through the canal up to Paris, barges had first to navigate the Loire successfully. And the Loire is 'the least navigable of all France's major rivers' as one guide to the French waterways puts it. In fact today, with the exception of the last seventy or eighty miles of river to its mouth, there is now almost no part of the Loire that is officially navigable by commercial traffic or even pleasure boats. A map of France's inland waterways has a large blank where the Loire should be.

The situation had been different in earlier times. The Loire was 'one of the great highways of France for over 2,000 years' according to another guide. The Romans used the river far up into its higher reaches and a string of towns along its banks have a Roman past. But its waters were always difficult to negotiate. The flow is low through most of the year, the river spreading and wandering across a wide bed between shifting banks of sand and gravel and little islands. Large parts of the river are often very shallow – just a foot or so deep. This is the Loire of my first meeting as a teenager that I remembered when in Blois. And then there are the floods that suddenly turn the river into a wild torrent of the sort that had destroyed Blois' old medieval bridge – a river that is impossible to navigate.

Finally, in the first half of the nineteenth century, the problem of navigation was solved, at least as far as the connection between the canals at Digoin and Briare was concerned. The Canal Latéral à la Loire was constructed not far from the left bank of the river, running between the two towns for a hundred and thirty miles, a huge undertaking that was completed in 1838. This was the canal I looked down at from my lunchtime halt.

Or rather, the problem was almost solved. Barges still had to cross the river to get from the Canal Latéral on the left bank over to the Canal de Briare on the right bank. This involved a difficult passage of half a mile down and across the river and an even harder one on the journey upstream – the barges had no means of propulsion of their own. The crossing was forever holding up traffic: often too little water, despite the dredging of a channel, or too much in time of flood. And so at the end of the nineteenth century, the Canal Latéral was extended a little downstream and the *pont-canal* at Briare was built to cut out the river crossing altogether, joining the two canals directly. Work began in 1890 and the bridge opened six years later. A great steel trough of water twenty foot wide sitting on top of fourteen huge masonry piers.

It might seem surprising that the investment was deemed worthwhile given the rise of the railways. France had over 20,000 miles of railway by 1890. Trains had been running on a line from Paris to Lyon and on south to the Mediterranean for thirty years. Digoin had been on the network since 1869. As in England, the railways had a substantial impact on traffic on France's inland waterways. After the arrival at Orléans of the line from Paris in 1864, the tonnage passing through the town's Loire port fell by about two thirds. However, many French canals continued to flourish. Indeed many were built in the nineteenth century during the railway boom rather than before it as in England where industrialisation began earlier. English canals were often dug with locks that would only take a barge with a capacity to carry about thirty tons – the classic narrowboat less than seven feet wide – and as a result they were severely exposed to competition from the railways. But the standard-sized lock on most French canals, codified in the late nineteenth century, is a substantial hundred and thirty foot long and seventeen foot wide, allowing for a vessel carrying some three hundred tons of cargo. This meant it was still economic to move heavy bulk loads by water. In the twenty years before the completion of the *pont-canal* at Briare, the tonnage transported on the Canal Latéral à la Loire increased by two thirds and 12,000 barges passed over the bridge in its first eighteen months of operation.

The French canals and rivers continued to compete with the railways and roads well into the twentieth century. Although their share of all inland freight fell, the total tonnage carried on the inland waterways carried on rising. Freight on the Canal Latéral only reached its peak in 1936 and on the entire system of waterways as recently as 1969. My father would have seen commerce on the French canals and rivers in full swing but his diaries are silent on the subject. Despite his wartime years in the navy, which he enjoyed despite the dangers, and a liking for ships, docks and sea travel in general, he never showed much interest in inland waters – other than as habitat for birds – or for smaller boats. As children, we could never convince him to take us on a canal holiday.

The larger navigations in France such as the Seine and the lower Rhône can take vessels as large as 3,000 tons and they still see a substantial amount of traffic. But the working barges have almost disappeared from the Canal de Briare and the Canal Latéral à la Loire. Their traffic today is the pleasure boats that I could see crossing the *pont-canal* from my vantage spot.

Lunch finished, I dropped down to the Canal Latéral and ambled along the towpath to the start of the *pont-canal*. Twin, dumpy twenty-foot art nouveau obelisks guard the entrance. From their bases emerge imposing head-high bronze sculptures of a winged griffin in the prow of a boat, oars protruding below, the bronze now green with age. Lamps on brackets in the form of boats adorn the columns above.

I walked slowly across the bridge on the towpath on the downstream side, looking onto the river below and a little sandy island mid-stream. I ran my hand along the railings, a design now familiar from countless little country road bridges and the crossings of the Canal de la Sauldre back in the Sologne: a balustrade joined to a final handrail above by periodic small metal circles. A row of ornamented standard lamps lines the bridge on either side, for all the world like street lighting. An identical pair of obelisks with their griffins guards the other end. Old photos show the aftermath when two sections of the bridge towards this far side were blown up in June 1940 as French troops retreated across the Loire.

Steps at the end led me down to the river and I headed upstream again. Not on the bank itself but parallel to the river, on the towpath of an old section of the Canal de Briare that has been out of use since the *pont-canal* was built – it had carried the canal to the final lock, the *écluse des Combles*, out into the Loire just south of Briare. A brisk march in the shade of a line of mature sycamores brought me there. I stood by the closed lock gates, above the now stagnant water, gazing out upriver over the half mile of sandbanks and gently moving current to the matching disused lock on the other bank, the *écluse de Mantelot*, the old entrance to the Canal Latéral. The view suddenly seemed forlorn in the haze of the sun in the dead of a hot afternoon; the now permanently shut lock gates with the ghosts of old Loire boatmen in the air.

The early evening brought birds familiar from life in Italy, a little flock passing high overhead, summer migrants from Africa to southern Europe. Like the vines by the Loir near Montoire, they made me feel that I really was progressing southwards. Bee-eaters. Despite the name, bee-eaters are not fussy about their insects. Wasps or hornets will do fine – these birds are *guêpiers* in France, from *une guêpe*, a wasp. As will dragonflies, butterflies, and cicadas, all seized in flight with long, downturned bills. Bee-eaters are often appreciated for their stunning, almost exotic, looks: their greeny-blue fronts, chestnut upperwings and heads, yellow throats, striking black eyelining. But for me it is their bubbling, far-carrying, contact call that is best, made in flight as they dart around far above in little groups, passing quickly from place to place on their broad, pointed wings, a repeated 'prruip, prruip, prruip…' that always makes me murmur 'bee-eaters' and look skywards. If I had to come back as a bird, I might choose bee-eater, despite the perils of the journey to and from my winter quarters. To buzz around all day with my friends, chatting sociably, showing off my finery. And I'd spare the butterflies.

* * *

After a night in the quiet little waterside village of Ousson-sur-Loire, I made up my mind to cut away from the river for a couple of days and explore the land to the east, towards an area on the border of Burgundy known as the Puisaye. Huge forests cover tracts of the Puisaye and the green of the woods on the map were a magnet, a promised mystery. The map marked a path that would take me out and back again in a giant zigzag, the red dashes once more pulling hard, returning me to the Loire twenty miles or so further south.

By mid-morning I found myself walking on a straight track with the remains of old rosy-pink cobbles emerging from its sandy surface soon proving hard on the feet. It ran for mile after mile through open countryside, hardly deviating from its line, dropping down into little dells, crossing streams, climbing slopes, relentless in its intent. Strung out on the map were the words, separated far from one other, '*Ancienne… voie… romaine*'. I was on a remnant of an old Roman road that ran up from Châlon, on the Saône, north-west across the hills to Briare. Before the Canal du Centre finally connected the two rivers, boats discharged their cargos at Châlon and mules then carried the goods overland to be loaded into boats once more at Briare and proceed on downriver. The road was thus part of an old route from the Mediterranean to the Atlantic, up the Rhône and the Saône, and down the Loire.

As I approached a lonely farmhouse, a large, burly off-white dog began to run parallel with me on the other side of a hedge, barking aggressively. I saw that it was not chained. Still, I had my stick and a shake or a tap or two on the ground had been sufficient to discourage dogs until now. But coming near the farmyard, to my horror it was joined by a pack of five or six others that roared out onto the track towards me, howling with rage. There was nobody about to call them off. My heart went to my mouth. My stick was useless. I might see off one but the rest could tear me to pieces at will. The dogs rushed up – and then, miraculously, stopped right in front of me, still baying furiously. I inched forward, keeping as far away from the farm entrance as possible. Then, slowly turning on my heels as I passed, I walked backwards beyond the gateway for thirty or forty yards until, one by one, the dogs dropped away, wandering back into the farm. Only the original dog was still with me now, just a foot or two away, barking continuously, until finally it too gave up and left me alone. I shook with relief. Later, I realised that these dogs were *patous*, Pyrenean mountain dogs. They are trained to do exactly what they had done so effectively with me – to rush at intruders, to intimidate and scare, but not to attack unless you threaten the flocks of sheep they guard or the dogs themselves. Had I tried to enter the farmyard the story might have had a different ending.

I stopped around noon at the end of the Roman road where it at last met a tarred lane. Unusually for this time of day I felt completely spent; a combination of the heat, the toll of the cobbles on the feet for the last few miles, and the close shave with the dogs. I dozed under a tree for a while but eventually pulled myself upright, had something to eat, and set off again, this time on a path that plunged quickly into the cool of the thick oak woods of the Puisaye.

I soon began to delight in the walking again, forging along a rutted track that wound its way among the trees through dark, earthy terrain. Recent rain had filled many of the ruts, some so big and deep that I had to leave the track to bypass them. At each step dozens of little frogs leapt ahead of me and launched themselves from the banks of mud into the water with pattering little splashes 'putt, putt, putt, putt...'. White Admirals everywhere – clouds rose up at my passage before gliding away down the track through what now appeared as an enchanted forest. I saw a red squirrel hop behind a log, an old dog fox slipping quietly away, and a large bird of prey that I could not identify cruising at head height between the trees – the elusive honey buzzard, I hoped, or perhaps a goshawk even, conjured up by the magic of the woods.

Emerging from the trees in the late afternoon, a bird call some way off brought me to a halt. A soft, quickly repeated 'oop, oop, oop'. Yes! Impossible to mistake. Like the bee-eater, another summer migrant to southern Europe. The hoopoe, scientific name *upupa epops* – the first word also its name in Italian. The onomatopoeia is obvious and it seems to be there in the French name too, *huppe*. But this means 'crest', reflecting the outrageous, huge fan-shaped feature on the bird's head that can be raised and lowered at will. Hoopoes are only occasional visitors to southern England, Gilbert White describing them as 'the most unusual birds I

111

ever observed in these parts'. My father's diaries record only sightings abroad, beginning with that first visit to France in 1939 to the Massif Central. Nevertheless, the shape of the hoopoe, crest raised, is familiar to generations of British birdwatchers and is one I knew long before my own first encounter. *A Field Guide to the Birds of Britain and Europe*, by Peterson, Mountfort and Hollom, was published in 1954 and remained in print for fifty years, a landmark work translated into a dozen other languages – a neighbour in Italy had a copy and I'd seen it on a shelf in a B&B further north in France. It was Father's only field guide. The outline of a hoopoe is embossed on the spine of his first edition and also on the later one I bought in my twenties – the bird remained on the cover in some form throughout the book's life. You don't need a second look at a field guide to identify a hoopoe: striking black and white barred wings and tail, a pinky-orange head, shoulders and chest, a long, slightly downward-curved, slim beak, and that extraordinary prominent crest, pinky orange again with black tips. Similar in size to a blackbird although much more slender. In my mind's eye, hoopoes are always as Gilbert White wrote: 'they march about in a stately manner'; in his case feeding on the walks of his Hampshire garden, in my memory grubbing and probing for insects on country tracks in Italy. That evening, I went to sleep in my B&B near St-Amand-en-Puisaye listening to the 'oop, oop, oop... oop, oop, oop... oop, oop, oop' of a lone male that went on and on calling, proclaiming his territory, before the welcome sound of steady rain on the roof took over.

I woke briefly at six to hear another sound beneath my window, the scrunch of gravel as my companion at supper the night before set off as he had intended. Sisto was the first walker I had met in a month, a retired nuclear engineer who was walking westwards for a few weeks from his home in eastern France, following the route taken by Joan of Arc to find the Dauphin at the French court at Chinon. We talked into the night, first slowly – on my side – in French but then more efficiently in Italian when Sisto revealed he had left Italy with his parents when a child. I had doubted that he would be up and away at what he said was his usual starting time – Sisto looked askance when I reported nine or ten o'clock starts, saying that he finished his walking not long after midday so as to avoid the heat of the afternoon. I felt rather amateur and vowed to do better, although it was some time before I put this resolve into practice and could overcome the desire to lie-abed on waking, linger over breakfast, pack leisurely, and only slowly get underway. Sloth complements vigorous exercise perfectly. Even when sleeping in the open I found it easy to doze on long after the sun was up.

I headed back towards the Loire, arriving at the river in the early evening at Cosne-sur-Loire – I was quickly getting used to the 'sur-Loire' endings. My diary records the afternoon sparingly as a 'long hot slog', underlining why I should have taken a leaf out of Sisto's book. Much of the countryside was now quite open again. Fields of pasture shorn of their grass, the newly made hay in big round bales waiting to be collected. Others with crops still ripening. But pockets of woodland once more produced huge puddles and multitudes of White Admirals. Taking a shortcut down a long farm track across an open hillside in the morning, I complimented myself on my map reading before arriving in a valley bottom at a deep brown muddy stream swollen by the overnight rain, too wide to jump. There was nothing for it but to wade across, the water over my knees. I should have read the map more carefully – the track had passed through '*Les Champs du Gué*', the fields of the ford.

It was a Saturday and approaching the little village of St-Vérain towards midday, sporadic excited shouts reached me while I was still some way off. What on earth was going on? It sounded so bizarre that my first, and uncharitable, guess was that the yells came from patients from a mental hospital on an outing. A poster revealed all. The village's *comité de fêtes* had organised a *concours de pétanque*, a boules tournament. The first boules that I had seen and yet more evidence of progress through France – *pétanque* is above all a southern game. It was a serious affair, singles matches (*tête à tête*) starting at eight-thirty in the morning and doubles (*doublette)* at two-thirty, with food and drink laid on. The whole village seemed to be there, young and old, in a large sandy space surrounded by lime trees outside the church, a building of neatly fitting limestone blocks with a deeply recessed Romanesque doorway. Lots of youth, clacking their boules together in a macho way, and the shouts I'd heard were the cries of joy or disappointment following particularly good or bad throws. I was tempted to change my plans for the day but I had set my mind on reaching Cosne that evening. I stopped for a break a couple of hours later, sitting under a tree at the edge of a field of rapeseed close to harvest, the yellow flowers of May long gone, looking out over the valley of the Loire again with distant views of forests beyond.

* * *

In early August of the long, hot summer of 1976, my parents crossed over the hills further south from the valley of the Saône and drove north, down this part of the Loire valley. Father wrote of the 'terribly dry country, everything here is like tinder, trees shedding their leaves and looking dead – even in the woods the undergrowth is drooping... the Loire stagnant and very low'. The weather and the countryside were both some way off that state in the summer of my crossing of France although June was turning out unusually warm.

A few miles short of Cosne, my parents encountered 'something unexpected – Sancerre on top of its twelve hundred foot limestone hill with its vineyards spread around the sides. A tremendous view... It must be the only hill of its size in this part of France.' Douglas Goldring, on his 1913 journey down the Loire, likewise described his reactions on first seeing 'the surprising, dominating peak of Sancerre... The sudden appearance cannot fail to make a profound impression. It is the return of the grandiose to the landscape, in a place where you had not expected it.'

It was not much less surprising for me, coming south from Cosne in the opposite direction. I was still on the right bank of the Loire, the eastern side, and as I came out of a belt of woodland, suddenly there was a little hill-topped town high above me on the other side of the valley. I was half-tempted to cross the river on the bridge at the foot of the hill, over to the left bank, and climb up through the vines and the pockets of trees to see the views from the top, described by Goldring as being 'across an expanse of country that is apparently boundless... the three provinces of Berry, Nivernais, and Orléanais lie outspread before you'. But such side trips are not undertaken lightly when you are travelling on foot, especially when it's hot. Nor, having yet to discover my father's and Goldring's accounts, did I realise at the time quite how good the views would be. Instead, I pressed on towards Pouilly-sur-Loire, Sancerre's near neighbour on my side of the river, a few miles south and the home of an almost equally famous white wine, made like Sancerre from the Sauvignon Blanc grape – Pouilly-Fumé.

I was already among the vineyards. Soon, as the path took me up the side of the valley, they were everywhere.

Nothing else, vines in every direction. Vines trained low, barely a foot off the ground, in the classic French way – *vignes basses* – that always surprise me after years of seeing vines trained high at head or shoulder height in Italy. They were planted in what at times looked like scree, the soil was so stony. I had thought to sleep in the open that night, among the vines, but the stones would have made for a hard bed. And luckily I had changed my plan as it was clear that the weather was also changing. A thunderstorm was building. Huge dark clouds appeared over the hillside to the east. The wind rose and then backed, a sure sign that rain was coming fast. I hurried on, jogging down a track into a hamlet, and just managed to get under a railway bridge before the skies opened and the deluge began.

The rain swept down, lashing the tarmac angrily before bouncing back up into the air. It poured and poured. The road running under the bridge became a torrent and the pavement on which I stood a riverbank. To pass the time, I tried to go through the different ways of describing heavy rain that I had learned before leaving England, which I could now use in the B&B that I had found in Pouilly for the night: *il pleut à verse* (it's pouring), *il pleut des seaux* (it's raining buckets), *il pleut des cordes* (it's raining ropes), and the elegant *il pleut comme une vache qui pisse*. And the phrases describing the consequences: *j'ai pris la flotte* (literally, 'I caught the fleet', but *flotte* is also used to mean water), *je suis mouillé* (I'm wet), *je suis trempé* (I am soaked). The storm raged on but eventually slackened off to gentle, steady rain. Time to get going again. Up out of the collection of houses and over hillsides covered once more with vines on all sides, muddy rivulets of water running down the track. Cresting a rise, I could just see Pouilly below in the murk of the rain and cloud, the church steeple prominent against a silver grey background of the river beyond. I arrived at the B&B at the same time as a pair of cyclists, fellow guests, each of them like me, *trempé*.

That evening in a restaurant I drank a glass of Pouilly-Fumé as an aperitif. Was it 'smoky', as its name suggests, or 'minerally, gunflinty' as one website describes that it can be? Or, perhaps, 'displaying a grassy and grapefruit character' that apparently would make it indistinguishable from a Sancerre? I didn't mind – it just tasted first-rate and a switch to some rough red felt as if I was giving insult.

The next morning I walked out of Pouilly past a roundabout at the entrance to the village that was planted with rows of vines. Is suitable land so precious or was it just a way of proudly proclaiming Pouilly's fame? And then the vines were all gone. The geology had changed. And the geography – the flat lands had returned, with fields of maize, wheat and even that staple of cool, damp climates, oats.

'Think of all those wine areas you'll walk through!' people had said to me before I left England. I had been in France a month and had seen pockets of vines here and there. But Sancerre and Pouilly was the first serious wine-producing district I had crossed and it had taken less than a day to do so. I had missed the big vineyards of the lower Loire, striking the river for the first time above them at Blois. I would not be going anywhere near the great wine regions of Bordeaux in the south-west, Alsace in the east, or Languedoc, Roussillon and Provence in the south. I had cut down through France well below Champagne, which lies to the east of Paris, and I was now passing to the south-west of the vineyards of Burgundy. I would be following the Rhône for a while in July but far to the north of the area where Côtes du Rhône is produced, although I did not realise it yet. It would be another two weeks before I saw a serious concentration of vines again. Bad planning? Bad luck? It turns out that France has under two per cent of its total land area in the cultivation of grapes, less than for either buildings or roads. Unless you choose your route across France with a bit of care, you're unlikely to spend much time among the vines.

* * *

'*Vous aussi, vous êtes un pèlerin?*' – You too are a pilgrim? – asked a middle-aged couple with large rucksacks, as I sat on the steps of the priory church of Notre-Dame in the town of La Charité-sur-Loire, an easy day south of Pouilly on the right bank of the river. Well, I thought, through life.

La Charité lies on one of the four main pilgrim routes across France that head for Spain and Santiago de Compostela. For a short while I would now be on a *chemin de St Jacques*, on the path that starts at the great Benedictine abbey in the town of Vézelay, fifty miles to the north-east, and then slants down south-west through Limoges and Périgueux before joining two of the other routes to cross the western end of the Pyrenees at Roncesvalles. The footpath for the next two days, 'The Way' as the routes to Compostela are known in English, now had proper signs rather than being marked just by flashes of red and white paint on a convenient object, the signs including an abstract representation of a scallop shell, the badge of Compostela pilgrims.

The priory at La Charité, built in about 1100, was founded as its most important offshoot by the abbey of Cluny, a hundred miles away to the south-east and for a long time the greatest monastery in Europe. La Charité's name comes from the aid given by the monks to the passing pilgrims. The priory church had been enormous, second only in all of France to that at Cluny, but fire and the Wars of Religion destroyed much of both the church and the surrounding monastic buildings. The original nave is no more.

I had been on the church steps waiting for my wife, Tina, and our friend Honi who were joining me for a few days. They arrived in the early evening, with a car. One of them walked with me each morning while the other drove, carrying our gear – including my rucksack. After lunch they swapped around. (Lunches returned to the standards Andrew had maintained in Normandy.) And with them came the second volume of *War and Peace* for my lunchtimes when they left again. The car also brought tents which we put up each night in campsites on the banks of the river, campsites largely empty of campers at this point in the early summer other than Belgians, Germans and, especially, the Dutch.

The landscape in this part of the Loire valley is restrained, which explains the surprise recorded by my father and by Douglas Goldring on seeing the hill at Sancerre when travelling north, downriver. Nevertheless it makes for pleasant and easy walking. The stretches of path near the river showed the Loire at its lazy best; the Loire that had been so trying to navigate before the building of the Canal Latéral; the Loire full of shallows, threading its way through the sand and gravel past the little islands thick with purple loosestrife, scrubby willow and alder, carving out huge meanders, some of them now cut off as oxbow lakes. Honi, a geographer, was in her element. Even here, far, far upriver, the islands sheltered colonies of nesting terns, birds that I now learned to have the same 'sea swallow' nickname in French, '*hirondelles de mer*'.

Just in from the riverbank we came across a pair of huge birds, three or four foot tall, foraging in a field of newly mown grass; long dagger-like red bills, white bodies and black and white wings, their gangly legs largely hidden behind the heaped-up rows readied for baling, making the birds look strangely stunted. What luck! Storks. This pair were far from their normal summer breeding grounds further north and east in Europe and must have decided to call it a day on their way up from Africa, stopping in these Loire river flats. White storks, *cigognes blanches*. They had been a constant presence for Patrick Leigh Fermor in his slow progress across Hungary and Romania in the spring and summer of 1934 after a first sighting by the Danube: 'now they were everywhere, and all the following weeks I could never get used to them.' He described their social calls made by clattering their beaks 'like flat sticks banging together: a dozen courtships in one of those riverside hamlets sounded like massed castanets'. I longed to hear this sound and to see their huge nests of twigs and sticks and I scanned the rooftops in the villages we passed through afterwards. But no.

Usually, however, our path was well away from the river, sometimes by a few miles, and we passed through a mix of deciduous woods and farmland, hay everywhere being made or already baled. *Prairial*, the month of the meadow, was drawing to a close – we were fast approaching *Messidor*, the month of harvest. Most of the time we kept to the east of the Loire but one day our way took us to the other side of the river and we walked along the towpath of the Canal Latéral for a while, passing an encouraging, old round stone marker that recorded ninety-seven kilometres from my first meeting with the canal at its start at Briare.

The mixture of different types of walking gave a good variety of butterflies. I got a clear, close-up sighting of a Comma in a woodland ride, its frequent habitat. This butterfly has an orange and black pattern to its upperwing that I already knew, bearing some similarity to that of a fritillary, with the wing having a distinctive jagged edge as if pecked by a bird. But it was the very different underside that I had not looked at properly before: the clearest of tiny white comma-shaped marks set amongst the dull mottled brown, giving the butterfly its name. Its French name is entirely different, *Robert-le-Diable*, from a legend about a Norman knight who thinks he is the son of the devil. Why this story became associated with the butterfly is unclear; the explanations offered are unconvincing – the shape of the wing outline or the colours of the upper wing.

The naming in French of another butterfly that we began to see, a true butterfly of summer, was more obvious. The *demi-deuil* – 'half-mourning' – lives in open grassland and has a simple chequered black and white pattern that is impossible to confuse with any other butterfly. It had almost the same name in England when first described in the late seventeenth century: 'Our Half-Mourner'. But from the 1800s the English name has emphasised the white in its colouring rather than the black. The Marbled White is a butterfly I remember seeing as a child with my father and brother one day on a steep sunny slope in the Dorset downs. In my memory the hillside was alive with Marbled Whites and every sighting of them transports me back to that scene, probably the first time that butterflies caught my interest. To my delight, Father recorded the July afternoon in 1968: 'a hot sunny picnic with Andrew and John along the escarpment between Dogbury Gate and Batcombe... permanent chalk grassland with its rock rose, trefoil, harebell, yellow and white bedstraw, thyme, potentilla, milkwort... plenty of butterflies – meadow browns, marbled whites, a common skipper and an undoubted white letter hairstreak.' Only the Marbled Whites stayed with me.

The towns along the Loire also held our interest in their different ways, each providing something to discover, W. H. Hudson's 'observables'. The largest of them came first.

Nevers lies just upstream of the confluence of the Loire with its biggest tributary, the Allier, and was the capital of the surrounding pre-Revolution province of Nivernais. 'Nevers makes a fine appearance, rising from the Loire', wrote Arthur Young coming from the south on New Year's Day 1790. 'But, on the first entrance, it is like a thousand other places', he continued disparagingly. My first entrance was from the north, away from the river. Walking into Nevers this way felt like coming into Blois: the town is all on the right bank, the suburbs stretch two or three miles away from the river, and large parts of town are down at heel – indeed, like Blois, Nevers has a *zone urbaine sensible,* a ZUS, an urban area classified as in difficulty. Indeed it has three of them. A 1970s guidebook to the Loire says that the town was aiming to double its population, which instead has fallen by a fifth.

But Young missed the point and my introduction to the town was likewise a poor guide. It may be that the old heart of Nevers is not exceptional but like so many other provincial French towns it is certainly good in an absolute sense and one should take pleasure from this rather than lamenting the lack of something truly special. And in fact Nevers boasts a fine ducal palace and an impressive cathedral. Father wrote of the latter having 'an apse at each end, the western one and crypt below being Romanesque, the rest of the church being a light, wide and high decorated Gothic'. The west apse has a huge twelfth-century fresco of Christ that runs across the ceiling, which my parents would have admired during their brief stop in the town while heading north in the hot August of 1976. But it also has something I loved that they would not have seen: the cathedral's windows were destroyed in an Allied bombing raid in July 1944 and they were not replaced with new designs until after my parents' visit. The three windows in the western apse were the first to be done, in the late seventies, in an abstract design of wavy blue and white horizontal bands contrasting strikingly with the fresco above. The other windows, in the nave, the transepts, the choir, and at the east end were completed progressively in the next twenty-five years by other artists in a range of designs and colours – some geometric, others figurative, with reds, blues, oranges and yellows. It is a bit of a mishmash but it works and as in Gien I thought the combination of old architecture and new glass was stunning. Outside, the narrow street that runs around three sides of the building is overhung by enormous gargoyles, crouching animals, their necks reaching out, ready to leap.

Next was the small town of Decize, which I later found out was the birthplace of Maurice Genevoix, the author of the Sologne's *Raboliot* – the *lycée* is named after him. Father noted 'a good market – cheeses and sausages'. We too were there on market day, but it was the enormous array of upright kilo bundles of white asparagus being sold direct by the grower that caught my eye, the table otherwise bare, the produce firmly declared in large letters on a prominent sign as '*Bio*', organic. The stalls clustered in the small square, dominated by a mid-nineteenth-century clock tower, over a hundred foot high, proudly inscribed with '*République Française*' and underneath the familiar '*Liberté Égalité Fraternité*'. An imposing early-twentieth-century post office reminded me of the one I had admired back in Normandy in Alençon. Just down from the square, a shady promenade of towering plane and lime trees, first planted in the late eighteenth century, stretches for half a mile towards the campsite on the bank of the Loire where we pitched our tents for a night.

The Loire is joined at Decize on its right bank by the Aron and another canal begins here, using the Aron's valley. Like the earlier Canal de Briare, the Canal du Nivernais, built slowly in the first half of the nineteenth century, connects the Loire with a tributary of the Seine. A large weir was thrown across the Loire to create enough deep, slow-moving water to allow barges to leave a lock from the Canal Latéral on the left bank and cross the river to enter the Canal du Nivernais, thus avoiding the problems that had plagued the longer crossing downriver at Briare before the building of the *pont-canal*.

Canals were on my mind at Decize. I would shortly have to take a decision on the way ahead. I wanted to get to Roanne, higher up the Loire, before finally leaving the river behind and striking east across the hills to the Rhône. But there would soon be no marked footpath to take me there. The obvious route would be to follow the Canal Latéral south-eastwards to Digoin and then its continuation, the Canal de Roanne à Digoin, which also tracks the Loire, due south up to Roanne. This is what I had planned to do when looking at maps spread out on the kitchen table back in England. From the point where I would need to put this plan into action, a couple of days ahead, it would be about fifty miles of canal towpath.

The canals might seem to offer much to the walker. Quiet, easy progress, undisturbed by motor car or lorry, with the little shops and bars that service the pleasure-boat trade and the hotels and restaurants in all the towns that the canals pass through. You could walk right across France on canal towpaths. But it would be a rather dull crossing of the country as far as the actual walking is concerned. A few miles of the Canal de la Sauldre in the Sologne and of the Canal Latéral had been enough. It had soon become boring. Too regimented, too straight. The thought of fifty miles of it was making my heart sink.

Leaving Decize, Honi and I climbed a hillside above the Aron that gave a huge view south and east. An information board pointed out the names of the distant hills. There on the horizon ahead, in a dark wooded band, were the Monts de la Madeleine. They form a 3,000-foot-high ridge running more or less north-south, the north-east corner of the Massif Central – a last finger stretching up from the vast area of mountains and high hills in central southern France that I had always intended to skirt around to the north. Roanne lay on their other side. The map showed the footpath I had been following since Briare leaving the Loire and heading up towards them. They beckoned. Even the name, with its alliteration, seemed seductive. Once or twice since starting from the Channel, I had felt just a little envy of the Compostela pilgrims, no decisions on the route ahead to be taken, always following The Way. But more often not, with finding my own way being part of the fun, and now I experienced the rush described by Frédéric Gros of the 'vertiginous freedom' of choice of the walker at a crossroads. Looking more closely at the map, I saw that I could climb the Monts de la Madeleine from the west on a variant of my current path. This continued on south along the ridge but I could no doubt then find a way down the other side to arrive at Roanne. Good. I would leave the canals below.

* * *

Tina and Honi left me at the little spa of Bourbon-Lancy. I stayed in a B&B in the lower part of town opposite the grand hotel, 'Les Thermes', that occupies a former convent built in the eighteenth century next to the baths. Two elderly *curistes*, people taking a cure, sat at separate tables at breakfast. One was just finishing her two-week stint and greeted the other with a hearty '*Bonjour, jeune homme*'. The night before, the town was filled with people who had come for La Fête de la

Musique. This, my landlady told me, is a national celebration across France each year on June 21, introduced in the early 1980s by the long-standing Minster of Culture, Jack Lang, and now celebrated in many other countries as 'World Music Day'. Groups and solo artists of various kinds were playing in the squares and outside the few places to eat. The pizzeria in the centre of town got the blues and was packed, with a queue outside. Down at the large family restaurant near my B&B where I finally found a table, we got music more suited to the *curistes* – an enthusiastic crooner in a lurid purple suit moving around the tables. He was still going strong when I turned in not long before midnight. A travelling funfair was also in town: teenagers jostling for rides on the dodgems, shooting galleries with huge fluffy toys as prizes, hard faces in the crowd, the noise and colour all familiar.

A morning's walk took me to a bridge over the Loire, here flowing west for a short stretch, and so to the village of Diou. In July 1940, I would now have been crossing the new *ligne de démarcation*, from the *zone occupée*, under the control of the Germans, into the *zone libre*, Vichy France. It was a line that would quickly become a closely guarded border, only to be crossed with a permit. Or rather, I would have been able to reach the *zone libre* in July that year if the bridge over the river had still been standing instead of having been blown up by French army engineers. In that month and those that followed I would have met a stream of people trying to come the other way – the refugees from Paris and the rest of northern France who had formed the Exodus of May and June, now trying to return home. The destruction before the armistice of bridges across the Loire by the retreating French army slowed up these return journeys. And not everyone was permitted by the Germans to go back to their homes in the north. Jews were quickly a forbidden category. The

Vichy government turned swiftly on the Jewish population too. By the end of July, French nationality could be removed from recently naturalised Jews and from October a decree prevented any Jew from working in a range of public sector jobs. Internment of foreign Jews in detention camps in the *zone libre* also began. The day before, still in the *zone occupée*, I had been within a couple of hours walk of the village to which Irène Némirovsky had fled from Paris in the Exodus, where she had started to write *Suite Française*, and where she was arrested by French police two years later.

On the other side of Diou, another bridge carried me across the Canal Latéral. I stopped to look down from the parapet onto the still water and the towpath I was now avoiding and then headed on towards the Monts de la Madeleine.

5

Rich and poor

'*Auvergne – la pauvreté continue de progresser*', read the headline in the local newspaper, *La Montagne*. Poverty is still rising. The message was displayed on a sandwich board outside the one shop in Montcombroux-les-Mines. The Auvergne – an old, pre-revolutionary province with one of France's elected regional governments from the 1980s – is at the heart of the Massif Central, traditionally one of the poorest parts of the country. Montcombroux-les-Mines is at its eastern edge among rolling hills of small cattle farms, hills that would lead me on to the Monts de la Madeleine ahead.

The shop was a welcome sight in the late afternoon after a warm day's walk up from the Loire valley. A sign advertised that it was a grocery, a newsagent, a tobacconist, a *dépôt de pain*, and *un point multi-service* – the services listed included photocopying, fax, internet access, mail order, home delivery, and cash withdrawal for customers of Crédit Agricole, the traditional bank of farming communities. Two tall tiers of metal racks stood outside full of big blue bottles of liquid gas, one rack advertising Totalgaz and the other Butagaz. I stocked up with food and wandered along the other side of the road to sit in the shade on a bench outside the *mairie*. On the way, I passed a small post office that was open for two hours each morning Tuesday to Friday and for an hour on Saturday. A poster advertised a van selling pizzas in the next-door village on Friday evenings, noting that with a loyalty card an eleventh pizza would be free.

The *mairie* was a fine, small two-storey limestone building set back from the road behind green-painted iron gates and matching railings hung with boxes of geraniums, its tall windows surrounded in red brick and flanked by shutters in the same green as the railings and gates. A single dormer window in the centre of the red tiled roof incorporated a clock in its little gable. As is common for a *mairie*, the building also housed the village school – an old inscription on the stone above the door showed it had been the school for boys. At five-thirty, a woman emerged and locked the door behind her. She was the *mairesse*, the mayor. After exchanging pleasantries I asked if there was a bar in the village. No, it had closed a year ago. And how many pupils were there in the school? Eight. But there were eleven the year before she quickly added.

The mining of coal that gives the village the tag to its name ended in 1950. A small factory opened in the mid-1960s, making rubber (*caoutchouc* in French, a word which always suggests to me a tempting combination of chocolate and liquorice). The factory still provides some employment but I counted just a dozen cars in the car park. Throughout the last quarter of the nineteenth century and the first of the twentieth, there were around thirteen hundred people living in the commune of Montcombroux-les-Mines. By the late 1970s there were six hundred. This was when the rural exodus in France as a whole finally ended, but in 2017 the commune's population was down to three hundred and thirteen.

* * *

The day had begun a few miles from the Loire at Saligny-sur-Roudon, a village on one of the river's tributaries, by the war memorial – a dark granite obelisk topped with a crowing rooster, the surrounding railings hung with troughs of vigorous pink and red geraniums. I walked south under clear blue skies along lanes and tracks, through woods, past farms – the 'whit, whit-whit', *paye tes dettes*, of a quail coming from a field of grass waiting to be cut – gently climbing to the village of St-Léon. From a vantage point of a little summit just outside the village, huge views stretched away west and east and back down north, far on beyond the Loire to the high hills of Morvan, some sixty miles away in central Burgundy, hills you cross if you drive south-east from Paris on the *autoroute* towards Dijon or Lyon. Five minutes later, around the other side of the hill, another sight made me gasp – away in the distance in the haze to the south-west was the chain of extinct volcanoes that lie beyond the city of Clermont-Ferrand. The horizon was dominated by the highest mountain in the chain and one of the best known in the Massif Central: the magnificent cone of the Puy de Dôme, nearly 5,000 feet high. After six weeks of walking, I felt a sudden shift from the lowlands to the highlands even though I was still not quite there.

There was a bar in St-Léon, curiously empty and a bit forlorn on a weekday lunchtime, nobody taking advantage of the advertised *resto' rapide*. It had a small, sad-looking corner of groceries inside and a rack of gas bottles outside again, the bottles this time from Antargaz and coloured orange. At the end of the nineteenth century, the commune of St-Léon had fourteen hundred inhabitants. By the Second World War there were a thousand. Now, after a continued decline, there are less than six hundred.

Just below the village, I had passed the *lavoir*, the public washhouse, set at the side of a field and surrounded by a barbed-wire fence to keep out the cows. A plain, rectangular open pool had the usual sloping surround on which to beat and drain the clothes, made of cement. The pool was fed by a little rush-filled stream at one end and drained underground the other through a grate to a culvert taking the water under the road until it emerged into a meadow as a stream again. In one corner, the cement surround was covered by the rusty corrugated-iron roof of an open shed-like structure that provided at least some shelter for the user. It was one of the simplest *lavoirs* that I had seen: no architectural merit, no decorative feature, purely functional.

I had been looking out for *lavoirs* since landing in Normandy, partly as a little game with myself when passing though any village – 'spot the *lavoir*'. But the one at St-Léon made me think more about their history and their place in rural life, perhaps because of its very lack of adornment. And I was now in an area where the social and economic history, of poverty, of ill health, of hard upland living, meant that it was easy to be interested in clues to past and present living standards.

The *lavoirs* illustrate how far the standard of living in rural areas in France has risen in recent decades. Only one in five rural homes had running water in 1946 and it was a good while after the Second World War before the *lavoirs* were no longer needed. Of Trôo in the late 1960s, the village on the Loir where I had found only a baguette dispenser, Geoffrey Grigson commented: 'It is the old women without a machine in their houses, except perhaps an electric coffee-mill, who still take in the washing of the well-to-do or of Parisians down for the summer and for weekends. They pull the washing in a trailer – a *remorque* with bicycle wheels – down to the cold spring water of the washing place.' To my surprise, I could find no mention in my father's diaries from the 1970s of seeing *lavoirs* in action. Too much attention instead to church architecture I thought. Or was it just that *lavoirs* were still so 'normal' that he did not think them of interest? A friend with a house in Normandy wrote telling me of *lavoirs* in service at that time: 'When we first arrived in 1975, the *lavoirs* were in active use. The old lady who lived in our house was the *blanchisseuse*, but she had only an outside tap and no electric power. She did the laundry at the *lavoir*. Like many, it is fed directly by a spring, and for some of our neighbours it was the sole source of water. Their use continued well into the 1980s.' The *lavoir* in St-Léon looked as if it could have seen even later use.

The coming of piped water to the vast majority of houses in rural areas, together with rising incomes, led eventually to washing machines in the home taking over from the *lavoir* down the lane. Alongside that progress, ending the relentless toil of washing by hand, something was lost – a meeting place for working-class women, from which men were excluded. Somewhere to see friends, to pass on news, to share problems. Of course, any regular meeting spot of this type that people are obliged by circumstances to use can also be a place of hierarchy and conflict – in Zola's *l'Assommoir* a Parisian *lavoir* is the scene of a terrible fight involving the main character.

The *lavoirs* are also a reminder of earlier progress in living standards in both town and country. Many date from the second half of the nineteenth century and were part of a push to improve public health. Around this time, the design of rural *lavoirs* often changed from being merely functional to become expressions of civic pride, taking their place alongside the *mairie* and the elementary school; as an architectural historian has put it, *lavoirs* 'became prime manifestations of the towns' sophistication and wealth', with another writer commenting on them under the heading of 'Mayors with ambitions'.

By this yardstick, the basic, unadorned *lavoir* at St-Léon suggests a poor nineteenth-century village, the recurring picture of living standards in rural Auvergne at that time. In 1836, Adolphe d'Angeville published a collection of maps of France, his famous *Essai sur la statistique de la population française*, showing that the inhabitants of *départements* to the south of a line drawn from St-Malo in Brittany to Geneva in the Alps had lower literacy, were worse fed, were shorter, and had higher mortality. There was a north-south divide, in favour of the north. The *départements* that made up the Auvergne and the rest of the Massif Central featured prominently on d'Angeville's maps as among the least favoured parts of the south. (One of the results of the poverty in the Auvergne meant that it was a prime region for Parisian wig makers trying to buy hair.) However, by the start of the twentieth century, the south was on the way to catching up. The new roads and railways of Napoleon III's Second Empire helped stimulate the south's economic development. Elementary education was made compulsory throughout France in 1882, closing at least in principle the literacy gap of the south with the north. And records of the heights of potential army conscripts show young men from the Massif Central starting to converge in stature on their northern counterparts, reflecting improvements in nutrition and health.

Nevertheless, catch-up was incomplete. The chapter on the region in a book from the 1970s on French social and economic geography starts firmly: 'The Massif Central forms the most extensive rural problem area in France.' And in *France in the 1980s* the journalist and lifelong Francophile John Ardagh commented gloomily on 'people [who] eke out a living from useless polyculture… a patch of vines for the family's vinegary own wine, a cow or two and some mangy chickens, cabbages struggling to grow on a hillside'. He also noted the lack of *remembrement* in the south – the consolidation of land holdings – compared to the situation in the north, such as in the huge arable landscapes of the Beauce that I had passed through in May, citing the example of 'a goat-breeder with eighty-five acres split into fifty far-flung parcels'.

* * *

What about living standards today – how poor really is the Auvergne now? On the face of it, not that poor when compared to the rest of France, at least according to the official statistics. Poverty is slightly lower in the Auvergne than in the country as a whole when measured by a yardstick of low household income. The highest poverty rates are found in another southern region, Languedoc-Roussillon, which runs from the eastern Pyrenees around the Mediterranean coast to the Rhône; in the most northerly region in France, Nord-Pas de Calais, bordering Belgium and the Channel, an area of past coal mining and former textile manufacturing; and in Corsica. (I refer here to the regions that existed before their re-organisation in 2016.)

But the overall figure for poverty in the Auvergne masks the variation among its constituent parts. Inner-city areas, including in its capital, the large city of Clermont-Ferrand, have the highest poverty rates, double those in most other urban areas. However, the Auvergne's 'isolated' rural communes have high rates too. A *commune isolée hors influence des pôles*, to use the full title, is a small rural commune classified by the national statistical office as being outside the influence of a reasonably sized centre of employment. In other words, a rural area without much work of its own and not within normal commuting distance of a town with jobs. About five per cent of the population of France live in these communes. Montcombroux-les-Mines is classed as a *commune isolée*, as is St-Léon.

The official figures for poverty, measured in terms of low income, need to be interpreted with care. They take no account of the differences in the cost of living between different parts of the country. On the one hand, some prices are higher in rural areas, meaning that living standards are worse than indicated by the poverty rate. The big blue and orange bottles of liquid gas on sale in Montcombroux-les-Mines and St-Léon must provide more expensive energy than a mains supply in a city. And small village shops cannot exploit the economies of scale of a large urban supermarket. On the other hand, housing costs are usually lower, especially in areas where the population is still in decline as in the two villages in question. Home ownership is much higher among the rural poor in France than among the urban poor – fewer poor people in the countryside have to spend their income on rent.

For a traveller on foot, the most striking feature of isolated villages that signals lower living standards is their lack of amenities and, especially, shops, bars, and restaurants. As a walker passing through, these are the things that you want most and like someone living in the village who cannot afford a car you don't have the option of just driving off to the nearest town to get to them. (The same is true of entertainment like cinemas or nightclubs but that is not something high on the wish list of many walkers.) The inner cities certainly have other problems including higher crime. However, at least the urban poor don't have to go far to shop – and may have a wider choice of schools for their children. In each village I walked through on my way to the Monts de la Madeleine, any conversation quickly led to stories of a closed bar, of the baker about to retire, of the small size of the school and so on – stories underlined by plenty of evidence of former shops and little hotels or restaurants, their fading names still painted on the walls of the buildings, together with the ever-present sign '*à vendre*' on houses for sale.

Part of the job of a commune's *maire* or *mairesse*, the mayor, is to fight against this decline. France is often thought of as the quintessential centralised nation, power firmly concentrated in Paris. This ignores a policy of decentralisation dating to the 1980s that led to the creation of the regional governments and a reduction in the powers of the *préfet* of each *département*, the prefect, an official appointed by the President to be the representative of the central government. And in the commune and in the figure of its mayor, the French state has long presented a highly decentralised face. France has some 35,000 communes, the great majority put in place at the Revolution with boundaries that have remained unchanged since. No other country in Europe has anywhere near so many 'bottom tier' local authorities. Italy, for example, with a population only a little smaller than that of France, has just 8,000 communes. There are vast numbers of very small French communes, their ranks swollen by the rural depopulation of the nineteenth and twentieth centuries. More than a half have fewer than five hundred inhabitants – St-Léon's total of somewhat less than six hundred people means it is larger than most and Montcombroux-les-Mines with a little over three hundred is a respectable size by comparison with many. Almost one in three communes have fewer than two hundred and fifty people living in them and over 3,000 have less than a hundred. Six have nobody at all. These are a special case, villages entirely destroyed in the battle for Verdun in the First World War and never rebuilt. But another twenty communes have less than ten people. Moreover, the French commune is far from being a mere symbol of local autonomy; it 'matters' and is a much more important body than the lowest tier of local government in rural England, the parish council. For example, the communes are responsible for local planning, water, sanitation, waste collection, local roads, school buses and the maintenance of primary school buildings – none of which is the responsibility of an English parish council.

I had passed through many small communes in the previous weeks. Walking into a tiny village and seeing a *mairie*, my reaction in the early days was one of bewildered amusement. How absurd, I thought. What on earth could the mayor of a commune of fewer than a hundred people do? How inefficient! But as time passed, I began to see the small communes in a different light. They mean that someone firmly within the state hierarchy has the job of fighting for the village, to try to protect local services. The mayor is not just an elected representative of the state with a tricolour sash to officiate at weddings and to open fêtes. His or her role in maintaining a supply of bread may not be the most important task but it illustrates the point. In Chaon, in the Sologne, where Jay and I had bought bread from the secretary of the *maire*, the commune's website described efforts to keep a *boulangerie* going. In Ousson-sur-Loire, south of Gien, my B&B landlady lived opposite the *mairie* and said that she had been asked by the mayor to act as a *dépôt de pain*.

I wish I had talked more with the *mairesse* of Montcombroux-les-Mines. About the problems facing the commune, what she could do to lessen them, and about the resources at her disposal. How, for example, might she try to persuade the Ministry of Education to keep the village school open, despite having only eight pupils? What would be her response if the one shop looked as if it would close? As the mayor of a commune of less than five hundred people, she was paid six hundred and fifty euros a month – not a salary for a full-time job. She had an elected commune council and probably a part-time secretary but no other administrative staff to help carry out her substantial list of responsibilities. A large slice of each commune's budget is derived from local taxes, so poorer communes have less money despite additional support from central government. Recent years have seen communes given incentives to group together and pool their resources for agreed common services and the great majority of the smaller ones now do so, relieving the burden on any individual mayor. A sign on the edge of the village told me that Montcombroux-les-Mines is one of fourteen communes in a *communauté de communes*. But actual merger has been rare until recently.

The key problem facing a *commune isolée* like Montcombroux-les-Mines is a lack of jobs. With more jobs, there would be more money around, more demand for a *boulangerie* or for a bar. Fewer people would leave. The population might even rise. In *Village in the Vaucluse*, the American sociologist Laurence Wylie wrote a detailed account of rural life in the 1950s in the commune of Roussillon, some twenty-five miles east of Avignon in the Luberon hills of Provence. Like Montcombroux, Roussillon has a past history of mining, in its case of ochre – an orange pigment of iron oxide used in dyes and paints. Ochre mining had collapsed in

Roussillon by the time of Wylie's year in the village after the discovery of a cheaper, synthetic alternative. The commune's population was half of what it had been in the late nineteenth century. Wylie describes being offered a windmill and the hill on which it stood for ninety dollars. Times were tough for Roussillon. But the commune has since boomed due to tourism – the ochre cliffs are now a draw. A recent book about the village, taking Wylie's story forward, is titled *From Rocks to Riches* and the population is now back at a level not seen since the 1880s.

Montcombroux-les-Mines is less favoured. Tourism exists in this part of the Auvergne but on nowhere near the scale of the Luberon. However, after my visit I learned of Montcombroux's big hope for the future, which the *mairesse* would surely have mentioned had we talked more about the village's prospects. A Dutch group of investors have bought the old chateau outside the village together with several hundred hectares of land, and have persuaded the commune and the *département* to allow them to build a twenty-seven-hole golf course, a ninety-six-room hotel, a riding centre, and three holiday hamlets comprising four hundred villas and apartments. The total investment is said to be in the order of a hundred million euros. The commune council voted nine to one in favour, swayed, one presumes, by the promised sixty permanent jobs along with all the additional spending of the new golf-playing tourists and second-home owners. The development should also sharply increase the commune's tax base.

Maybe it will work out – that the demand forecast by the developers really will materialise. The scale seems fantastic. Our village in Italy on the edge of the Apennines saw a similar proposal thirty years ago, a project still mired in controversy – heads shake with a knowing smile when '*il golf*' is mentioned.

The golf course was built and is still there but the original developer and the next company to take over the business both went bust. Much of the associated development has not taken place and a new road built through the area as part of the project is now crumbling, eaten away by landslips and never opened to traffic. It transpires that the proposed development in Montcombroux also has a long history, stretching back to 1989 when the chateau and land were first acquired with the aim of creating golf course and holiday village by a Japanese company that eventually sold the property on to the Dutch without starting anything. It remains to be seen how the story will end.

* * *

The old chateau at Montcombroux is destined to become a club house for the golf course, with a restaurant and an indoor swimming pool. I passed several other chateaux on my way to the village that were all still in private hands. None of them was open to the public. A stone's throw from the war memorial at Saligny-sur-Roudon, where my day began, was a fairy-tale little castle in apparently perfect condition with a fourteenth-century round tower and a graceful main building from the sixteenth century, punctuated with tall windows. All, including the tower, topped with elegant, steeply pitched, slate-covered roofs. Next, half an hour's walk short of the humble *lavoir* at St-Léon, the farm track I was on ran by the entrance to a massive, slightly tatty, rambling fortified manor from the sixteenth century with a big courtyard, extensive stone outhouses and two great round towers at each end of the main building, all again with steep roofs, this time covered in rose-coloured tiles sprouting moss and lichen. On its own, surrounded by farmland, no cars or machinery in sight, it could have been a scene from before the Revolution. Then, half an hour on past St-Léon, a small nineteenth-century, plain flat-fronted chateau, less obviously attractive than the previous two and its roofs less steeply pitched, but pleasantly set in modest grounds behind gates and railings with several large cedar trees.

It would have been fun to have tried to find out more about the owners of these chateaux. Has the Napoleonic code's principle of partible inheritance resulted in the houses being shared by siblings or cousins, none of whom is actually resident in the commune? Do their owners spend lives entirely separated from the village or are they important landlords with a number of local tenants, engaged in the commune's problems and future? And vice versa – what is the attitude of the locals to their neighbours in the big house? John Ardagh wrote of aristocrats having 'to devote part of their new industrial incomes to the upkeep of their cherished family châteaux' but of 'the great families' still enjoying 'their own exclusive social world, inviting each other to formal cocktail parties or an occasional ball or banquet with echoes of past glories'. Meanwhile, as he put it, 'the rest of France tolerates and ignores them'. My Normandy friend urged me to read Daphne du Maurier's *The Scapegoat* in which an Englishman travelling in France replaces his double, the aristocratic head of a dysfunctional family with a failing glass-works. A family retainer tells him: 'For you people at the château life is full of complications. Sometimes I wonder how you live at all.'

I left Montcombroux-les-Mines in the angled shadows of the early evening and began to muse about the impact of the Revolution on the distribution of wealth in France. Surprisingly, it seems to have been modest. It has been estimated that only ten per cent of land changed hands, largely property confiscated from the church and from those aristocrats who fled abroad. Rather than redistributing this land, the state then sold it off and it was the larger farmers and *bourgeoisie* who could afford to buy rather than the peasants; in Zola's *La Terre*, Old Fouan laments that his grandfather did not have the money that would have allowed him to add to the family's holdings. Many nobles held onto their property – the Meilheurat family built the chateau at Montcombroux a few years before the Revolution and kept it until selling up for the golf development. Those who fled were compensated in 1825 by the restored Bourbon monarchy for at least some of their losses through the famous *milliard des émigrés* – a billion francs-worth of government bonds. The French economist Thomas Piketty, in his best-selling *Capital in the Twenty-First Century*, summarised the situation by saying that 'the magnitude of the changes initiated by the French Revolution should not be overstated', going on to argue: 'France remained the same society, with the same basic structure of inequality, from the *Ancien Régime* to the Third Republic, despite the vast political and economic changes that took place in the interim.' His comment on the Third Republic, which lasted from 1870 to 1940, refers only to the period up to the First World War. Piketty estimates that the share of total wealth – land and other assets – of the richest one per cent of the French population reached a high of around sixty per cent in 1910, compared to just under fifty per cent in the first half of the nineteenth century. Then, in the upheavals of the twentieth century – war, financial crisis, war again, reconstruction, the end of the Fourth Republic – this share of the top one per cent fell to little more than twenty per cent by 1970.

And, skipping closer to the present, what about the last twenty or thirty years – how have the rich fared since the France of the 1970s and 1980s of which John Ardagh wrote?

Piketty's figures show that the richest one per cent saw a small increase in their share of total wealth, from 22.0 per cent in 1970 and again in 1980 to 24.4 per cent by 2010. Any comparison of France with other countries is fraught with problems of differences in the nature of the available data and in the definition of wealth. But Piketty argues the changes in France over the last two hundred years in the share of the richest one per cent to have been similar to those in Britain and writes that in the late nineteenth century: 'inequality of capital ownership was only slightly greater in Britain than in France... even though Third Republic elites at the time liked to portray France as an egalitarian country compared with its monarchical neighbor across the Channel.' In both countries, what he calls a 'patrimonial middle class' emerged in the twentieth century owning a significant share of national wealth as the share of the richest fell.

* * *

I wandered along a quiet lane from Montcombroux, the road rising and falling as it worked its way from one little valley to another. It was a perfect evening and I was looking for somewhere to sleep in the open. The hillsides were dotted with small pastoral farms, each likely looking field turning out to have cows or someone on a tractor making hay or to be too close to a farmhouse for comfort.

I reached the little village of Bert, tucked down in a valley, population of the commune two hundred and fifty, a continuous decline from the peak of eleven hundred in 1891. The limestone west end of yet another Romanesque church glowed golden in the warm still air, tower and squat steeple rising up out of the valley bottom into a deep, blue cloudless sky. Nobody was about. Who knows what discord might have lain behind closed doors but on the streets in the lingering of the day Bert was at peace, a complete peace.

I passed another little village school that I later discovered to have fourteen pupils. Not far to the south in this part of the Auvergne is where the engaging 2002 documentary *Être et Avoir* was made, following several months in the life of just such a school, with about a dozen pupils and a single teacher in his penultimate year before retirement. The film starts in winter with the school bus picking up children from surrounding farms in blustery snow. And it ends on the last day of the school year, with the quiet, endlessly patient, bearded teacher, Monsieur Lopez, the son of Spanish immigrants, holding back his tears after saying goodbye to his pupils – kisses on each cheek from most of them – several for the last time as they move on to secondary school. The film was shown at Cannes, was nominated for Best Film and Best Director in the French film industry's annual César awards, and had considerable success at the box office. It is better not to know the coda, Monsieur Lopez suing the film-makers for a share in the profits, unsuccessfully.

An information board in the village told me that I was now moving over one more border: from the land of the Oïl, the language that became modern French, to the land of the Oc, where the old language Occitan of the south of France was spoken and is still used as a second language by perhaps half a million people. Hence Languedoc, the former province below the Auvergne, and the post-2016 region that combines the former regions of Languedoc-Roussillon and Midi-Pyrénées: Occitanie. In another documentary about twenty-first-century life in the Massif Central, *La Vie Moderne*, focusing on several farms further south in the Cévennes, one octogenarian comments approvingly that it is only Occitan that is understood by his dog.

But at this point, with the evening wearing on, I was more interested in finding somewhere to bed down for the night. A long, carefree day was beginning to look as if it might end in the frustration of a fruitless search for a good sleeping place. Of course, it doesn't really matter where you sleep as long as it is dry, you are warm enough, and nobody – or no cow – is going to disturb you. But it's an unsatisfying end to a grand day in the open to have only a mediocre spot for the night. After casting around unsuccessfully along one road leading out of the village, I tried another that climbed a steep hill past the cemetery and it quickly produced a suitable site, a little fallow corner of a small field of ripening wheat with a hedge hiding me from the road and a view over the hillsides I had passed earlier where a tractor was still working back and forth. I ate provisions I'd bought in Montcombroux, read for a while, and was in my sleeping bag waiting for the night sky, bats flickering about above me, before the church bell in the valley below struck ten. A first-quarter crescent moon moved towards its setting. Venus, Jupiter and Saturn, low down, came out and then the first star appeared right above me – Arcturus, perhaps, I thought – before I quickly fell asleep.

I awoke early to a glorious morning. A heavy dew had soaked the land and I spread my sleeping bag out to dry in an already warm sun while slowly packing up. Then it was back down the hill, past the cemetery again and into the village. At that point I found that Bert had a bar, overlooked in a side street the evening before. It was open. Coffee at the counter, the friendly *patronne* chatting with her regulars as they dropped by to pick up bread and newspapers.

My way out of the village led up from the valley bottom on an unsealed road through a forest of pine and chestnut, the road still deep in shadow and the treetops above glistening in the sunlight. The road was being carefully re-made, a digger with an enormous front blade delicately grading the surface to get the right camber to encourage run off to one side rather than rain washing downhill. A large roller was slowly compacting fine, pinky-orange gravel, new pre-cast drainage channels neatly inserted at angles across the road at regular intervals to catch the water that the camber failed to take away. It all looked in perfect condition. If every country road were like this rather than asphalt, I thought, road walking would be really quite pleasant – especially under such a beautifully cool canopy of shade.

The asphalt returned after a mile or two, and with it came open higher ground and views once more south-east across hills towards the ever-nearing Monts de la Madeleine. A day of minor roads, tracks, woodland paths, farmland, forest and hamlets – one with the ubiquitous Romanesque church with portal covered in a spectacular display of pink roses. And so by late afternoon to my destination, a B&B in a chicken farm on the edge of the village of Droiturier. I was not the only guest. Two other walkers, Yves and Joëlle, were going in the opposite direction to me. They had started a couple of weeks earlier near the source of the Loire, to the south in the Cévennes highlands, and were walking north back to their home west of Sancerre. But they were not carrying rucksacks – their gear was all on the backs of two much-loved donkeys.

It was Joëlle's birthday and the next day it would be Yves's. And since it was June 24, it was also my saint's day, dear from our life in Tuscany less for it being my *onomastico*, my 'name day', which traditionally serves as a second birthday, but rather because the feast of San Giovanni is the day to pick green walnuts to make *nocino*, walnut liqueur, with fireworks in Florence in the evening as John the Baptist is the city's patron saint. The little chapel of St Jean des Bois in the Normandy woods that I came across with Andrew in my first week would be having its one mass of the year. The French, like the Italians, recognize name days and Brigitte, the warm and voluble farmer's wife, embraced me enthusiastically with kisses on both cheeks. So we three guests all had something to celebrate and Brigitte and her husband, Roland, helped us enthusiastically. We ate duck, the wine flowed, and Yves produced a bottle of champagne that he had hidden in one of the donkeys' panniers. The conversation swung this way and that, everyone tolerant of my stumbling contributions, Yves teasing me gently on my repeated failure to correctly pronounce the word for 'more', *plus* – sometimes the 's' is silent and sometimes not. Yves fell to talking with Roland about the old Route Nationale 7, the main road from Paris to the Mediterranean in the pre-motorway era, the *route des vacances*. South from Paris to meet the Loire at Briare, up the Loire and then from Nevers up the Allier, and next east towards Lyon, passing a mile or so to the south of where we were at Droiturier. The conversation focused on the traffic jams as holidaymakers poured south along the N7 in July and August. The hold-ups became so famous that there are now annual festivals to celebrate them, Roland told us, such as at Lapalisse just to the west of Droiturier, people coming from all over France in classic cars of the era and pretending to be in a traffic jam, police in period uniforms overseeing the chaos.

The next morning we were all up early as another hot day was forecast. Yves, Joëlle and I left together, they and the donkeys turning north at the farm gate towards Bert and I south to climb the Monts de la Madeleine, passing first under a new section of N7 dual carriageway, the traffic running smoothly.

* * *

By late morning, I had reached the village of Arfeuilles, the main ridge of the mountains still a couple of thousand feet above. Arfeuilles is a large rural commune by French standards – a population of six hundred and fifty. But again, there has been a continuous fall from the late nineteenth century. The peak came in 1881 with over 3,500 inhabitants. As Yves had told me the previous evening, houses for sale were everywhere to be seen together with the fading signs of past *boulangeries*, *charcuteries*, *épiceries* and bars, all gone. However, the village had a pretty face as well with boxes of red geraniums and pink petunias hung on several footbridges crossing a little river. And it is still big enough to support a few shops, which I had hurried to get to before they closed for lunch. The forecast heat had come about and I passed a long hour in the shade of a little garden that surrounds the war memorial, recovering from a faster than normal morning's march.

Then it was steep uphill to climb a lateral ridge that led me on upwards, in and out of woodland and open pasture, following a series of tracks and paths. Huge vistas to the west and south-west began to unfold in the open stretches, away to the distant Puy de Dôme and the other peaks in the volcanic chain beyond Clermont-Ferrand that I had first seen from outside St-Léon, stretched out in a line on the horizon. The sun beat down, sweat poured off, but I began to feel the elation of walking in higher land, stopping repeatedly to take in the view.

I climbed on, now deep in the forest that covers much of the Monts de la Madeleine, largely a mix of beech and pine. The decision to avoid the canals and seek the higher ground had proved a good one and I felt rather proud of my discovery of this little known corner of the Massif Central. But almost inevitably, reading my father's diaries back in England showed that he had arrived before me, passing through the area with my mother by car in the 1970s. 'Winding little roads. Quiet – an occasional *auberge*. Partly pine-forested but also high, rolling deciduous wooded farmland – hay, cattle and some corn.' In one village they were drawn into the *cortège* of a large funeral: 'on the wide open *place* the farming families from all corners of the Monts de la Madeleine were congregating in their dark suits, meeting, shaking hands and kissing. What a wonderful spot in which to finish one's life and to be remembered, high up in this ancient church.' The entry concluded with what I thought a surprising judgement of the landscape: 'very like South Wales, Wye to Abergavenny.' For me, these mountains resemble more the Apennines in the part of Tuscany where we used to live. Working my way upwards on a steep stony track through beech woods felt like a hot afternoon from an earlier life. The heat became too much and I clambered down to a stream to dip quickly in a freezing pool by an abandoned mill, the old metal wheel still there on the side of the building, rusting away among the bushes. The late-afternoon sun was now at my back and my shadow stretched out in front on the path, mimicking my every move. The gradient in time levelled out and I came to a little hamlet at a crossroads where I spent the night in an upmarket B&B run by a friendly Dutch couple in what had been the old school house, its design very similar to the building that had housed the *mairie* and school in Montcombroux-les-Mines. I went to sleep thinking of the contrasts in such a day. At one point, plodding uphill, muscles complaining, dust and dirt clinging. At another, a sudden halt at an enormous view of valleys and hills rolling on into the distance. And now of lying clean in a comfortable bed and full of good food (mustard and salmon soup, filet mignon, cheese of course, and tiramisu).

But I was not yet at the top and the next day I carried on up a track towards the crest of the main ridge, the going quickly becoming steep again. The forest was being actively managed and in a couple of places huge swaths of trees had been clear-felled, perhaps a year or two before, in each case a belt some sixty or seventy yards wide stretching far down the mountainside; and in their place a great purple carpet rolled downhill, thousand upon thousand of foxgloves in full flower. I neared the top and followed a little path up through the woods to the summit of one of the peaks on the ridge, almost running the final bit in my urge to look down on the other side of these mountains that I had first seen on the horizon a week ago from that hillside outside Decize. Nothing! I was still enveloped by short beech trees. Hence on along the ridge, now on a new well-made dirt road that it quickly became clear had been built to allow construction of a line of half a dozen huge wind turbines. I stopped at the second of these, its arms inert in the still heat of the day far above me on its tall slender column, and followed a faint path through the woods to the east. This led to an open patch on the edge of the ridge and there finally below me was the view I had been waiting for.

An immense vision – down east over the wide Loire valley again, a couple of thousand feet below, the river clearly visible a dozen or so miles away together with the large town of Roanne, on the river, my destination for the next day. Beyond in the haze and forming the horizon, a line of blue hills that I would then need to cross, separating the valley of the Loire from that of the Rhône and its great tributary the Saône. I stared and stared, 'like stout Cortez... silent, upon a peak in Darien'. In the right conditions in winter you can see from the Monts de la Madeleine to Mont Blanc, two hundred miles away to the east. Even without that further vista of my journey's end, the sight of everything before my eyes and the sense of the raw geography – the ridge I was at last now on and all the land laid out below me – rooted me to the spot.

I eventually shook myself free, turned and followed the ridge and its dirt road on south for two or three more miles past the other turbines. A windmill is the same in French as in English, *un moulin à vent*. Not so with the wind turbines. 'Turbine' focuses my reaction on the functionality, the engineering. But in the French name the wind is all. Aeolus, the keeper of the winds in Greek mythology, gives us *une éolienne*. The graceful lilt of the word rolling off the tongue conjures up the slow turning of the blades, although not to be seen that day on the Monts de la Madeleine. A sign I saw later proclaimed '*7 éoliennes = 20,000 foyers*'. A quick check confirmed that *un foyer* here is not a cinema or theatre entrance hall but a household or home, literally 'a hearth'. The right choice of word to finish the equation, the energy of the wind replacing that of the fire.

The road emerged from the forest and the ridge flattened out into an open heath with the same huge view to the east. I settled into the shade of a boulder by a solitary scrubby little beech tree and did not move for the next two hours.

Had I known then what I discovered a couple of days later in Roanne, I might have spent part of those two hours criss-crossing the heath, looking down from side to side, intent on trying to find a particular insect. The Violet Copper is a small, rare butterfly of upland areas; the *cuivré de la bistorte*, the 'copper of the bistort', the plant on which its caterpillar feeds that pushes up a bottle-brush column of pinky-white flowers on a spindly stalk. The butterfly is absent from Britain and found only locally in the rest of western Europe, this particular piece of heath on the Monts de la Madeleine being one of those places. Photos show it to be a bewitchingly beautiful insect, the brown and orange upperwing distinguished by a distinctive and vivid violet sheen. A book resulting from an academic symposium on the butterfly is beguilingly entitled

Jewels in the Mist, referring to the damp conditions that the bistort and hence the Violet Copper prefer.

I did not see a Violet Copper on that or any other day. But later in the afternoon, as I started to pick a way downhill on paths and tracks into pine woods on the eastern side of the ridge, I saw two other butterflies. One was another upland species, seen only in Britain in the Scottish Highlands and the Lake District – and our only true mountain butterfly. Medium-sized, with a dark brown upperside to its wings and with orange patches containing dark spots towards the rear edge. A Mountain Ringlet, a *moiré de la canche*, labelled affectionately by one writer as 'that dusky denizen of the high hills'; *moiré* means 'iridescence' or 'shimmering' and *canche* is matgrass, which grows in tufty clumps on poor upland soils. Then an orangey-brown butterfly in the skipper family feeding on a white bramble flower, this one a Large Skipper I thought – but small in relation to what we usually think of as a large butterfly. Common in southern Britain and throughout the rest of western Europe – a *sylvaine* in French, reflecting one of its habitats of woodland rides and clearings, although as with the White Admiral back in the Sologne the etymology is maybe clearer to the English, with Sylvaine now a French girl's name to match Sylvain for the boys. Skippers of this colour are easy to identify from other butterflies since at rest they hold their forewings and hindwings behind them at different angles and as a result look a bit like the feathering of a dart or an arrow. And with their prominent heads and fat bodies like other skippers, they also seem a bit like moths. Indeed some guides say the skippers are not true butterflies at all and sit somewhere between the two, forming a separate superfamily within the Lepidoptera, the order of insects into which butterflies and moths are classified.

A third butterfly, sitting quietly in sunlight on a bush, foxed me. Small with dark brown, almost black, outstretched wings, a tiny, delicate fringe of white on their tips. Beautiful... But what was it? And then I slowly realised it was not a butterfly at all. Looking closely I saw its antennae lacked the all important clubbed ends of the butterflies (more like hooks in the case of some of the skippers). So it really had to be a moth this time, one of the group that fly by day. My phone's butterfly app included some of these and after a bit of digging around, there it was. The Chimney Sweeper moth, common in both Britain and continental Europe, and known by the same profession in French, *un ramoneur*. I'd never taken any interest in moths. The only one I knew already by name was the enchanting Humming Bird Hawk-moth, also a day-flyer, which does not seem like a moth at all – more like a bumble bee with bigger wings, no buzz and an enormous proboscis as it hovers, wings whirring a-hum, probing flowers. But 'systematists have arrived at the conclusion', declared my grandfather's old field guide, 'that there is no actual line of division between moths and butterflies' and a century later that still seems to be the general view. The French worry less about the distinction, butterflies being *papillons de jour* and moths *papillons de nuit* even if day and night evidently do not provide a hard and fast dividing line. Moths. A slippery slope. Although I will almost certainly never see them all, the fewer than sixty of British butterflies at least feels like a number I can get to grips with. But there are a good 2,000 different moths to be found in Britain and two or three times that many in France.

Down and down I went through the pines. The air became ever more redolent with the scent of resin and on rounding a corner I saw the cause, a massive yellow, tracked cutting machine at rest on a large slope of fresh tree stumps, still oozing, the trunks stripped of their side branches but not yet piled. In time I got to the bottom, to a hamlet where I sat resting in the shade against a wall of the little church, drinking water, oblivious to the house martins popping in and out of their mud nests that clung to the eaves above until one of them shat on me.

I pushed on up over a lateral ridge and then finally emerged from the woods at the village of St-Haon-le-Vieux. Smart houses. Everything up together. Another world to St-Léon, Montcombroux-les-Mines, and Arfeuilles. The population of St-Haon-le-Vieux has increased by more than half since its low point in the 1960s and is now back up to its pre-First World War level. The village is just twenty minutes' easy drive from the centre of Roanne – and work. And a different agriculture to the other side of the Monts de la Madeleine with a substantial belt of vineyards on the last of the slope before the wide Loire valley bottom. I found lodgings for the night in the outskirts of the village with a young couple of *vignerons* who were producing Côte Roannaise, a red wine made mainly from the Gamay grape like Beaujolais over the hills to the east. Not that vineyards producing wine with an *appellation d'origine contrôlée* necessarily mean rich farmers and rich villages. My hosts told me quietly of the hail in a recent year and of the late frost in another, sudden happenings that had set them back.

The next morning, after breakfast under a big acacia tree, an easy half-day's walk across the fields brought me to Roanne. I passed within a half a mile of a little aerodrome. It was a Saturday and a skydiving club was practising. I sat watching in the shade of a hedge as a little plane climbed higher and higher in circles, engine straining, before it levelled out and then after a few seconds, puff, a parachute suddenly opened way below and then quickly afterwards, puff, puff, a couple more. The plane landed and ten minutes later took off again and the same sequence unfolded. I watched time after time, trying to predict when and where the parachutes would open, always getting it wrong. At last, I got to my feet and walked on feeling very lucky. The skydivers had one sort of freedom and I had another.

6

Heat

The sun glared down, pitiless. Mid-morning but the temperature was already soaring towards the heights of the previous day. What would it reach – the high thirties? Forty even? Any conversation later on would surely turn to the heat if it didn't start with the subject straightaway. I was walking along a level track but the sweat still poured out of me. Rivulets trickled down my forehead, out from under my straw hat and down my face. My shirt was already soaked and clung everywhere. The backs of my knees oozed. My hazel stick slid through my hand, oily smooth. I looked ahead. The only shade for the next mile was the occasional tree every few hundred yards. Progress became spasmodic – my aim was just to reach the next tree where I could stop for a moment. *Thermidor*, the revolutionary calendar's month of the heat, had come early. And it was doing its rebellious best. This was *la canicule,* the heatwave, which for ten days that summer gripped France like a vice.

It is easy to complain about walking when it's hot. I joined in willingly in the daily grumbling about *la chaleur*, the heat, the standard topic in shops, bars, hotels, restaurants, indeed with anyone I met, accepting gratefully the sympathy often given to me as *un marcheur*. The usual parting encouragement to walkers was at last appropriate – '*Courage!*' There is a big difference between walking in temperatures in the mid-twenties, already tiring, and those ten or more degrees higher – temperatures that, literally, sap you. You drink huge quantities of water to replace what is coming out. I can remember days when I drank five, even six litres. A note scribbled in my diary at noon one day laments: 'Need water but only water hot', my second water bottle – the first one long empty – having cooked up in my rucksack. This was the only part of my journey when I had to knock on a door to ask for help, to ask for water.

However, a heatwave beats persistent rain. In her book *Rain* on walking in 'English weather', as the subtitle puts it, Melissa Harrison makes a good argument for the joys of a wet day's outing. And the occasional shower or thunderstorm on a walking holiday is fine. But rain day after day ruins everything. 'The most patient people grow weary at last with being continually wetted', wrote Stevenson. Rain eventually soaks you despite any waterproof – it just gets in somehow. Or the waterproof makes you sweat anyway. Unlike with the heat, you cannot just spread your shirt on a bush at lunchtime, or hang up your washing in the evening and find it bone dry in the morning. Your boots become sodden and remain that way – putting on damp socks and wet boots is especially dispiriting. There are either no views to be had, the rain shuttering out all, or at best murky landscapes, drained of colour, merging with the grey sky above. Few birds, no butterflies, flowers beaten down, vegetation everywhere dripping. Lunchtime stops become only brief pauses, huddled under a tree or an overhanging rock. Sleeping in the open becomes a misery, even with a good bivvy bag, and you try very hard to avoid it. I may have been unlucky to have the *canicule* during my crossing of France but I was fortunate to have little rain.

And some pleasures come with the heat too. The solidarity felt with all you meet, transcending barriers of language. A cold drink in a bar or café becomes something absolutely perfect, impossible to better – you cannot imagine how it could be so good – the nectar of the gods. The inferno of the day is replaced with the delicious contrast of the cool of the evening and, even better, the early morning. That cool is only relative – the temperature may never fall below twenty degrees even in the hours before daybreak – but you luxuriate in your temporary escape from the oven. How good it is to be in shorts and shirtsleeves whatever the hour, however late or early. And if you adapt your use of the day to the weather, as finally I managed, you experience that new sensation of getting up in the dark while the world sleeps on, quietly moving about preparing your pack, and then stepping out into the still of the dawn.

* * *

The *canicule* arrived while I was in Roanne. I stayed in a hotel near the railway station for two nights, giving a first full day off since Gien, nearly three weeks earlier. A rest day again in a Loire town, a month since arriving at the river at Blois. The first night I was bothered persistently by a mosquito that was thriving in the heat. At last, enraged, I jumped out of bed in the early hours, turned on the light, and eventually got it. But the red splat showed that it had got me first.

My hotel was on the western side of town, the bulk of which lies to the west of the river, and my first priority after checking in was to hasten on east and see the Loire again. The river still hooked and reeled me in. I headed through town to the main bridge, a long, early-nineteenth-century construction in stone with seven arches, which replaced earlier wooden crossings swept away in floods. Looking out across the water, the river seemed little smaller than it had on first sight all that time ago. 'It is here a good river... at a vast distance from the sea,' commented Arthur Young in 1789 on passing through Roanne. As if to emphasise this importance, over five hundred miles from its mouth, the river gives its name to the surrounding *département*. Moreover, not a name that combines or qualifies the Loire, as elsewhere. It is not 'Loire-Atlantique', 'Maine-et-Loire', 'Indre-et-Loire', 'Saône-et-Loire', or 'Haute-Loire' – it is simply 'Loire'. And here in Roanne, I would at last be leaving the Loire for good.

Roanne is where serious navigation of the Loire begins, whether by the lateral canal that I had declined to walk along in preference to crossing the Monts de la Madeleine, a waterway extended south to Roanne from Digoin in the 1830s, or by the river itself in earlier times. Above Roanne are gorges, now dammed. A leaflet I picked up in the tourist office claimed that the port of Roanne was once the second largest in France, such was the significance of river and canal for trade, notably in coal from mines to the south at St-Étienne, the capital of the *département*, and in the textiles for which Roanne was long famous. 'Many flat-bottomed barges on it, of a considerable size,' noted Young about traffic on the river. The town centre is a little way from the water, presumably due to the risk of flooding before the dams upstream were built. Roanne is not a Blois or a Gien with a chateau and church on high ground dominating the river and its location lacks any other obvious physical charm. It is just a town built on the level in the valley bottom.

On his journey down the length of the Loire in 1913, Douglas Goldring quickly dismissed Roanne: 'with the best intentions in the world, I could not discover any redeeming features.' I explored in earnest the next day, a baking hot, dead Sunday with much of the centre closed, the buildings lining the streets like the walls of a furnace. I too did not fall in love with the town. The main church underwent an unfortunate restoration in the nineteenth century and all that remains of the old chateau is a square sixty-foot-tall tower. However, Goldring was too quick in reaching his verdict and there are certainly bits of Roanne worth seeing. I tried to get inside a large, early-seventeenth-century Jesuit chapel, said to have a most impressive interior. It was locked but I could still admire the simple, light, classical facade with its small twin towers topped with cupolas poking up on each side of the central pediment. I liked a long, three-storey, late-eighteenth-century building that now houses the sub-prefecture, with tall windows and white-painted external shutters – although it was the shade of a huge cedar of Lebanon behind the railings of the grounds outside that I really wanted. The nineteenth-century development associated with canal and railway produced riches that not only gave the church its makeover but also led to some fine public buildings, such as the imposing Second Empire *hôtel de ville* and the nearby neat little neoclassical *théâtre municipal*. I passed a stone town house built in the twentieth century, shortly before Goldring's visit, its art nouveau front decorated with little sculptures and delicate railed balconies. And, with sightseeing done, if you really want to splash out while in Roanne, you can try a long-standing, three-star Michelin restaurant, one of only a dozen or so outside Paris in all of France. I ate well – a local speciality of potato pancakes, *râpées de St-Étienne*, and an enormous salad – in somewhere much more humble, sitting at a table on the pavement in a narrow little side street under the hot night sky.

* * *

Late that evening I crossed the road from my hotel to the station. A tall, dark-haired man got off the last train from Lyon, well tanned with stubble beard and broad smile and carrying a battered blue rucksack with an old camping mat crammed on top of a sleeping bag. '*Allora, basta con questa natura, storia, eccetera – mi stavi aspettando per gozzovigliare!*' Riccardo had arrived, an old friend from Florence. No more nature or history, we were going to carouse. With some effort I dragged my mind from French to Italian but kept on mixing up my languages, much to Riccardo's amusement. We would now strike east from Roanne, out of the valley of the Loire, over the high hills I had seen from the Monts de la Madeleine, and then down into the valley of the Saône and the Rhône.

We set off the next morning far too late after talking into the night and dawdling over breakfast. A final crossing of the Loire on the last day of June, with both a twinge of regret and a glow of anticipation, and we started out through Roanne's eastern suburbs under a cloudless sky. But try as we might, we could not pick up footpaths to take us in the direction that we wanted to go. This was one of the few stretches of my route across France where there was no suitable GR path and maps marked no useful local substitutes; it ended up my only day spent entirely on tarmac. We soon started labouring in the heat and at our first brief stop in shade Riccardo immediately went to sleep, a knack he would demonstrate repeatedly. We traced our way uphill on a network of lanes past fields on the lower slopes where the grain harvest had started, great round bales of straw waiting for collection on the shaved stubble. Wide views opened up back over the Loire valley and to the Monts de la Madeleine on the horizon beyond, the *éoliennes* I had walked beneath three days earlier just visible, their arms still not turning. We had booked no beds for the night, Riccardo insisting we were on a *zingarata*, a carefree gypsy jaunt. We both had sleeping bags he declared. What would happen would happen. My suggestion of looking ahead was deemed far too Anglo-Saxon, although by our lunch stop Riccardo said the one thing he must have that evening was a shower. An hour or two before sunset, we came hot and grimy to the large village of Thizy, with luck found a cheap, friendly little hotel, ate outside on the terrace, and were in bed by nine, showered.

From then on we became more serious about our starts, rising as early as we could force ourselves in order to make some decent progress before the day hotted up. From Thizy, we worked up and down a tangled series of wooded ridges, each at around 2,000 feet. The afternoon was spent in the shade on top of one of them, snoozing and reading, whiling away the worst of the heat. Another ridge took us over a watershed; six weeks after crossing the Forêt d'Écouves in Normandy with Andrew, north of Alençon, I was finally out of land drained by the Loire or one of its tributaries. Water now flowed not behind, north and west to the Atlantic, but ahead, east and south to the Mediterranean, with all that this meant in terms of progress made and another part of France slowly opening up.

The trees we had been among since our afternoon halt rolled back and we stopped towards sunset on an open hillside just below the crest of yet another wooded ridge. A village huddled in the valley below, church with tower and little steeple prominent, and beyond, out in front of us, were more hills still to be crossed, covered with a patchwork of woods and high pasture. The slanting rays of the departing sun bathed the scene, capped with a sky as clear as it had been all day. We repeated our simple picnic lunch, this time helped down with a bottle of wine we had picked up along the way – hardly carousal but it made a welcome change from warm water. The air finally cooled, helped by a gentle breath of wind, and we got into our sleeping bags as dusk was falling.

I was about to drop off, lying on my back gazing vacantly at the sky above, when a pair of birds came out of a tree close behind and flew quickly and silently across us in the gloaming. They looked a bit larger than a blackbird but smaller than a pigeon, with long, pointed wings and narrow wedge-shaped tails. I couldn't think what they were. The wrong shape for an owl. I thought no more of it and began to drift off. Suddenly, a strange sound came from trees some way off to my left in the direction in which the birds had gone. 'Trrrrrrrrrrrr, drrrrrrrrrrrr, trrrrrrrrrrrr, drrrrrrrrrrrr', a fast, loud chur, alternating occasionally in pitch, each note held for maybe ten or fifteen seconds at a time. The sequence went on for a minute or so. The same noise came again several times, always the same rising and falling sound, the change always coming abruptly. The call of the quail in a field of wheat had puzzled me back in the Sarthe but now I knew straightaway what this sound must be. Only one bird could be responsible. I had never heard it before, but this had to be the cry of a nightjar.

The nightjar or the mysterious 'goatsucker', believed to take milk at night from the udders of goats and cows. And still its name in Italian, *succiacapre*, and its scientific name, *caprimulgus*. But the nightjar eats only insects, especially moths, hoovered up with its mouth held wide as it hunts on the night airs – its French name, *engoulevent*, comes from an old word meaning 'to swallow greedily'. The bird is entirely nocturnal, spending the day crouched motionless along a tree branch or sitting on the ground, relying on camouflage to escape attention – with grey-brown, mottled plumage, it seems just a piece of dead wood – and emerging only in the twilight that foreshadows the true darkness. It is a bird of heaths and of the edges of pine woods: another of its old names is the fern owl, celebrated in John Clare's haunting, short poem 'The Fern Owl's Nest'. ('The weary woodman rocking home beneath his tightly banded faggot wonders oft while crossing over the furze-crowded heath to hear the fern owl's cry…')

My father wrote of first hearing a nightjar as a teenager in the late 1920s, on a night-time excursion with my grandparents to the North Downs to see the sun rise on Midsummer's Day, and then of not hearing one again until the war when he was stationed for a while with the navy at Chatham. Nightjars are migrants from Africa that reach southern England in only modest numbers, their population much reduced by the decline in heathland. Sixty years after his first encounter, he made an effort to hear the bird again 'before it is too late', although reading this I wondered whether he was referring to himself as much as to the nightjar, whose numbers are now recovering a little. At dusk, on midsummer's eve again, with 'a Cheshire cheese-coloured full moon' rising over a heath in southern Dorset, 'I walked up through the pines to the top of a ridge where the trees stopped. Suddenly, magically, so faint that I hardly believed it, a reeling rattle began.' He wrote of this renewal of meeting with the nightjar as having 'the old youthful quality' of the excitement at first hearing and identifying new birdsong. I felt that excitement keenly on our ridge top in France. I had at last heard the reeling rattle of the nightjar.

* * *

It was not yet five o'clock. The moon, one day off the full, had risen from behind the hills while we slept and ranged over us like a searchlight in the small hours before falling away out of sight again. Night still ruled at this southern latitude but its reign was ending – the black outline of the hills to the east was crowned with a stripe of orange merging into the darkest of blues above. We packed in sleepy silence, the light rapidly increasing and the forms of the ridges and valleys around us becoming clear. The blue lightened and slowly other colours came into the world. The fields below began to show green and the woods started to lose their obscurity. We were away quickly and it was wonderful to be up and walking at this hour with the 'strange exhilaration' that Stevenson reported when rising at dawn after his night among the pines of the Cévennes: 'a solemn glee possessed my mind at this gradual and lovely coming in of day.'

We threaded through dark pine woods, the darkness slowly surrendering as beams of light forced their way with increasing vigour between the trees. A wide swath of the horizon now had the orange band, lighter than before. Finally, an hour after we had woken, a yellow sun peeped up through the orange behind a hill ahead. All around us swiftly changed, the dimness everywhere of twilight replaced by gleaming, bright, fresh sunshine on the hillsides to the west contrasted with the dense shade of the slopes in front to the east and in the valley below. The blue of the sky, again cloudless, sharpened and deepened again. Far away in a now lit-up field, a herd of creamy-white Charolais cattle were on their feet, each cow boasting a brand new shadow behind.

We walked on, dropping slowly on farm tracks and then more steeply, arriving at a village in a valley bottom at seven. There was a bar and it was open. Perfect, coffee. But the *boulangerie* was closed for the day. We waited an hour for a little *épicerie* run by a young Vietnamese couple to open, only to find its shelves strangely empty and devoid of anything we wanted to buy. We had lost an hour of the early-morning cool and the day was starting to heat up again.

Our route east took us through a quiet side valley on a forestry track, climbing up the hillside through oak woods towards yet another ridge a thousand feet above. The gradient was easy, so easy that it lulled us along and we missed the path we wanted that somewhere at the head of the valley turned off steeply uphill between the trees. The track zigzagged back and forth as it gently wound its way up the opposite valley side, and we grumbled to each other about walking further than we would have had to on the missed path. First the lost hour waiting for the *épicerie* and then this. It was too much. Eventually the track flattened out and contoured along through the woods. It widened as it passed a spring emerging out of the hillside through a pipe, the water trickling down into a stone trough. Still grumbling we stopped to take a breather and shed our rucksacks for a few minutes. '*Già fa un caldo boia,*' Riccardo grunted indignantly as the sun blazed down on us – it was already 'hangman hot'.

Looking around, I saw a large, dark-coloured butterfly settle on the ground on the other side of the track and wandered over to take a closer look. And then I stared, unable to believe what I was seeing. The undersides of the half-closed wings were a mixture of grey, white, and reddish-brown, with one large eye-spot of concentric circles of orange, black and, at its centre, white. I could just see dark brown or black colouring with white patches on the uppersides, the colours of a White Admiral. But it was too big to be one of those – it seemed huge – and the underside markings were distinctive in any case. It was a butterfly that I had doubted I would ever see, whether in England, France or anywhere else. It was a Purple Emperor.

'A sighting of this magnificent insect represents the pinnacle of ambition of most butterfly enthusiasts' starts the entry to the Purple Emperor in my field guide to British butterflies. And in his absorbing account of trying to see all of Britain's fifty-nine species in one summer, *The Butterfly Isles*, Patrick Barkham writes that 'no other butterfly has attracted so many names, tributes and epithets', devoting a whole chapter to it. My introduction to the Emperor was my father reading to me and my siblings *Brendon Chase* by 'B. B.', the pen name of Denys Watkins-Pitchford, our family copy an old first edition from 1944 with sun-faded green covers and the author's own stunning dark, full-page scraperboard illustrations. Three brothers run away from their aunt to live in a forest in southern England. The elderly local vicar blunders through the woods one day in hope of finding his first Purple Emperor, and manages a brief encounter with one on the wing. He goes home jubilant – '*He had seen a Purple Emperor!* He could think of nothing else.' The image stuck and I had dreamed of thinking the same.

The Emperor is powerful and aggressive with 'the morals of an orc', as one seasoned observer has put it. Males will even try to chase off birds from their territories. Its French name fits the bill, *le grand mars changeant*, after the god of war. And it is very hard to see. Purple Emperors spend their time in woodland in the treetops, feeding on sap and on aphid honeydew left on leaves. Females almost never descend to the ground. Males may occasionally come down, alighting to obtain moisture and salt from mud, dung, or dead animals, the latter preferences only adding to the butterfly's reputation. My grandfather's guide reports 'the insect's rather depraved taste for the juices of animal matter in a somewhat advanced state of decay'. Laying out rotting meat on a forest ride is a recognised way of attracting the Purple Emperor – B. B.'s vicar thinks to return 'with a very ripe rabbit and hang it up on one of the oaks'. But many people's sightings are nevertheless just of the butterfly in flight, high above them. A website devoted to the Emperor warns: 'this is not an insect you will stumble upon, unless you are blessed with extraordinary luck. He must be sought out, in suitable country, and even there the untrained eye may totally fail to spot him.' And here one was, right in front of me on the track.

In line with its reputation for the unsavoury, my Purple Emperor was crawling intently over a discarded cigarette butt. I rummaged in a pocket for my phone and then fumbled desperately to turn on the camera app, my hands already sweaty now seemed to be sweating even more. The Emperor was unconcerned, even regally disdainful, as I crouched down at his side. After completing a close inspection he eventually left the fag end and moved on to investigate a pebble nearby. I took photos until he eventually spread his wings – displaying the glorious purple sheen on the uppersides that is found only on the male, the iridescence, the *changeant* – and in the same instant took off, flying with purpose up and away towards the tree canopy above. If we had been more alert, I would never have seen him. We would have taken the path that turned off below.

* * *

Towards evening, we crossed our last ridge, came down out of the woods and found spread out before us a landscape of gentle low hills falling away to the great, wide valley beyond of the Rhône and the Saône. But it was not the geography that most impressed the eye. It was the vines. Vines everywhere, carpeting the land, rolling over the slopes. We'd happened on the very heart of the production of Beaujolais. Late sun lit up the rippling flow of the lines of light green vines, the little hamlets and villages dotted here and there, and the dark background of woodland on the higher ground we were leaving. Work was in progress in the vineyards pruning foliage to let the sun get at the grapes and to stop excess growth taking away the plants' strength. I had naively assumed the job was still done by hand but here was a man sitting atop a motorised pruner that spanned each row of vines on tall spindly legs.

We arrived at the village of Oingt, its smart appearance belying its porcine-sounding name: restaurants, a pottery shop, an art gallery, but nothing much for the locals. The buildings were constructed of a golden-coloured local stone known, suitably, as *pierres dorées*. This, according to the headline in the local newspaper, has attracted the attention of '*les experts UNESCO*' who were considering giving this part of the Beaujolais area the status of a 'Global Geopark'. The label would probably help the restaurants and the galleries, but it is less clear that it would bring back other shops. A poster in a window of the pottery shop gave advice about the *canicule*. Drink water regularly (agreed). Eat properly (ditto). Don't drink alcohol (hold on). Avoid physical effort (now there's a problem). We ate little that evening out of choice, despite the poster's instruction, both of us too hot and tired after a long day, and then began to look around on the edge of the village for somewhere to sleep in the open once more. But instead we stumbled on a B&B. Ahh… a shower again, clean sheets.

We had wandered east from Roanne across the ridges in an unplanned manner, our route determined by whatever paths we could find as we went along. Had we been aiming for any particular destination I would probably have chosen Vaux-en-Beaujolais, a village just a few miles to the north of Oingt. This was the setting for the hugely successful satirical novel *Clochemerle*, written in the 1930s by Gabriel Chevallier, which follows the ructions in village life after the installation outside the church of a urinal, *un pissoir*. The BBC serialised the book on television in the 1970s and the memory of its picture of a bucolic, rural inter-war France stayed with me, probably more so than was justified given the satire. Looking at the Vaux-en-Beaujolais commune website now, a visit would only have led to disappointment. The village all looks so neat and tidy, like Oingt, and unsurprisingly the Clochemerle name, the book's characters, and Chevallier are all milked heavily in the commune's efforts to attract tourists. The square is dominated by the advertising of a wineshop called the 'Cave de Clochemerle' and an ornate, old-fashioned *pissoir* has been placed in the square's centre.

Clochemerle was translated into two dozen other languages, has sold millions, and was followed by two sequels. But Chevallier was capable of much more serious work than a rural farce with greedy peasants, voluptuous landladies, and a priest who drinks two litres of Beaujolais a day. Before achieving success with *Clochemerle*, he wrote an autobiographical novel based on his time as a private in the infantry in northern France during the First World War. *La Peur* was published in English only in 2011, dropping the definite article for its title, *Fear*. It is a bitter anti-war statement, the bitterness directed especially at the disregard for human life of mid-ranking officers and generals. Chevallier held back nothing in his description of the horrors of trench warfare. The clinging stench of putrefied flesh when a pickaxe goes through a body buried in the mud. The constant clambering past corpses in order to get anywhere. The sight of a field covered in blue as his section arrives at the forward trench to support an attack, with the realisation that the blue is the uniformed bodies of comrades killed in the first wave of the assault. And the fear that seems in particular to have led to the book's title, the terror of artillery bombardment day after day after day. It would be facile to think that Chevallier turned to a light-hearted send-up of country life just to push his memories behind him. Whatever the reason, the gulf in subject matter between the two books demonstrates his versatility as a writer, although on re-reading *Clochemerle*, I wondered if there was some bitterness there too, beneath the satire.

* * *

A map of France's geography shows a long, wide valley stretching north from the delta of the Rhône in the Camargue. The valley rises up the map between the Massif Central to the west and the Alps to the east, narrowing a bit to the south of Lyon but then opening out again as your eye moves on up past Dijon and beyond, the Burgundy hills on the left and the Jura mountains on the right. At first sight, it looks as if this is all the valley of the Rhône. But a closer inspection shows that in the northern half, the valley has been created by a different river, the Saône, and the Rhône is nowhere to be seen. What has happened to it? Look closer and you see that the Rhône rises well to the east in southern Switzerland, drains the northern slopes of the Matterhorn and neighbouring peaks, flows into Lake Geneva, and then on exit carves its way between the Alps and the Jura, tacking westwards before turning sharp left to the south, through ninety degrees, at Lyons, at exactly the point where it is joined by the Saône. This was the valley that we now had to cross.

Another day east from Oingt, through yet more vines, brought us down to the valley bottom not far north of Lyon. The mighty Saône stretched northwards, to be connected about sixty miles upriver by the Canal du Centre over a low point in the Burgundy hills to the Loire at Digoin. Further north again other canals allow passage from the Saône to the Seine, to the Marne and even to the Rhine, the last of these thus linking the Mediterranean with the North Sea. We slept in a chalet in a stifling campsite by the side of the Saône, our sleep postponed by a long and desperate struggle with the lock after returning late from supper, the camp office long closed. We took it in turns to fiddle with the key, silently cursing and laughing in the dark, each accusing the other of gross incompetence as our efforts became ever more frantic. A night outside with the mosquitos loomed but finally the door gave way.

We were now back in territory where there was an obvious route to take, a GR. It led east across a wide, flat area that lies to the north of the Rhône as the river makes its way west from the mountains towards its confluence with the Saône. La Dombes is a low plateau of boulder clay, some thirty miles across, east to west and north to south, dotted with hundreds of little lakes. Like those of the Sologne, the lakes are almost all man-made, created by monks in the Middle Ages in the dips in the clay to stimulate a fishing industry to supply Lyon. And as in the Sologne, with the lakes came mosquitoes and malaria. Absentee landlords and poor soils played their parts as well and so La Dombes became another long-standing area of sickness, child death, short lives and destitution. The 1996 film *Ridicule*, which won the prize for best film in the Césars, tells the story of a local aristocrat from La Dombes – one who cares – going to the court of Louis XVI to seek the backing of the King to drain the malarial swamps and improve the life of the peasants. It ends with the Revolution and the drainage work finally starting. But the film's action is firmly set in Versailles – this is not another *Raboliot* with all its scenes of the watery landscape of the Sologne. And the drainage work can't have got far. Writing in 1859, a local engineer summarised the area: 'sadness, loneliness, disease and poverty, that is La Dombes.'

The malaria is now long gone from the 'land of a thousand ponds… its treasures of fauna, flora, patrimony, gastronomy', as a tourist brochure promotes La Dombes, emphasising its tranquillity and in particular the huge range of birds. It would be nice to recount the joys of moving slowly through this quiet area of water and wildlife, and when planning my way across France back in England I had looked expectantly at the red line of the GR on the map snaking its way between the little lakes. But in the main the crossing of La Dombes was just a long, hot struggle. This is largely open country, without the woods of the Sologne. After the cool of an early-morning start from our campsite by the Saône, we trudged most of the day through lengthy treeless stretches, heads down, willing ourselves on. The green lakes seemed surprisingly uninviting. Records show it was thirty-eight degrees that afternoon in Lyon. A road sign at one point twisted the knife with a warning of 'verglas fréquent', frequent ice. A pair of scavenging black kites cruised back and forth not far above for a while, tails twisting this way and that as they ruddered their way around a small patch of sky, looking down on us hopefully.

At the halfway point, Riccardo left me at a smart commuter village after a celebratory supper to round off our time together, taking the train south to meet his family who were joining him from Italy. '*Vai, torna alla tua natura – e attento alle serrature!*' he ordered on boarding the train: 'Go on, back to your nature – and mind the door locks!' Alas, he missed the better of the two days needed to cross the plateau. The second day produced more shade and the going was easier. At one point, in woods, I passed the stunning little thirteenth-century chateau of Montellier, built of brick, its perfect red towers and turrets poking up through the trees. The same family has owned the chateau since a few years before the Revolution and the familiar green post box of houses in country areas at its entrance in the lane had a certain style – a handwritten label stated that the inhabitant was '*Richard du Montellier*' above the usual request for no junk mail, '*Pas de Pub. Merci*'.

* * *

I met the Rhône the next day at noon outside the small town of Lagnieu. The river had just finished a long run to the north-west in a final zigzag after leaving the Alps and was now turning back sharply to head towards Lyon. Wooded ridges studded with forbidding limestone bluffs rose abruptly a thousand feet up on the eastern side of town, a last thrust south of the Jura. They shouted 'high ground' in a way that I had not been expecting, despite it all having been very obvious from the map. The eastern edge of the great Rhône-Saône valley. The Alps and the last part of my journey were suddenly close and the realisation was unsettling. I didn't feel quite prepared. The flatlands were finished. I had to confront the mountains now. Real mountains.

But not just yet. I was not going to climb those ridges above me. I had always meant to when making my plans but I could never settle on a route. The paths marked on the map were not quite heading where I wanted and the geography beyond seemed intricate and a little baffling. And climbing now in the heat of the *canicule* held no attraction. I decided to walk instead along the Rhône for a couple of days, on the narrow strip of land between the river and the high ground to the east. I would be heading upstream, on the right bank, tracing the river back up the length of that north-westerly run that ended at the point where I was standing.

This arrival at the Rhône in early July felt quite different to that bright, fresh windy afternoon back on the first of June when I reached the Loire at Blois. There, the sky had been full of seabirds wheeling in the wind, the colours everywhere vivid, the little waves capped with white horses. Here, under the deadening heat from a midday sun, the colour was washed out of the land, no birds around, the air still, and the river looking big, deep, powerful, and very slightly ominous. The surface of the water had an oily calm as the current slipped by. Not the *taureau furieux*, the 'raging bull' as the Rhône is sometimes called, but nevertheless a little menacing. A small jolt to the world and the waters of Lake Geneva would come pouring out and I would be swept away down to Lyon and beyond. The scene before me was also strangely lacking in any evidence of river traffic. No boats, no navigation markers. This was not the Loire with all its shallows and sandbanks that so hindered its use over the centuries – it was the Rhône for heaven's sake. After all, below its junction with the Saône at Lyon the Rhône is a major waterway. Cruise lines offer week-long trips on huge tourist boats down the valley to Avignon and the delta. Enormous barges carrying up to 3,000 tons come upstream. Not far north of the Lyon junction, I'd looked down from the bridge over the Saône that Riccardo and I had crossed at sunrise after our night in the campsite chalet and had seen the red and green navigation buoys guiding boats and barges that arrive from the Mediterranean going north or that are heading south to the Rhône and the sea. It all seemed a bit odd.

A few miles further upriver, at the village of Sault-Brénaz, the situation became clearer. There, either side of a long, three-arched nineteenth-century stone bridge, two rocky bands stretch across the Rhône forming lines of rapids. The river drops seven feet in the course of about a hundred yards – *sault* is an old spelling for the French for a 'jump'. The rapids of Sault-Brénaz are just one of the barriers to navigation on the upper Rhône. Gorges – as the river fights its way out of the mountains – other rapids, and huge surges of rain or melt water all combined in the past to severely limit traffic. In contrast to the Loire, a fast, full current characterises the river even in normal times. Nor were these problems unique to the upper Rhône. Surges originating in the Alps kept on going downriver. And until the 1970s, the stretch from Lyon to the sea, now extensively canalised, also presented huge hazards as the river dropped over five hundred feet in these last two hundred miles, a much greater rate of descent than for other major European rivers. A 1950s guidebook of the Canoe Club de France said of the Rhône: 'strictly speaking, it is not a river: it is a great torrent.' The *taureau furieux*.

Efforts were made on the upper Rhône to overcome these problems and the evidence was there to be seen at Sault-Brénaz. I walked the length of a tall stone quay, several hundred yards long, that still carried great iron mooring rings, each almost a foot in diameter measured by my boots. Some of the boats that had come upriver this far simply loaded up with stone from the quarries in the nearby cliffs to the east and did not confront the 'jump'. But others struggled on up, hauled by teams of horses, and later by steam. And in the middle of the river, running through an island, was a short section of canal with a lock, built to circumvent the rapids, that opened in 1890. However, competition rose from rail and road. By the 1930s, river traffic on the upper Rhône beyond Lyon had died out.

The post-war canalising of the river south of Lyon came with various hydroelectric schemes to exploit its relatively steep descent. The upper river has also seen low barrages thrown across it for the same purpose, including one at Sault-Brénaz in the 1980s on the other side of the island that carried the now disused little canal. Attempts have been made to encourage pleasure boating higher up as stretches of the river down from Lake Geneva became navigable once more. But the barrage at Sault-Brénaz has no lock and together with a similar barrage thirty miles upriver it is an effective stop to the passage of all but smaller craft. The Compagnie Nationale du Rhône, which runs the hydroelectric schemes, reports on its website that a *'chariot transbordeur'* can carry your boat around the barrage at Sault-Brénaz if it is no more than nine and a half metres long and three tonnes in weight. But in two days of walking I saw no boats on the river. Maps of the French waterways still show a straight blue line coming up the Rhône-Saône valley, past Lyon, and on towards northern France, with a blank space to the east where runs the upper Rhône.

* * *

The 2006 film *Indigènes* ('Natives'), released in Britain as *Days of Glory*, tells the story of Berber volunteers from colonial Algeria who join the Free French army and take part in the invasion of southern France by the Allies in August 1944. The landings on the coast of Provence, two months after those in Normandy, were followed by a swift advance up the Rhône valley with Lyon liberated by early September. The film was a commercial and critical success, winning prizes at Cannes and at the César awards and a nomination for the best foreign language film at the Oscars. It did much to draw attention to the discrimination against the wartime colonial troops and to the French government's subsequent treatment of veterans from the former colonies. But soldiers from her African empire had fought for France in the Rhône valley during the Second World War long before 1944. A plaque on the riverbank at Sault-Brénaz, just before the bridge, told of the part played in June 1940 by troops not from North Africa but from West Africa, the Tirailleurs Sénégalais – 'Senegalese Sharpshooters'.

The Tirailleurs Sénégalais came not only from Senegal, France's original African possession, but also from the other colonies that made up the huge confederation of French West Africa, including Mauritania, Mali, Niger, and the Ivory Coast. By the time of the German invasion in the spring of 1940, over 100,000 Tirailleurs Sénégalais had been recruited into the French army, largely through conscription, of whom about two thirds saw service in the defence of France. The plaque at Sault-Brénaz commemorates the *tirailleurs* who on June 19, 1940 first blew the bridge to prevent the Germans crossing over to the left bank, the western side of the river at this point, and then for two days fought successfully to prevent a pontoon bridge being constructed in its place.

The German army swept south in 1940 even more quickly than the Allies pushed north up the Rhône in 1944. Paris, three hundred miles away to the north-west, had been taken less than a week before the events recorded on the plaque I read. Pétain had already announced to the nation on June 17 that he would seek an armistice and the fighting at Sault-Brénaz took place just six days before it came into effect. The plaque does not recall the fate of the defenders of the bridge other than saying that they withdrew south towards Grenoble. Not far to the west, outside the village of Chasselay, near Lyon, just a few miles south of where I had crossed the Saône with Riccardo, about two hundred other Tirailleurs Sénégalais from the same regiment had fought on until they ran out of ammunition. On surrendering, they were separated from their white officers and shot. Nazi racial ideology viewed black soldiers as inferior, unworthy opponents and research has suggested that perhaps as many as several thousand captured black troops were massacred that summer. In all, about one in four of the Tirailleurs Sénégalais serving in France in 1940 lost their lives during or immediately after the fighting.

Reading the plaque at Sault-Brénaz, looking out at the bridge, not for the first time I thought of my generation's luck in never having had to fight and of the success of the former combatants in Europe in avoiding war again. About the only thing I had in common with the poor *tirailleurs* in their defence of the crossing was the heat – June 1940 had also been sweltering hot. That evening, I chanced on more evidence of the tragedies of war, a leaflet in my hotel for a museum commemorating the Jewish children and their teachers who lived nearby in the village of Izieu for a year from April 1943. Two black and white photos showed happy groups of children grinning at the camera, one with the Jura mountains behind that had been to the east of me all day, the other taken in front of the schoolhouse that was the children's home. The children had come after the Germans moved south into the *zone libre* of Vichy France following the Allied invasion of North Africa in November 1942. France east of the Rhône was occupied at this time by the Italians and many Jews in Vichy fled to the relative safety of the Italian zone, including the refugee school that came to Izieu. But after the fall of Mussolini and the Italian armistice in September 1943, the Germans took control of this part of France too. Six months later, the forty-four children and seven adults of the Izieu school were deported to A͏u͏schwitz, bar one child who jumped out of a window and ͏/͏ garden. One adult returned. And no child.

* * *

I was away the next morning before six. A steady march up the right bank of the river on the *levée* where sheep were grazing. I felt full of vim. The going was easy, it was beautifully cool, and there was always something to look at. A multitude of swans, dozens and dozens of them, floating serenely. An old car, its boot yawning wide, head down and half-submerged in the river. The occasional building over on the other bank catching the gentle, early-morning sunlight to best effect. A chateau with square tower and steeply pitched red tiled roof. A cement works. A nuclear power station, smartly painted in yellow and white together with its great, grey cooling tower. Towards nine o'clock I found a café for some breakfast in a riverside village and saw from the map that I was making good progress. I thought I could do anything, walk any distance – all I had to do was to continue along the riverbank. I should have taken more notice of another flock of sheep, already tightly huddled in the shade of a tree and hardly stirring as I passed close by. They knew what sort of day was coming.

The land between me and the high ground to the east suddenly shrank as the path took me through woods a little way in from the river. I lost my way, crossed some pasture and pressed on through a short marshy field that ended in tall reeds. Pushing the reeds apart, I found I was on the bank of a stream, clearly too deep to wade. But there was a submerged rock towards the other side that would serve as a stepping stone for one foot to hop on if I could jump that far. I threw my rucksack over to the opposite bank, took a couple of steps back for a better take-off, and then rushed and leapt after it, only the boot placed on the rock filling with water. Hah – done! Success further boosted my belief that this was going to be a day when all would go perfectly. Walking alone gives you the freedom to think all sorts of things that aren't so and to make plans that ·wards turn out to have been foolishly ambitious.

Farmers were drawing water from the river for their now head-high maize. A great drum of the thickest hose I'd ever seen, the drum standing tall above the crop, ever so slowly winding in the hose, almost imperceptibly, pulling in the sprayer set on a three-wheeled frame. Tuff... Tuff... Tuff... Tuff...! An enormous jet of water emerged at forty-five degrees, rotating in jerks in a huge arc above the rows of plants. I scarcely bothered to dodge the spray when it strayed onto the path.

I ploughed on. On along the riverbank, on past apple orchards and walnut groves, leaves hanging limp, on through small villages dozing in the heat, none of them with bars that were open, dogs barely raising themselves from their slumber to bark as I went by. It was now ferociously hot. Had I come across a hotel or a B&B I might have stopped for the day, but probably not – I had rigidly set myself the target of reaching the little town of St-Genix at the point where the Rhône emerges from the mountains and starts its north-westerly run to Lagnieu. The afternoon hours passed slowly and the temperature continued to rise. This was the day when I knocked on a door to seek water. I began to flag. I crossed the river on another bridge blown up in 1940, lumbered up a short, modest slope the other side that felt like a mountain, and slept for half an hour under an old apple tree in a field by a farmhouse. I trudged on down lanes, past houses and gardens of boiling little hamlets, past fields baking in the sun, and with frequent stops struggled along a final two-mile stretch of hot, wide track through woods to stumble at last into St-Genix. The town is on the Guiers, just short of where it joins the Rhône, and all of St-Genix youth was basking on rocks by the side of the water in the early-evening sun, occasionally taking a dip to cool off. A thermometer outside a chemist showed it was still thirty-five degrees.

A shop directed me to a hotel, but for no apparent reason it was closed. My spirits sank further and I wondered wearily what to do. Buy some food – and water – and head out of town again to cast about for a secluded corner of a field? The town surely could not run to another hotel. But suddenly I chanced on one, an old building set back a bit from the road by the river and surrounded by trees. However, it too seemed shut, undergoing work. In desperation I approached the front door where I could see someone standing outside who looked as if she might be the *patronne*. She was. Was the hotel open please? No, she was sorry, it was not. Then, seeing my tired and grubby state and obvious disappointment, she paused. Well, perhaps it might be… And with grace and charm she and her husband, the chef, took me in. A huge, cool, simple bedroom. A bath. Supper under the trees. I could scarcely believe my luck.

Usually I never bothered to measure how far I walked in a day. Too easy to become obsessed with the figure and to compare it with how I felt. But for once I checked. Pushing thirty miles. Madness.

* * *

Twenty-four hours later the *canicule* came to an abrupt end. From St-Genix I carried on wearily up the Rhône, as it flowed down through the mountains, to the little town of Yenne, putting off yet again the time when I would have to climb in order to move further east. I wanted to reach the city of Chambéry, a jumping-off point for the Alps beyond. To do so I needed to cross a steep ridge of low mountains, the Mont du Chat and its southern extension, the Montagne de l'Épine, the extremity of the Jura range – the peaks of the cat and the thorn. (The *autoroute* takes you underneath this ridge if you drive east from Lyon towards the Fréjus road tunnel into Italy.) The obvious route would have been the direct one, due east from St-Genix, leaving the Rhône behind and heading straight up into the hills. But worn out from the day before and befuddled by the heat, I decided mindlessly to head north in a long loop, up the river again, adding on many more miles, and then to cross the mountains the day after at their lowest point. It meant another hot day plodding up the riverbank. At Yenne I was joined for the next day by two friends, Patrick and Judy, who were on their way home from the Alps. Left to their own devices they would have surely tackled the high point of the Mont du Chat ridge, which runs up to nearly 5,000 feet. But they kindly fell in with my suggestion to sneak over a low col at less than half the height, after which we would head back down south to Chambéry.

That evening, as we stayed in Yenne in the seventeenth-century buildings of a Capuchin friary, now a hostel, it began to rain. Not heavily, but something was changing. The morning brought a new world. The heat had gone. We left the Rhône, climbed gently to the col on tracks and minor roads, and there, down on the other side below us, was France's largest natural lake, the Lac du Bourget, ten miles long and up to two miles wide. The spa town of Aix-les-Bains lay on the opposite shore under a lovely, cool grey damp cloud that blotted out the mountains beyond. Out for supper in Chambéry, I even put on a jersey.

7

Mountains

One, two, three… forty-seven, forty-eight, forty-nine, fifty
– *don't look up* – fifty-one, fifty-two, fifty-three… I toiled
slowly up a hillside high above Chambéry, head down,
silently counting off double paces. A method of last resort.
The slope stretches on up above you relentlessly, progress
seems minimal, and you wonder if you are ever going to get
to the top. Knock it off in chunks. Tell yourself that you will
count to fifty before looking around again. Keep your eyes on
where you are putting your feet. But when you finish, don't
look up – just carry on counting. Then repeat when you get
to a hundred. When you start, you fool yourself that it is only
fifty pairs of steps so the number to be reached does not seem
too far off. By the time you get bored with the game, the
gradient has often slackened a bit, or the terrain has changed
in another way, or something else has happened to break up
the ascent. And when you do at last look around, you see you
have made some height.

* * *

Patrick and Judy continued on their way home when we got to Chambéry. Had this been the mid-nineteenth century, my walking would have been over, too – I would have finished crossing France. For in Chambéry, I was in lands of the old duchy of Savoy. The Savoyard state originated in the tenth century and from an early date spanned both sides of the Alps, on the west down to Chambéry and on to the Rhône – the duchy of Savoy itself – and on the east to Turin and on towards Milan – notably the duchy of Aosta and the principality of Piedmont. From the early eighteenth century the state also included the kingdom of Sardinia, from which the head of the house of Savoy took his most important title. The duchy of Savoy was only incorporated definitively into France in 1860 when the then king of Sardinia, Victor Emmanuel II, gave up the western part of his lands in return for France's support against Austria, becoming in the next year the first king of the newly unified Italy. Suitably, Chambéry, now in the French *département* of Savoie, is twinned with Turin, the city that replaced it in the middle of the sixteenth century as the Savoyard capital. 'Savoia', a name from life in Italy. Exiled after the 1946 referendum that ended the monarchy, the *casa Savoia*, the former Italian royal family, still features regularly in the gossip columns.

I took a day off – it proved the last of these rest days and as relaxing as the first back at Alençon. 'Very simple and delightful' wrote Hilaire Belloc of Chambéry in a letter in 1922, 'like all places that have been capitals, it is dignified and has a spirit of its own'; although eight years later after another visit he was commenting crustily about the noise: 'every young man in France has bought a motor bicycle in the last eighteen months and rides it with the exhaust out and leaves it standing for half an hour banging like a battery of seventy-fives.' The centre of town has a relaxed feel. Pedestrianised roads and squares full of tall, gracious Italianate buildings with shuttered windows, albeit with post-war infill after a large Allied bombing raid in May 1944 aimed at the railway. (How many places had I passed through that saw the same that year?) Red flags with a white cross, the flag of Savoy, everywhere in evidence. Mountains high above the end of each street. The weather had quickly improved again but the great heat of the *canicule* did not return. It was bright and sunny and I enjoyed the same 'rest in that cool mountain air' as Belloc did on his first visit, even seeking out the sun at times to warm myself up. I came across a plaque to Jean-Jacques Rousseau, who spent several years living on a hillside just outside the town with his lover and benefactress, Madame de Warens. 'If there is a little city in the world where the pleasures of life are experienced in an agreeable and friendly commerce,' he said, 'it is at Chambéry.' I wandered about, drifting here and there, seeking out nothing in particular, taking pleasure in friendly commerce in the cafés, reading, writing up my diary.

But as I lazed around Chambéry, idling the day away, I needed to settle on a course forward for the morrow towards my final goal: the southern flank of Mont Blanc. There the Col de la Seigne would carry me into Italy. I had not really planned this passage through the Alps. The logical next step was Albertville, to the north-east, the town named after the father of Victor Emmanuel II. How to get there? The easy way would be to keep firmly to the low ground. As Arthur Young reported when he passed through Chambéry in 1789, 'the mountains though high recede; the valleys are wide'. Those wide valleys would provide a simple route to skirt around the mountains. In a couple of days I could reach Albertville by marching first south-east through one broad valley to reach the River Isère, before turning north-east upriver through another. It would be a virtually level walk – a rise of little more than two hundred feet. But I would have with me the *autoroute*, other roads, the railway, and a string of settlements and development along the valley floors.

Ambling around town, I kept on gazing up to the crags of the surrounding high ground – vast limestone cliffs far up above that form the ramparts of the Massif des Bauges to the north and east of Chambéry and the Massif de la Chartreuse to the south. These ranges are part of the 'Prealps'. Formally, they are just curtain-raisers, the foothills to the real thing further east – but foothills that reach over 6,000 feet. Seen from below they appear to be huge flat-topped plateaus, guarded by those enormous cliffs, although I realised this to be an illusion and that valleys with little mountain villages lay within. The wilds were calling. This time I would embrace the mountains rather than avoid them as I had when leaving the Rhône. I decided to strike directly north-east from Chambéry, up into the Massif des Bauges, pass through the mountains more or less as the crow flies, and then drop down again to Albertville.

* * *

Hence the counting of steps on a hillside above Chambéry. The decision to head for the high ground had been taken lightly. The lure of the hills, a quick check on the map for paths – and no attention to the number of contours. Now I was paying for it. Four thousand feet from the town in the valley bottom to a col high in the walls of the Bauges. More than a climb from sea level to the top of Snowdon. As I laboured uphill, my rucksack loaded with more food and water than usual, it seemed as if all the weeks of walking from Normandy had been for nought. The muscles in my legs screamed, lungs gasped, heart thumped. Twenty miles a day in the plains seemed simple by comparison. I had forgotten what it was like to climb up and up and up. How could it be this hard? The gradients appalled and I slipped and slid on the toughest bits as I thrust and pushed on my hazel stick. I thought back to walking with my father in his sixties in the Pyrenees as he crept slowly up the steepest slopes, me ahead waiting impatiently. Now I understood.

But bit by bit, I got higher and higher, at first passing the occasional old farm building in a mix of stone and wood, then leaving any habitation far behind as the minor path I was following wound its way skywards across the open mountainside. And the views got better and better. Down to Chambéry, further and further below. Across to the extraordinary stark outline of the cliffs of the Massif de la Chartreuse picked out against a cloudless blue sky. It all felt surreal. I had become so used to walking across the lowlands, week after week, with the exceptions of the brief foray over the Monts de la Madeleine, half the height of these Prealps, and the Normandy and Beaujolais hills. There was a dreamlike quality to the morning beneath the panting and the struggle. These uplands were a different world. Was I really here? A prospect of the higher peaks of the Alps proper to the east started to emerge, giving an exhilarating first sight of the permanent snows, shimmering in the distance. At last I reached the col, a mere nick in the skyline, a narrow defile through the cliffs. I gulped in the clean mountain air. The endorphins kicked in, Frédéric Gros's 'drunkenness on the peaks, the high passes where the body explodes'. Looking back down to the valley far beneath in the heat haze, it all seemed worthwhile. Easily worthwhile – it felt fantastic.

I was now high up among alpine meadows, carpeted with flowers that I could not start to name – blues, yellows, pinks, mauves – and grasses of all manner of types and heights. And butterflies. Fritillaries flashed by too fast to be identified. Mountain Ringlets again, as in the Monts de la Madeleine, and the somewhat larger but similar looking Scotch Argus – another northern butterfly in Britain that I would never see near home in the south. And a favourite from life in Italy, the Scarce Swallowtail – 'scarce' as very rarely if ever seen in Britain and in fact unrelated to the true Swallowtail, which it only marginally resembles. An outrageous butterfly, thoroughly deserving of its French name, *flambé*. Large, shaped like a hand-held fan, with great zebra stripes of black and very pale yellow radiating out from the back of the body, plus two parallel tails sticking out the rear and a mesmerising, lilting flight.

The alpine pasture, the *alpage*, is grazed in the summer by dairy cows brought up from farms in the valleys below, from June until mid-October a farmer I chatted with later in the day told me. On the climb up I stopped to admire an inquisitive herd of Abondance cows, thrusting their heads over a fence, with their mahogany brown hides, white bellies, feet and tail ends, and white heads with great brown eyepatches. And not far down from the col into the valley on the other side, I passed a little open-sided four-cow mobile milking parlour on wheels that must have been hauled up by a tractor, the four stalls neatly packed in under a corrugated iron roof.

That evening, in the small village of Aillon-le-Jeune, deep in the Bauges and still up at 3,000 feet, I ate the cheese made from the milk. I slept in a *gîte d'étape*, a simple self-catering hostel with no resident warden, this one owned by the commune. (An *étape* is a 'stage' as in the daily stages of a walking holiday – or the Tour de France.) I paid my modest fee in the *mairie* and found I had the place to myself and could take my pick from the half a dozen bunk beds in each of the two little dormitories that opened off the communal kitchen. The *gîte* was above a *fromagerie*, which not only made cheese but sold it, too, in its shop, the only one in the village. I bought a good amount of Tome des Bauges, one of the less well known of the Savoy cheeses, made with the milk of Abondance and Tarentaise cows. It has a slightly moulded, edible, dusty grey rind and a fairly firm pale yellow interior, similar to the better known (and double-m) Tomme de Savoie. I happily jettisoned the packaged cheese I had bought doubtfully early that morning in Chambéry in a small supermarket. (Carrot-coloured Mimolette, from up by the Belgian border – not the strong, salty, hard Mimolette Vieille, aged for a year or more, but the rubbery, rather tasteless Mimolette Jeune.) I had not taken cheese seriously until this point, appreciating what was put in front of me in restaurants and B&Bs but rarely remembering names or seeking out anything particular in shops. There is a lot to learn if you want to be a connoisseur of French cheese. De Gaulle, commenting on France's diversity, famously once asked: 'How can you govern a country that has two hundred and forty-six different kinds of cheese?' It was bread, cheese and tomato again for supper, at the kitchen table, but what a cheese – the Tome des Bauges was ambrosia. The *fromagerie* also provided yogurt for dessert and a bottle of light Savoyard red to wash everything down, a Mondeuse from the wide valleys joining Chambéry to Albertville. Life was good.

The morning after, I climbed back up to another col to cross over to another valley. Not so big a climb as the previous day since the valley floors within the Bauges are much higher than those of the wide encircling canyons outside the ramparts. And most of it also less steep. Another day of alpine meadows with flowers and butterflies and distant mountain views. And the 'dong... dong... dong...' of cow bells, slower and deeper than the 'ding... ding... ding...' of sheep or goats on the move. The sound travels a surprising distance and you may have to scan the hillsides for a while to spot the source.

* * *

By late afternoon I was down in a valley bottom again at another small settlement, École. It was hot and I spent an hour in the shade on the terrace of the village bar before wandering over to look at the church, set back at the corner of a crossroads opposite the *mairie*. A simple stone memorial stood outside, a few yards from an old water trough into which a pipe let fall a constant trickle giving a gentle backdrop of sound. It was headed: '*École – à ses martyrs victimes de la barbarie nazie.*' Twelve names followed, with their ages. One was seventy. Three were just sixteen. And underneath the simple statement: '*Fusillés sur cette place le 6 juillet 1944.*' The twelve had been shot, right there.

The *maquis*, the French resistance, played an important role in helping disrupt rail and road transport throughout France in the run-up to the Normandy landings of June 1944. This action continued vigorously following the Allied invasion but in another part of the Prealps further south, the Massif du Vercors, which lies beyond the Massif de la Chartreuse overlooking Grenoble, things went much further. On July 3, a declaration was made by the local *maquis* that the French Republic was restored in the Vercors, that this part of France was now liberated. Four thousand *maquisards*, many only newly recruited, then defended the massif as a redoubt against the German army. The hoped-for Allied support from the air never came. Instead, within three weeks massive numbers of German troops overwhelmed the Vercors, ironically some arriving by glider. Over six hundred *maquisards* and two hundred civilians were killed, many in cold blood in the brutal suppression that followed, although the main bulk of the fighters managed to melt away and to reform to subsequently harass the enemy after the Allied landings in August further south on the coast of Provence.

Alongside the tragedy of the Vercors, other smaller atrocities took place across the mountains that summer. The deaths at École on July 6 were one example. German troops were scouring the Massif des Bauges for *maquisards* and found an arms cache nearby. The entire male population of the village was assembled at three in the afternoon. In front of them, in the space between the church and the *mairie*, twelve men and boys were shot one by one. First, the seventy-year-old, who was the mayor, and then the others. In vain, the village priest had begged to take their place if they were set free. Much of the village was then burnt.

Looking at the memorial, it was impossible to square the horror of that afternoon with the neat, sleepy little village under a blue sky in which I stood. Did the victims hear the same trickle of water into the trough? The same far-off sound of cow bells? I was in École less than a week after the annual anniversary of their deaths. A sign on a wall showed that the space between *mairie* and church is now the *Place des Fusillés*. I thought of similar memorials I had seen in villages and hamlets in the Apennines north of Florence. These commemorate the victims of reprisals against the Italian partisans in the spring and summer of the same year, as the Germans slowly retreated north in the face of the Allied advance up Italy. Alongside sadness and incomprehension, the only suitable reaction is 'Never again' and an overwhelming feeling of gratitude for the peace of the last seventy-five years in this part of Europe.

* * *

It was a Saturday and École had a *fête* that evening with food and fireworks. But I had a long way to go if I wanted to make it to Albertville the next day. I discussed my dilemma with the young owner of the village bar who had revealed himself a keen walker. After hearing my planned route, he shook his head sadly. He was sorry, he thought I needed to set out. I reluctantly shouldered my rucksack and headed off on a quiet metalled road up a wooded valley that would lead me to the climb to a col through the outer walls of the Bauges. The road led beside a river that tumbled down over rocks between the trees and from time to time I passed families lazing in a patch of evening sun, children playing in the water, laughing and shouting. The gradient was easy and when after half a dozen miles the road stopped at a locked barrier, allowing access only to forestry vehicles, I had already gained a thousand feet.

The way ahead was now a faint footpath winding abruptly up the forested valley side. That could wait for the morning. Instead, I cast around for somewhere for the night. My dislike of sleeping in woods has one exception: when next to a mountain river. The noise of running water close by all night is one of the best of sounds. It lulls you as you lie waiting to drop off. It keeps you company when you wake in the small hours. It greets you in the morning. I hunted about for a suitable spot. The valley had narrowed and there was no level ground above the riverbank. The best prospects looked to be on the other side of the water. The river was strewn with boulders and smaller stones and was only ten or fifteen feet wide and at most a foot or so deep. I crossed over, jumping from rock to rock, and eventually found a tiny beach of pebbles right by the water. There was just room to stretch out, the soles of my feet against one rock and my head just short of another. I could reach to put my hand in the water as it bubbled by. The weather was set fair – the level was not going to rise in the night. My insulation mat seemed even thinner than usual but removing the odd larger stone from among the pebbles helped. Protruding branches of beech trees on either side of the river framed a patch of sky above and an hour or so later I slid into my sleeping bag, lay on my back and looked up at the stars, listening to the runnel over the rocks. It seemed one of the best beds I'd had since leaving England. As night came and I drifted off to sleep, I could just see both the Plough and the Little Bear standing clear above.

I was awake at six, chilled by the layer of cool air slipping down over the river. A rousing dash of icy water in my face, a bit of bread and fruit, a quick packing up, and I was away. Above the still dark woods, the early-morning sun doused the higher parts of the mountainside in bright yellow light, cliffs hundreds of feet high with gullies in shadow still harbouring here and there a stripe or two of old snow.

After a couple of false starts I found my bearings and climbed steadily through the woods on the little-used path, up the steep valley side, every now and again having to pick my way delicately across small landslips where the earth and rock had fallen away. The path led higher and higher, still in the trees, until finally emerging into *alpage*. The grass was dotted here and there by plants with large lily-like clumps of leaves from which a stalk rose up three or four feet carrying several distinct layers of small yellow flowers. It didn't take long that evening to identify this as Yellow Gentian – the bitter-tasting roots are used to make Suze, a popular *apéritif*. Soon I was on the col, here a broad saddle rather than the narrow cleft through which I'd entered the Bauges. It was just nine o'clock.

Not a cloud was in the sky and the views were still clear of haze. Looking back, the nearby ridges obscured the rest of the massif. But looking forward, I saw an enormous snow-covered mountain standing clear in the distance to the north-east. Neither sharp peak nor spire, but a steep-sided dome. After a few seconds, there, I realised, at last was Mont Blanc. It appeared far closer than the thirty miles shown on my map. Italy lay on the other side. I was standing on a col at 5,000 feet, far above the normal daily world. Way below in the valley bottom in front of me, Albertville was plain to see, a toy town in miniature, its roofs glinting in the morning sun. But looking out towards Mont Blanc it was as if I was merely on the edge of a trench dug into the surrounding landscape. The mountain top was over 10,000 feet above me. Two miles.

The descent to Albertville was as bad as the climb from Chambéry and it took almost as long. Brutally steep for much of the way, loose stones often strewn across what was now a well-used path. Descents do not have that same air of anticipation as climbs. You just want to get down, to get it over with. There is never the same satisfaction as you gauge your progress. I have no equivalent of my trick when climbing of counting steps. I groaned as I rounded corners in the path to find yet another section falling away beneath me, shockingly abrupt. Down, down and down, the gradient rarely relenting, knees begging for mercy, my stick too short to be much use as brake or support. I think I've always been slow downhill – in the same holiday in the Pyrenees when I waited for my father on the climbs, he used to skip ahead below me like a mountain goat. Now as if to rub it in, a pair of teenage girls, so similar as to be identical twins, shot past me, running down the mountainside, deftly stabilising themselves as they went with flicks of walking poles held in either hand.

Towards the bottom I passed a sign warning those coming up of the danger of rock falls – *risque de chutes de pierres* – and that use of the path was strongly discouraged in winter due to avalanches. 'Stay humble in the face of the mountain', it urged. But eventually I neared the valley floor and the first houses of outlying villages. I stopped under a plum tree with Mont Blanc in full view, its snows now shining brightly in the midday sun, finished off my three-day-old bread and the last of the Tome des Bauges, and dozed for an hour, flaked out.

* * *

If Chambéry is a gateway to the Alps, as guidebooks and websites will tell you, Albertville, on the Isère, is an entrance door beyond. The mountains to the east are no longer just Prealps. These are the real thing. Several of France's best known ski resorts sit high above the Isère valley, further upriver – Méribel, Courchevel, and further again, La Plagne, Les Arcs, and finally, amongst the headwaters under the border with Italy, Tignes and the eponymous Val d'Isère. Albertville itself was the host city for the 1992 Winter Olympics. These ski areas are all to the south-east of the town, which sits at the apex of a sharp bend in the Isère. Having run north-west for twenty miles, the river here turns and rushes to the south-west towards Grenoble beneath the cliffs of first the Bauges and then the Chartreuse, before zigzagging north of the Vercours eventually to join the Rhône. But the way forward to Mont Blanc from Albertville is to the north-east, away from the Isère, through an area known as the Beaufortain, which is largely free of organised skiing.

Sitting outside a café in Albertville in late-afternoon sunshine, full of expectation for the finale of the high tops, I thought about why my father had returned time and again to the Pyrenees but had never tried the Alps. He was not a skier but why had the vast opportunities for summer walking never drawn him? His shelves had a good selection of Alpine mountaineering books such as Frank Smythe's 1930s classic *An Alpine Journey* about a six-week crossing of southern Switzerland – Smythe was a leading inter-war climber and a member of three Everest expeditions – and the famous first volume of *Peaks, Passes and Glaciers*, published by the newly-established Alpine Club in 1859. The latter was a large red book with a gold embossed design on the front cover that captivated me as a child – two climbers roped together on a steep slope of snow and rock, the one above with ice axe raised, felt hat crammed on his head, and jacket caught in the wind, the one below waiting, flattened against the mountainside, knapsack on his back and carrying the ice axe's forerunner, an alpenstock, a long pole with a spike.

My memory of Father's own explanation of his constancy to the Pyrenees is that he said they were walkers' mountains and that he was a walker and not a climber. There is no pass on the frontier ridge between France and Spain that is so high that it cannot be reached in summer without crampons and ice axe – we had crossed one of the highest together at just under 10,000 feet. In this sense, you can go anywhere in the Pyrenees, unrestricted by permanent snows. And he was right that these are mountains worth going back to, time after time. Summarising the French landscape after his three journeys criss-crossing the country in the 1780s, Arthur Young declared: 'there is no doubt that the Pyrenees are more striking than all the other mountains of France; their verdure, their woods, their rocks and their torrents have all the characteristics of the sublime and the beautiful.' Sublime is a word used loosely nowadays. But Young was writing after a debate over its definition among eighteenth-century philosophers such as Burke and Kant. The sublime was something awe-inspiring, terrible to behold but a source of pleasure in the knowledge that the observer was safe from threat. According to Burke, it was the cause of 'the strongest emotion that the mind is capable of feeling'. For the Pyrenees to be sublime was high praise.

However, the Alps of course also offer a vast range of enticing possibilities for the walker. I had long suspected that the main reason my father stuck to the Pyrenees was people. He wanted to walk where others did not go and the Pyrenees have always been much less popular than the Alps. For many years, the only walking guide in English remained his beloved Belloc's *The Pyrenees* – still an excellent account today of the geography and of the issues to be confronted in mountain travel – supplemented by Charles Packe's 1860s climbing guide in which the author lamented the 'inundation of our own countrymen' in the Alps, 'who meet you at every turn', urging the reader to try the Pyrenees instead. Even Smythe, in *An Alpine Journey*, harked back to earlier times, saying his aim had been to 'recapture something of the charm of mountain travel... which breathes from the pages of *Peaks, Passes and Glaciers*...[away from] the elaborately mapped, meticulously guide-booked and scientifically run Switzerland of today'. For Father, the mountains were like the beaches that he sought for us in my childhood – best if other people weren't there and access meant a walk.

At the time, that hunt for the empty spaces often frustrated us children, and I think also our mother – she shared Father's love of nature but was drawn more to domesticated landscapes than to the sublime. Summer holidays could be in various far-flung corners of the British Isles and the self-catering in rough dwellings, some with no running water, at times would have seemed like little holiday to her. But Father's search had its positive effect. It opened my mind to the possibilities of not staying with the throng, of what the remote offers, of adventure. Here I was, near the end of a journey of a lifetime, much of it far from the crowd even if little had been in the real wilds. Would I have struck out through the Bauges alone without that childhood primer? Perhaps, but Father's introduction had signed the way.

That evening I went to the train station to meet a friend. I grew up with Richard and our fathers were friends too, our houses a hundred yards apart. (I can think of at least one popular Dorset beach where I had swum with his family but not mine, one not needing a decent walk to arrive.) Richard is my oldest friend, the right company for the end of the journey, this last stretch around Mont Blanc. He had just finished cycling the length of the Rhine – different muscles he argued when I outlined the week ahead and I thought back to that tiring day off by the Loire on the bike borrowed in Blois.

The next morning we worked our way slowly up a sunny hillside in and out of woods, with views opening out behind across Albertville to the walls of the Massif des Bauges that I'd struggled down the day before and to the flat top of the Massif de la Chartreuse further south – looking for all the world like Table Mountain, uprooted from the Cape and transported north to Europe. Once more, there were butterflies galore. What I decided was a Black-Veined White, a butterfly that became extinct in England in the 1920s when my father was a boy (my grandfather's Edwardian field guide already noting that 'this species has seemingly always been somewhat uncertain in its appearance'), although I remember him sometimes taking an optimistic second look at passing Small and Large Whites. And several stunning Dark Green Fritillaries, one of the commonest fritillaries in Britain, the green referring to the background colour of the undersides of the wings (although it is often more lime green than dark). I like their French name, which emphasises the big, shiny, off-white blobs dotted across this background, *grand nacré*, 'large pearly'. Plus another day-flying moth, wings spread wide at rest, from among the few listed by my phone app – the Speckled Yellow. The name is a perfectly appropriate description for what I learned to be a very common insect, a yellow background to the wings with many small dark-brown patches, but I prefer what I read to be the French, the equally apt *panthère*.

Rounding a shoulder on the hillside, Mont Blanc stood in front and remained thus for the rest of the day. I had not thought about it before coming to France, but I now appreciated that we were approaching the mountain from what was probably the best direction. The Mont Blanc massif runs for about thirty miles along an axis from the south-west to the north-east. Coming from either the French side, from Geneva up to Chamonix, the village below one end of the Mont Blanc tunnel, or up the Aosta valley in Italy to Courmayeur at the tunnel's other end, you are approaching the flanks of this massif. It is true that Mont Blanc, at nearly 16,000 feet, can be seen as the highest point in the ridge. But ten other peaks are of over 13,000 feet; the two closest on either side, Mont Maudit and Dôme du Goûter, are only eleven hundred and sixteen hundred feet lower. Viewed from either the approach from Geneva or up the Aosta valley, Mont Blanc does not stand out always as exceptional. But coming from the south-west, in line with the massif's axis, we were seeing a mountain that seemed isolated, utterly dominant, towering over the landscape, even if this was an illusion – the lower peaks on its far side hidden from view and the ones on our side foreshortened and blending into a ridge that led up to the summit.

In the evening, we watched the sun set slowly on the mountain's face, still some twenty miles away. The shadows in the sunlit valley beneath us lengthened, the lines of the wooded ridges that climbed the valley sides becoming more pronounced as the darkness grew beyond each fold in the land. A thin band of light cloud drifted across the face of Mont Blanc, a delicate grey scarf around the mountain's shoulders, the summit above and the snow slopes below all clear and brilliantly white, lit up by the now tiring sun. Then the sunlight left the valley beneath us completely, the ridges and the shapes of the hillsides now less distinct as everything became an even shade of dark green in the failing light. At the same time, the colour on the snows of Mont Blanc began to redden, at first just the slightest of tints and then deeper and deeper as the mountain shed its scarf of encircling cloud and the setting sun exposed its whole bust, everything below now in shadow.

* * *

How wonderful to watch the sunset standing instead on the very summit of Mont Blanc, all of Europe beneath you. When a student, I toyed one summer with the possibility of climbing the mountain with a trekking company but it came to nothing. The view from the top at the day's end was described in the nineteenth century by one of the early presidents of the Alpine Club, Sir Leslie Stephen (the father of Virginia Woolf), starting with the prospect back towards from where Richard and I stared upwards and then turning around to look beyond:

> The long series of western ranges melted into a uniform hue as the sun declined in their rear. Amidst their folds the Lake of Geneva became suddenly lighted up in a faint yellow gleam. To the east, a blue gauze seemed to cover valley by valley as they sunk into night and the intervening ridges rose with increasing distinctness, or rather it seemed that some fluid of exquisite delicacy of colour and substance was flooding all of the lower country. Peak by peak the high snowfields caught the rosy glow and shone like signal-fires across the dim breadths of delicate twilight.

Stephen next depicted the spread into Italy of the huge shadow of Mont Blanc itself. The Aosta valley below him, where at its head at Courmayeur I would finally finish walking, was 'swallowed up ridge by ridge' as the shadow crept eastwards.

I was spellbound by Mont Blanc. I could not stop looking up and trying to capture its image on my camera phone, failing in photo after photo to do it justice. For years, the mountain had been just the thing up above the seven miles of post-war road tunnel that we drove through into and out of Italy, between Chamonix and Courmayeur. 'Mont Blanc' had meant the tunnel – either a quick but dull transfer between two countries, without any real sensation of crossing a major geographic divide, or a long, frustrating wait in traffic tailing back from the entrance on one side or the other. Now the mountain had come into its own – the tunnel no longer existed for me. As Richard and I got nearer and nearer in the coming days, my reaction was the same every time we lifted our eyes to its snow-covered form.

I was in danger of developing what *The Times* in 1855 labelled as 'Mont Blanc mania'. 'Mont Blanc has become a positive nuisance', it thundered the following year. The mountain was first climbed in 1786, from Chamonix. Alongside interest in scaling the peaks, the Alps were becoming fashionable as a source of the sublime, including for the writers and artists of the Romantic movement. Wordsworth came to see Mont Blanc in 1790 followed by Byron and Shelley a quarter century later. (By contrast, Coleridge wrote his 'Hymn before Sun-rise, in the Vale of Chamouni' without leaving England.) 'Far, far above, piercing the infinite sky, Mont Blanc appears – still, snowy and serene', wrote Shelley in his resulting poem, before going on to emphasise the awe the mountain invoked in him: '... how hideously its shapes are heaped around! Rude, bare, and high, ghastly, and scarred and riven.' Mont Blanc's glaciers got the same treatment: '[they] creep like snakes that watch their prey.' That description is too sinister for me, although when you drive up to the entrance of the road tunnel on the French side you can see how it might fit the Glacier des Bossons, which seems to hang coiled above you. Artists came and drew and painted, among them Turner twice and then Ruskin repeatedly over the course of fifty years. By the mid-nineteenth century, a tourist industry was well underway in Chamonix, helped by rising middle-class incomes and the development of the French roads and railways. Many more people back in London were introduced to the rock and snow and ice of the mountain by Albert Smith's spectacle 'The Ascent of Mont Blanc', based on his climb in 1851. Smith's show ran for seven seasons with some 2,000 performances and it is estimated that they were seen by three quarters of a million people. The 'Cats' of its day.

And people still flock to Mont Blanc today in vast numbers. Each year, some 20,000 climb the mountain itself, provoking concerns about the environmental impact and the risks taken by the unprepared and the ill-equipped. (Two hundred climbers a year die somewhere in the Mont Blanc massif.) About 10,000 walkers every year are believed to do the Tour du Mont Blanc, a hundred-mile circuit of the whole of the massif that passes through France, Italy and Switzerland. The route crosses half a dozen major passes and involves over 30,000 feet of climbing, more than the height of Everest. It takes about ten days to complete but, extraordinarily, runners do the whole thing in one go in an annual ultra-marathon. The event's organisers limit the number of entrants to 2,500 and tickets sell out in minutes. Two thirds of runners usually finish. It's hard to believe but the winner completes the round in not much more than twenty hours.

My father would have hated all this. Not in the sense of resenting other people's enjoyment of the mountains, which he always welcomed. But the paths around Mont Blanc would have been the last place he wanted to walk. Much too busy. I was more relaxed about the prospect. I had already had the peace and quiet of the Massif des Bauges. And the stretch that Richard and I would do that actually formed part of the Tour was just a single day in France, up over the Col de la Seigne, and a day afterwards on the Italian side down to Courmayeur – our approach up through the Beaufortain was on paths that proved to be little busier than those in the Bauges. Moreoever, the 8,000-foot Col de la Seigne has a good pedigree in the history of trans-Alpine travel. It was long thought of as a possible crossing for Hannibal's elephants. That hypothesis is now out of favour with passes further south seen as more likely but the col was certainly known to the Romans, whose coins have been found near the pass – Courmayeur was the Roman 'Curia Maior'. The Col de la Seigne, as the first feasible pass at the south-west end of the Mont Blanc massif, continued to be used for many hundreds of years by travellers wanting a quicker route towards Lyon than offered by the lower Little St Bernard Pass a few miles to the south, over which a road now runs.

* * *

With more people walking in the mountains comes the infrastructure to cater for them. Refuges – larger versions of my *gîte d'étape* from the Massif des Bauges but staffed and with meals provided – allow you to carry minimal equipment and to stay high. We slept in several refuges, which varied substantially in size and character – those on the Tour being both the largest and the most crowded. A pleasing culture and camaraderie pervades the refuges. Boots and walking poles to be left in an anteroom, giving you the feeling that you are almost promoted to being a mountaineer shedding crampons, ice axe and rope. Everyone, young and old, was using poles. My hazel stick – my *bâton*, as it had been over the preceding weeks – seemed other-worldly, although on one occasion it drew admiring comments in halting English from a Japanese couple. Supper is taken sitting together on benches – one night we ate *tartiflette*, a filling dish of layers of potato, onion, bacon and the Savoy cheese Reblochon, and on another the Savoyard pasta, *crozets*, shaped in small squares (not very appealing to my mind but confirmation that we were approaching Italy fast). Talk around the table reveals where everyone has come from and where they are going, often conjuring up interesting possibilities – one evening we met a couple walking GR5, the path that threads its way through the Alps from Lake Geneva all the way down to the Mediterranean coast. Breakfast is a quieter and more hurried affair, everyone keen to get away. We drank this early coffee of the day from bowls, a habit that delighted me on first encounter as a teenager and one that I had only rarely come across in the previous weeks in the lowlands.

After our first night in a refuge, we dropped down to the little town of Beaufort, which gives its name both to the Beaufortain, the area, and to another Savoy cheese. Across the road from our hotel stood an imposing old four-storey stone building with wooden balconies and huge overhanging eaves. Seen in the summer, the overhang looks vastly too large. But it is of course there for the winter, to keep snow sliding off the roof well away from the house. Faded paint on the peeling render of the end wall spelt out 'Gendarmerie Impériale'. Which empire? It must have dated to the years between 1860 and 1870 following the final integration of Savoy into France and before the fall of Napoleon III and the birth of the Third Republic. Next door, built into the hillside, was the church, its great carved wooden double entrance doors reached by a flight of steps that carried elegant scrolled iron railings of the sort that I had seen repeatedly during my way down through France – a particularly fine example with ornate curls between each pair of uprights.

It was July 14, Bastille Day. In the late afternoon a group of children in period costumes paraded around the streets followed by three or four rather half-hearted, scruffy adult revolutionaries carrying pikes, red cockades in their bicorne hats. Later, a small brass band of a dozen or so played on the church steps beneath our hotel window, the players in black trousers or leggings and different coloured short-sleeved shirts – red, purple, lime green, orange, blue. It was my last town or village in France. The festivities were perfectly timed, as if they were a send-off. I went to bed early, falling instantly asleep, strangely tired after what had been only a modest day with almost no climbing. Shortly afterwards I was jerked awake by the deafening blast of what sounded like explosives going off outside the window... the noise of the commune's fireworks display a little way downhill, echoing off the facade of the church opposite. The thunderous booms and crashes continued and I knew that I should, like Richard, go and take a look. But somehow I could not make myself get up and had the experience of hearing a big set of fireworks without the view of them – the sense that is usually subsidiary at a fireworks display is hugely magnified in the absence of any sight of what is causing the bangs. The fireworks were followed by a rock band playing at volume until past two in the morning. The revolutionaries parading earlier may not have brought much credit to the town, but Beaufort knew how to party.

* * *

The valley was still emerging from the darkness as we left the next morning but the tops of the surrounding ridges were shining bright. A long day lay ahead. Some 5,000 feet to climb – up to a col and then keeping high, up and down, up and down, before another refuge for the night. The going was steep for the first couple of hours, up and up through thick woods. But it demanded less from me than similar gradients in the Bauges. Richard was proving a good pacer – it is easy to push on too fast when climbing alone. And with a companion you always chat a bit even when the uphill starts to bite, distracting the mind from the effort required. Spells of counting steps were few and far between.

By late morning we were out of the trees and had reached the Col du Pré, the Pass of the Meadow. It was well named. Here and throughout the next day we were among the high pastures again, the *alpage*. Vast grassy hillsides and huge bowls, dwarfing those of the Bauges, hay being made here and there on a few flatter bits. Herds of all-brown Tarentaise cows and once more the brown and white Abondance, the combination required for Beaufort cheese as well as for Tome des Bauges. Plus the sonorous ring of their bells clanging loudly close by or sounding faintly away across a valley. Little mobile milking parlours again, one at milking time with the cows barging each other aside in their urgency to get into the stalls to unload. And that evening, when we came to our refuge on another col, crossed by a road, milk churns ready for collection, a sight I had not seen since childhood – with the only difference that the metal churns now had plastic lids.

The *alpage* below us at the Col du Pré was even more extensive sixty years ago. The 1950s saw the damming of the headwaters of the Doron, the river that then flows down through a steep, narrow valley to Beaufort. The resulting reservoir, the Lac de Roselend, is some three miles long and up to half a mile wide, its waters used to generate hydro-electricity. Black and white photos from before the dam's construction show a huge open high-altitude basin surrounded by rocky ridges, the bottom full of meadow, much of it remarkably flat. In its centre was the tiny village of Roselend. Just a dozen or so houses, a couple of hotels, and a chapel. The images have a timeless quality and looking at them it is easy to be nostalgic. Simple beauty swept away by the tide of progress. But would the village have survived unchanged at this height? Farm employment was falling steeply. How much of that flat meadow would have been built on or covered in the tarmac of a car park surrounding a visitor centre? Was the reservoir a worse alternative to a ski station? The compensation given to local farmers apparently played an important role in the founding of the Beaufort milk co-operative.

And the lake, set among those rocky ridges, was a spectacular sight that day. Dropping down from the Col du Pré to skirt round above the reservoir's southern shore, a picture-perfect view of Mont Blanc opened up – dark green pine trees immediately below us, a deep turquoise of the lake, and beyond the now much closer white mass of the mountain.

By the evening of the next day, we had crossed the Cormet de Roselend, a pass that carries a minor road coming up from Beaufort. The road then winds below into a valley that runs down to the south to the town of Bourg-St-Maurice, which sits on the Isère beneath Les Arcs and La Plagne and the Little St Bernard Pass over to Italy. A group of cyclists had just made it to the top, emulating riders in the Tour de France – in recent years the Cormet has featured several times in one of the Tour's mountain stages. We dropped down from the pass on a path that curved away from the road around a quiet side canyon and we began to make out the entrance to the valley that would bring us the following morning up towards the Col de la Seigne and the frontier. The col itself remained tantalisingly out of sight but we could see the tops of peaks on the Italian side.

Down in the bottom of the valley huddled a small collection of buildings occupied only in summer, the hamlet of Les Chapieux – the 'Chapiu' of the nineteenth-century alpinists. Three or four houses kept company to a small low-vaulted chapel founded in the eleventh century, with room for just a couple of rows of short wooden benches. We stayed in one of the houses, now a large refuge. A well-organised, tightly run operation was doing a roaring trade. With people in cars who had driven up the valley for lunch from Bourg-St-Maurice or had come over the Cormet from Beaufort. And with walkers, lots of them. For in Les Chapieux we had finally joined the Tour du Mont Blanc. We lounged around on the terrace watching other arrivals. The walkers were of two types. Those who like us were carrying their own things. And those 'doing the Tour' with one of the companies that ferry their clients' bags each day from one refuge or hotel to another, often involving a lengthy roundabout drive. Minibuses and vans pulled up from time to time and drivers and their assistants wearing T-shirts with their firm's logo humped bags into the building. The walkers arrived in various states, some seemingly as fresh as a daisy and others looking all in, this not depending much on whether someone was carrying their own belongings or not. We had only met French walkers in the Beaufortain but here there were lots of fellow foreigners – Americans, Canadians, Germans, other Brits – although strangely, from what I heard spoken, no Italians. Preparation for re-entry into another world, I thought, a world that was not just French.

* * *

The last day in France dawned bright and clear. We were the first away from the refuge, in the cool, motionless air of the early morning. Cloud started to gather around Mont Blanc itself and threatened to creep from the Italian side over the Col de la Seigne, which we could soon see above us. But the forecast was reasonable. We were lucky – during the previous July it had rained on twenty-three days at Les Chapieux, someone told us the evening before, rain that was often snowstorms higher up; a weather report for the Bastille Day week that year warned of eight inches of fresh snow on the climb up to the col and the need to take care with ice. It was hard to imagine as we walked in shorts and shirt sleeves up the valley towards the final ascent to the col, first on tarmac – a last bit of the *chemin goudronné* that I had managed largely to avoid over the weeks – and then on an unmade road.

A mix of feelings ran through me. An immense sense of anticipation of finishing the crossing of France, of reaching Italy at last, a bookend to pair the excitement on starting out that May morning by the lighthouse on the quay at Ouistreham. But regret that the adventure would soon be over. No more the simple daily round of rising, walking, arriving, eating, sleeping. No more seeking out red and white flashes of paint or scanning the horizon ahead, wondering what lay beyond. No more occasional nights in the open, staring up at the heavens or waking to the break of day. No more evenings of French with B&B hosts or of meals in back-street restaurants after a cheery command to be seated, *'installez-vous!'* No more daily surprises of nature, of history. And no more *War and Peace* at lunchtime when alone; I'd almost finished my father's second little volume – Napoleon had won his pyrrhic victory at Borodino and in a week would be in Moscow, the brief high watermark of the French invasion before the disastrous retreat westwards with the onset of winter.

My journey had started in Normandy with the reminders of one invasion. And on leaving Les Chapieux it ended with the record of another. A title on an information board caught my eye and further investigation gave a final surprise: *'Juin 1940: une résistance héroïque.'* Surely the German army had not got this far before the French stopped fighting, deep into the Alps? After all, the plaque I had seen back at Sault-Brénaz, on the Rhône, recorded the actions of the Tirailleurs Sénégalais on June 19, just three days before the armistice was signed. There could not have been time for the Germans to get here as well? But the resistance had not been to the Germans. The invaders were the Italians.

After annexing Albania in the spring of 1939, Italy remained neutral at the outbreak of hostilities at the end of the summer between Germany, France and Britain that followed the German invasion of Poland. But another nine months later, with the collapse of the French imminent, Mussolini declared war on France and Britain on June 10. His hope was to seize territory quickly west of the Alps before the French sued for peace, telling his army chief of staff: 'I only need a few thousand dead so that I can sit at the peace table with the victors.' The Italian army had been far from ready for war and it was not until June 21, the day before French and German representatives signed an armistice document, that Mussolini ordered his troops into France. The invasion took place along the whole three hundred mile length of the border, from Switzerland down to the Mediterranean.

Here in the high Alps, the attacks included a thrust over the Col de la Seigne, with the immediate objective of taking Albertville. The Italian journalist and former partisan, the late, great Giorgio Bocca, wrote of the terrible irony in the resulting clashes around the Mont Blanc massif between the specialised alpine troops on each side, the Italian *alpini*, and the French *chasseurs alpins*, men who had climbed the same mountains, stayed in the same refuges, skied in the same competitions.

The Italians attacked along the front with an overwhelming numerical advantage, a force of some quarter of a million troops, outnumbering the French defenders by more than three to one. But the French had well-prepared positions guarding the passes – concrete bunkers and gun emplacements constructed over the previous decade. And they had the weather on their side – a heavy summer snowfall and bitter sub-zero temperatures of the kind that Richard and I avoided severely hampered the attackers, most of whom were ill-equipped for mountain warfare and short of supplies of all types. Three days later, the French signed an armistice in Rome. The Italians had hardly penetrated into France, their principal gain being the coastal town of Menton just across the border. Here around the Mont Blanc massif, the invaders fell far short of their objectives. Troops quickly crossed the Col de la Seigne but the map on the information board showed that the *résistance héroïque* held the narrow valley below and the Italians failed to reach even Les Chapieux. The three days of fighting along the front left six hundred Italian soldiers dead and another six hundred missing. French losses amounted to thirty-seven.

Just before the climb to the col, we stopped for coffee, in bowls once more, in an old-fashioned, wood-lined refuge towards the head of the valley. As a result we were overtaken by some of our fellow walkers from the night before who had come up from Les Chapieux in a minibus. We no longer had the climb to ourselves. But it didn't matter. This was going to be a great morning whatever happened. A final two hours up to the frontier, steep at first as we climbed out of the valley. People passed us coming down who had crossed over from the Italian side including one party with their belongings on two mules, immediately bringing to mind Yves and Joëlle and their donkeys from my way up to the Monts de la Madeleine – a recent email had reported their arrival home.

Tiny mountain flowers clung to the patches of shale and rock that began to replace the grass as we got higher – mauves, whites, blues and yellows. I thought a little sadly that I'd not learned much about French flora since landing in Normandy but at least it had never stopped diverting and pleasing. A fritillary that once more I could not identify. Several marmots scurrying over rocks on the hillside above us like big, burly grey squirrels but without the bushy tail. A panorama opened up back down the valley towards Les Chapieux and to the outline of the rocky peaks of the Beaufortain beyond. To our left was one of the glaciers that runs down from the south-west end of the Mont Blanc massif, one known perhaps rather unimaginatively as Glacier des Glaciers. At last the gradient eased off and I realised that the end was coming fast; a minute more and we suddenly saw ahead the col itself, a wide, open scoop in the mountain's flank with a head-high cairn of stones amassed by passing travellers and a patch of winter snow clinging on nearby.

We were met with 'a view of extraordinary grandeur', as the first president of the Alpine Club, John Ball, described the vista on the other side of the pass in his 1866 guide to the Alps. Turner had sketched it quickly thirty years earlier when he came over the Col de la Seigne, heading like us for Courmayeur – one of five little drawings crammed onto a single page in a small sketchbook now in the Tate, capturing with a few delicate pencil strokes the bare outline of the spectacle before us.

Down below is the valley called the Val Veni that runs away from you along the south-east side of the Mont Blanc massif to the head of the Val d'Aosta and, out of sight, Courmayeur. Three or four miles down the valley you can see the tail of the huge debris-strewn Miage glacier that comes off the massif, spilling out across the valley bottom to form a barrier looking like the back of a dam wall. Beyond the glacier and to the right, well below you, guarding the south side of the entrance to the valley, is the pointed top of Mont Chetif, a little mountain featured in several watercolours that Turner painted of Mont Blanc, looking back up from Courmayeur.

Much closer, about half a mile away from you on the left, are the twin Pyramides Calcaires sprouting from the valley side, small rocky limestone peaks joined by a saddle, their summits not much higher than you are at the col. To your immediate right is an immense grey ridge that forms the south side of the upper Val Veni – it never ceases to amaze how much wild, bare stony ground is about you at this height. And past the Pyramides on your left, past the Miage glacier, and far, far above, still thousands of feet above, is the great bulk of Mont Blanc itself with the snowy upper slopes and high rocky ridges of the mountain seeming to float in the sky. That day, as we gazed up, cloud swirled around the mountain, coming, going, coming again – the view constantly changing. What we thought was the summit peaked through from time to time but it was difficult to distinguish snow from cloud, the uncertainty adding to the drama of the scene before us. Towering dark storm clouds topped by patches of blue sky blocked out the views beyond Val Veni to the mountains behind, providing the backdrop.

It was a glorious sight, looking out of France into Italy. With one step more I was there.

Envoi

Le soleil s'est couché ce soir dans les nuées.
Demain viendra l'orage, et le soir, et la nuit;
Puis l'aube, et ses clartés de vapeurs obstruées;
Puis les nuits, puis les jours, pas du temps qui s'enfuit!

Victor Hugo

Another twenty-four hours down to Courmayeur. A night first in a large *rifugio*, a thousand feet below the col, once more full of different nationalities. Including now of course Italians. Many of them. A large, boisterous group, all male, had managed to arrive on mountain bikes, a huge effort given the paths. People from Milan judging by their accents behaving like, well, caricature Italians. Jabber, jabber, jabber! A hubbub of noise as they called back and forth to each other, heads thrown back in shouts of '*ragazzi*…!' – 'lads…!'. Hands moving vigorously in concert with mouths. Flirting with the female staff. Familiar, but still a bit of a shock, so used was I now to being among the French. André Gide reportedly said that French people are Italian people in a bad mood. Unfair, but it does at least suggest a greater restraint. And the Italians are not always like that, expansive, exuberant. The caricature is one viewed from abroad, but live among the Italians and you see another side. Pessimism, at times a defeatism even. A resigned shrug and the familiar comment '*siamo in Italia*' – we're in Italy, the standard explanation for something in the bureaucracy, in local government, in everyday life that doesn't work, something that can't be done, that cannot be changed. I never heard an equivalent in France. More a quiet pride in France, in the French, misplaced or not.

Down the next morning with other walkers past the great Miage glacier, remorselessly gouging out the southern flank of Mont Blanc, the mountain towering ever taller above us as we dropped in height. We had crossed another watershed on the Col de la Seigne and the milky torrent emerging from the Miage ice was rushing to the plains to join the Po. I had watched waters on their way to the Channel, the Atlantic, and the Mediterranean – now they were heading for the Adriatic. A last, short climb up over a shoulder out of Val Veni, round the back of Turner's little Mont Chetif. And then a steep, steep final descent on a path through the woods to Courmayeur, occasional views opening up below of the mountain-lined trough of the Val d'Aosta, the valley that I had driven up and down so often in the past, to and from the tunnel to France and, eventually, England.

Most of our fellow walkers took a chairlift down to the village, avoiding what looked to be just a knee-jarring plunge into the valley of a couple of thousand feet through the pines. But a sunny clearing on the south-facing hillside brought a reward. A breathtaking display, the best of the entire journey, better even than in the Bauges or on the slopes above Chambéry. Butterflies everywhere, species so numerous it was hard to decide where to look first. Several I had not seen in the previous weeks or that were entirely new to me. Several I did not recognise and still could not identify afterwards from photos. Fritillaries galore – the Dark Green again and the Spotted, absent from England. A male

Chalkhill Blue, a brilliant, almost azure body with wings of a pale sky-blue that turned to grey before ending in a thin black margin and a white outer edge; and a female, quite different with a brown upperside to her wings finishing with a row of orange markings at the rear before the same white outer rim. The Chalkhill Blue is a smallish insect and can be found easily on downland in southern England. But then we saw the much larger and improbably named Great Sooty Satyr, never to be seen back home, a butterfly that here was towards the northern edge of its flight lands: a male with its dusky, dark brown wings and a few small, black, white-centred spots. Plus a day-flying moth from the large burnet family, sitting on knapweed, black swept-back wings with red spots surrounded by the thinnest of white margins. And best of all, something I had dreamed of finding in the Alps. Apollos. Breathtaking large mountain butterflies with waxy white wings, black patches on each fore part and spectacular red eyes to the rear with white centres and black surrounds.

The first Apollo we saw was close to its end. Ragged, wings almost transparent where scales had been lost, the red eyes faded to orange. Perhaps it had managed to mate. There is just a single Apollo brood each year. Eggs are laid in the summer and hatch out in the spring. The resulting caterpillar then eats and grows, shedding its skin several times, and finally undergoes the metamorphosis into adult butterfly. My journey began long before this specimen had crawled out of its chrysalis and spread its wings to dry – it had probably emerged when I was somewhere near the Rhône or perhaps even when I was tackling the Massif des Bauges. And like the brief, stunning life in all its splendour of the Apollo on the wing, my walk started much earlier than the day I set out from the quay at Ouistreham. It was born as an idea, lying dormant for many months – or in a vaguer form for many years, disturbing the metaphor. It then hatched into something that needed at least some planning, although the effort I put in to this stage had been much less than that of the voracious caterpillar. And finally the plan had to be realised. The chrysalis? The critical step of transforming plan into action. Of deciding irrevocably to carry it out. And of packing a rucksack and taking that ferry to France.

What was now left other than the memories? Where had been the regeneration, the Apollo laying eggs for the future? 'Having nothing to do but walk makes it possible to recover the pure sensation of being, to rediscover the simple joy of existing,' argues Frédéric Gros, '… to marvel at the beauty of the day, the brightness of the sun, the grandeur of the trees, the blue of the sky.' To listen to the wind, to wait for the stars. To act on a whim, to not plan everything. Things to hang onto when the walking has stopped. It needs some effort as life back home re-establishes and you fall back into daily routines, spending more time inside than out. But you can hold on. Keep looking, keep listening. Out blackberrying in Hampshire a few weeks later, I surprised a friend by blurting out that the stubble field next to the hedge we were working down would be a good place to spend the night – I had been automatically eyeing up the possibilities. I told myself too that I would keep a rucksack ready packed near the door; this hasn't happened but something of that spirit survives.

I had also learned much as I walked, over fields, through woods, across rivers, up and down hills, over mountains, the red and white paint leading me on. In and out of villages and towns, into shops, bars, hotels and people's homes. At times with intent, pressing on towards the horizon, at times just flitting like the butterfly from place to place alighting where I would. It was impossible not to learn without closing eyes and blocking ears. Buchan's Jaikie Galt had been right, the earth was 'very spacious and curious'. I had taken in chunks of French history. I had stumbled into a little of the country's vast literature. I had a much firmer grasp of the physical and economic geography of a great band of France – the map had been filled in. My knowledge of butterflies had shot up. I had heard new birds. My schoolboy French had leapt ahead. I had learned more about myself, about the things that interest me most, and about the value both of companions and of time alone.

A day of Courmayeur, a resort town in both summer and winter. Smart hotels, restaurants, and shops selling Gucci handbags. I sent off a clutch of three-word postcards to hosts of various overnight stops: '*Je suis arrivé*.' And then we were on our way home, Richard by plane, me overland. An early morning bus under Mont Blanc to Chamonix, another to Geneva, the midday TGV to Paris, the *metro* across the city, and a train to Caen. A little more than twelve hours and I was back almost to where I had started. In a daze, I stared out of the window at France rushing by at what seemed an insane, an impossible speed.

I ate supper outside on a hot evening by the basin at the head of the Canal de Caen à la Mer. The next morning a bus would take me to Ouistreham and the ferry. My thoughts went this way and that. What would have been my father's reaction, had he been there in Courmayeur on our arrival? A steady, blue-eyed smile, half-moon glasses in place, a brief, firm handshake. A quick but warm 'Well done'. Then questions. Questions about the mountains. Had we seen a lammergeier – the bearded vulture – and what other birds of prey? (Defence – no binoculars.) What about the flowers, what was out? (Not much to say but report colours and shapes and sizes – ask about the butterflies please.) Huts were crowded around Mont Blanc? (You've got me there!) And what did

I think of the Maudes' *War and Peace*? (Good – but a little old-fashioned.) I had also learned about him and in reading his diaries later I learned more, connecting again across time, appreciating again his knowledge of the natural world, the pleasure and fulfilment he too had in walking, in travelling on foot, and his love of France, now rekindled in me.

Notes

Books with titles given in the main text are not mentioned below but are listed in the bibliography.

Prologue

The extent of tarmac road in France in 1913 comes from the French Wikipedia entry for '*route*' (other websites give the same figure). The Institut Géographique National map of all GR paths is number 903. The comment by Tony Judt about a French Rip Van Winkle is from Judt (1975) and the one that follows, referring to Balzac, from Wright (1964). Sutcliffe (1976) is the source for years when the urban population came to dominate in France, Britain and Germany. The numbers of tractors (and the importance of subsistence farming pre-war) are taken from Moulin (1991); the first figure refers to 1938 and I have calculated the ratio of tractors to farms using information on the latter for 1939 from Clout (1975). The share of employment in agriculture in the 1930s is from the magisterial study of French peasantry by Weber (1977), a figure given by other authors too, and subsequent numbers are my calculations from annual 'GraphAgri' publications of the Ministère de l'Agriculture; the 2015 edition also provides the figures for the comparison of average farm size in France, Germany and Britain. The new classifications of rural France (e.g. 'residential') and the importance of manufacturing in rural areas are described in Behaghel (2008). The Wikipedia entry for 'ultralight backpacking' reports conventional definitions of lightweight and ultralight backpacking as under ten kilograms and under five kilograms respectively; Belloc (1909) comments on weight.

1. Landing

The estimate of the number of civilians killed in Normandy in 1944-5 is from Dodd and Knapp (2008). Beevor (2010), among other authors, describes in detail the fighting in the Falaise Pocket while the account of the battlefield afterwards is from Eisenhower (1948). The 1947 *Guide Bleu* to Normandy is just the 1933 guide with an eleven-page insert describing '*changements et nouveautés*' while the picture of Falaise before its destruction is from Dearmer (1904). Edward Thomas's description of the wood warbler is in Mabey (2013). Belloc's comment in a letter on the shrine to St Thérèse at Lisieux is from Speaight (1958). The progress of Thérèse's sister, Léonie, towards sainthood can be followed at www.leonie-martin.fr (in the spring of 2020 the diocesan enquiry submitted a report on her case to Rome of over 30,000 pages). Moore (2011) reports de Gaulle's decision to give up smoking on Leclerc's death.

2. Walking alone

Robert Louis Stevenson's essay 'Walking Tours' is in Stevenson (1881). Smith (1975) tells the story of my father's convoy to Russia, PQ18. My grandfather's guide to butterflies is South (1906), described by Marren (2015) as the standard field guide for much of the twentieth century; Marren discusses at length the origin of butterfly names, as does Oates (2015). John Clare's description of the oxeye daisy comes from his poem 'The Fear of Flowers'. Richard Mabey (1993) tells of hearing a nightingale for the first time and gives details of the BBC's live broadcasts of a cello and a nightingale in the 1920s, which my father wrote of in his diary. Holt et al. (2012) is the source for the figure of a ninety per cent decline in the number of nightingales in the UK and Newson et al. (2012) discuss the impact of the rise in the deer population. There is a large literature on First World War memorials; I have drawn on Inglis (1992), Sherman (1994) and Scates and Wheatley (2014). I took figures for the total French population in 1914 and for its age structure from the website of the Institut National de la Statistique et des Études Économiques (INSEE), the French national statistical office. Figures for French and British war deaths (the total, the numbers year by year and the losses on August 22, 1914) come from Lafon (2014) and Prost (2014) and the same figures are given by Hastings (2014). Moulin (1991) describes the reasons for the heavier mortality among those from rural areas. The translation of a line from Ronsard's poem on the forest of Gâtine is mine. (A few of Ronsard's poems are included in the anthology in Grigson (1980); many more, with their translations, are available on the internet.) Grigson (1970) tells the story of how the phial of the tear of Jesus was said to have come to Vendôme and of its loss. The first phrase from *La Terre* that I cite is my translation from the French; those that follow are from Zola (1980). The prosecution of Zola's first English publisher is described by Horne (2015) who also reports the comment by Tennyson; the same author gave her view of Dickens and Hardy compared to Zola in the BBC Radio 4 programme *Front Row* on November 20, 2015. The labelling of laws on division of land by de Tocqueville is cited by Weber (1977) and the details of the legislation following the Revolution and the Napoleonic Code are in Law Library of Congress (2014). Resistance to *remembrement* and a continued preference for division stemmed in part from the view that division ensured good land was shared out and gave insurance against the local vagaries of frost and hail (Baker, 1968). The average size of holding in the 1891 survey of cadastral records is given in Roche (1951); Rozental (1956) discusses the enclosure movement in France; and the figure for the total number of hectares subject to *remembrement* by 2007 is from Philippe and Polombo (2009).

3. Town and forest

Belloc's 1923 description of Blois is in Speaight (1958). Brown (1994) places Saint-Saën's film score to *La Mort du Duc de Guise* in historical context and reports the seriousness with which the composer took the job. The definition of a ZUS is given on data. gouv.fr. The average incomes in the Blois ZUS and in the rest of the town are taken from DRJSCS Centre (2012) and refer to 2009. Robb (2007) describes the death of Alain-Fournier on the Meuse in 1914 and the discovery of his body in 1991; Robb also discusses the 'colonisation' of provincial France in the mid-nineteenth century (as does Weber, 1977, who notes the use of the word at the time in relation to the Sologne), although his focus is more on the resulting dramatic change in landscape in the Landes. I have drawn on Bardon (2011) in recounting the geography and history of the Sologne (including that of the Canal de la Sauldre) and the same source gave the ironic suggestion of Félix Pyat. Poitou (1978), who argues that the turnaround in living standards in the Sologne pre-dated the Second Empire, and Dobson (2010) report the infant mortality rates I cite; Girard and Daum (2010) are the source for the rate of rejection by the army of potential Solognot recruits (the same figure is given by Bardon). The increase in the Solognot population in the nineteenth century (forty-six per cent between 1820 and 1911) is given in a report of a December 2013 lecture by Christian Poitou titled 'Les Solognots du XIXe siècle' on the website of the archives of the *département* of Loiret (archives-loiret. fr); I took the figure for comparison with metropolitan France as a whole from the INSEE website (thirty-two per cent). The Victor Hugo poem that I mention is 'Fuite en Sologne'. The figure for pizza consumption is for 2016 and comes from an annual report from Gira Conseil. The history of poaching in France from the *ancien régime* to the twentieth century is recounted in Cameron (1996). Sales of *Raboliot* to 1985 are given in the 'Commentaires' by Francine Danin in the 1989 'Le Livre de Poche' edition of the book that I bought in the Maison du Braconnage at Chaon. The first of

Maurice Genevoix's books about his experiences in the First World War, *Sous Verdun*, covering August-October 1914, was translated and published in English in 1916 with the title *'Neath Verdun*. (The collection of five books was re-published as one volume in 1949 as *Ceux de 1914*, and was adapted for French television in 2014.) Alain-Fournier was killed on September 22, 1914 at Vaux-lès-Palameix, just to the east of the Meuse. Genevoix's entry for that day in *Sous Verdun* records that he was at Mouilly, which is two miles to the north. My figures for the numbers involved in the Exodus are from Diamond (2007), which is also the source for the diary entry (by Camille Bourniquel) for June 11, 1940 concerning the Loire bridges. The 2015 film *Suite Française* focuses on the second book in Irène Némirovsky's unfinished novel and does not cover her account of the Exodus in the first book. The battle for Gien is described in Pillard (1949), Champault (1982) and the 2015 diaporama *Bataille de Gien*, which can be found on YouTube. Douglas Goldring wrote of his journey down the Loire in Goldring (1913). The figures for French deaths from Allied bombing and the tonnages of bombs dropped on France and Britain are from Dodd and Knapp (2008) and Barot and Knapp (2014).

4. Heading upstream

The meeting of the Supreme War Council in Briare is described by Diamond (2007), who also deals with the return of refugees from the Exodus after the armistice. Eden's account of Reynaud's comment on Pétain are in his interview (in French – the translation is mine) for the 1974 documentary *La Bataille de France*, directed by Jean-Louis Guillaud and Henri de Turenne (available on YouTube). The British offer of political union with France is discussed in Shlaim (1974) and Streit (1958). The first quote about navigation on the Loire is from Edwards-May (1984) and the second from McKnight (2005), who also gives the history of the Canal de Briare, the Canal Latéral à la Loire and the Canal du Nivernais. The late-nineteenth-century standard governing the size of locks was the Freycinet gauge. Mauret Cribellier (1996) describes the history of the *pont-canal* of Briare. The figure for railway mileage by 1890 is from Robb (2007). The apparent impact on tonnage at the Orléans river port of the arrival of the railway is from a display board in the Musée des Deux Marines, at Briare. The figures for freight on the Canal Latéral and for the number of boats using the *pont-canal* are from Brucy and Velleret (2016) and those for total tonnage on French waterways from Le Sueur (1989). The percentages of land devoted to vines, buildings and roads are from the *L'utilisation du territoire en 2014, Agreste Chiffres et Données Agriculture n° 229*, published by the Ministère de l'Agriculture (they refer to Metropolitan France, ignoring the overseas *départements* and other lands). Patrick Leigh Fermor (1987) described his wonderment at encountering massed storks on the Danube and again in Leigh Fermor (2013) on seeing their southern migration at the summer's end. Wade (1979) is the 1970s guidebook reporting plans for the doubling of the Nevers population. Diamond (2007) and Moorehead (2015) describe the measures taken against the Jews from July 1940 by the Vichy government.

5. Rich and poor

Figures for the population of French communes, usually stretching back to the Revolution, are given in each commune's entry in the French version of Wikipedia. (Had I known this at the time, I would have had no need to ask in the Vibraye *mairie* for the pre-First World War population of the commune as described in Chapter 2.) INSEE provides an Excel file on its website of the population of every commune and my comments on the distribution of commune size are based on this. (I draw on the December 2019 version of the file that is based on 2017 census figures but using January 2020 commune definitions; there are 34,883 communes in metropolitan France in this file, a figure that may be compared with the 36,571 in the December 2015 version using January 2016 commune definitions, reflecting the recent rise in commune mergers.) Weber (1977) reports that in 1876 there were only six hundred and fifty communes with less than a hundred people, which may be compared to the more than 3,000 now. The comment on the architecture of rural *lavoirs* is from Roddier (2003) and that on 'mayors with ambitions' from Boogaart (2016). (There are photos of some 18,000 *lavoirs* from across France, as of June 2020, at the website www.lavoirs.org.) Moulin (1991) provides the figure on rural homes with running water in 1946. In constructing his maps of France, Adolphe d'Angeville built on earlier work by Charles Dupin and the contributions of both men are mentioned in Robb (2007). Zdatny (2006) describes the purchasing of hair in the Auvergne (see also Weber, 1977). The catch-up in height among potential conscripts from the Massif Central is analysed in Postel-Vinay and Sahn (2010); I am grateful to Gilles Postel-Vinay for confirming that the series in Figure 1 are mislabelled – the order from the top should read Massif Central, South West, North East, and East. Clout (1972) provided the quote on the Massif Central as a rural problem area. Figures for poverty rates in 2012 are taken from the INSEE website (the rates refer to the pre-2016 regions) and from a June 2015 'Flash' for poverty in the Auvergne (rates are again for 2012); poverty is defined as a household income below sixty per cent of the national median. Behaghel (2008) records home ownership among rural and urban poor. The monthly salaries for mayors of different-size communes are given on the website droit-finances.commentcamarche.com (I cite the 2020 figure for a mayor of a small commune). The INSEE website is also the source for information on the *communes isolées*. The French Wikipedia entry for 'Commune (France)' details the state's efforts to persuade communes to merge or to at least group and pool resources and responsibilities. The book *Rocks to Riches* is by Pringle and Schaefer (2012); Wylie (1974) uses the name 'Peyrane' for Roussillon in *Village in the Vaucluse*. Local government in France, including the decentralisation of powers to *régions* since 1982, is described by Knapp and Wright (2006). In discussing the proposed golf complex and associated development in Montcombroux-les-Mines, I have drawn on the report of a public enquiry available on the website of the *préfecture* for the Allier *département* from 2011 and on reports on the website of the newspaper *La Montagne*. The estimate of the amount of land that changed hands as a result of the Revolution is from Grigg (1980), my source also on who acquired the land lost by the nobility and the church. Piketty (2014) draws on a number of other authors when comparing wealth inequality in France with that in Britain and the USA, notably Atkinson and Harrison (1978) and Lindert (1986) in the case of Britain. The reference to Cortez on a peak in Darien is from Keats's poem 'On First Looking into Chapman's Homer'. Habel et al (2014) discuss the Violet Copper butterfly and the description of the Mountain Ringlet as a 'dusty denizen' is from Oates (2015).

6. Heat

Stevenson (1878) gives his view of persistent rain. The origins of the French name for the nightjar are discussed by Avenas and Walter (2007); the 'rattle' of the nightjar's call noted by my father is a description used by Wordsworth and Meredith amongst others. The 'solemn glee' of rising at dawn is from Stevenson (1879). My butterfly field guide is Easterbrook (2010) and the website from which I took the comment on the Purple Emperor was www. thepurpleempire.com, a site formerly maintained by Matthew Oates but no longer in existence; see instead the blog on this butterfly started by Oates and others, apaturairis.blogspot.com (from which comes Oates's comment on 'the morals of an orc'). Oates (2015) writes more about the Purple Emperor (noting that his introduction, like mine, came from B. B.'s *Brendon Chase*), and much more in Oates (2020). The nineteenth-century engineer's comment (my translation) on La Dombes is from Manceron (2006). The post-war development of the Rhône is described in Pritchard (2011). The comment on the river from the 1950s by the Canoe Club de France is taken from McKnight (2005) and the state of navigation on the upper part of the river on the eve of the

Second World War is described in Schiff (1936) and Aubert (1939). The attitude of the Nazi regime to black French colonial troops and the atrocities perpetrated on them in 1940 are detailed in Scheck (2006); Moorehead (2015) describes the coming of Jewish children to Izieu and how that followed the earlier protection of Jewish refugees in the Massif Central.

7. Mountains

The western lands of the Savoyard state were seized by France in 1792 but were returned in 1815 following Napoleon's fall. Belloc's comments on Chambéry are in Speaight (1958). Rousseau's verdict (my translation) was given in Book V of his 'Confessions', published in 1782, and Young's on the valleys surrounding the Massif des Bauges and on the Pyrenees is from Young (1929). Ashdown (2014) recounts the uprising of the *maquis* in the Vercours in July 1940. The action of the École village priest in July 1944 was detailed in an announcement in 2015 on the Chambéry parishes' website when a road was named in his memory in Bassens, a suburb of Chambéry (rue Chanoine Henri Féjoz); on his death in 2005 he was buried at his wish in the École cemetery next to the villagers who had been executed. Leslie Stephen's description of sunset from the summit of Mont Blanc is in Stephen (1871). The comment on the Alps by Charles Packe is from Packe (1867). The mania for Mont Blanc in the mid-nineteenth century is told in Hansen (1995), Fleming (2000), Macfarlane (2003) – from where I have taken Burke's words on the Sublime – and McNee (2015). Shelley's poem, written in 1816, is titled 'Mont Blanc: Lines Written in the Vale of Chamouni'. There is a huge literature on the location of Hannibal's crossing of the Alps. Ball (1870) gave the Col de la Seigne as one of six candidates in discussion at that time (another was the nearby Little St Bernard Pass, which has held onto more support). The possibility of the Col de la Seigne is discussed at length in Chaix (1855); de Beer (1955) championed a route much further south over the Col de la Traversette, just north of Monte Viso, an opinion strongly disputed by McDonald (1956) and Walbank (1956). This southerly route has recently found favour with Mahaney et al. (2017), as widely reported in newpapers in April 2016, but some sceptical reactions are summarised by Harrsch (2016). Mussolini's comment (my translation) on his need for several thousand war dead in June 1940 is reported by Bocca (2006), who also describes the fighting around the Mont Blanc massif. Ball (1870) described the view into Italy from the Col de la Seigne and Turner's quick drawing of this view is in his Val d'Aosta sketchbook from his Tour to the Alps, 1836, which can be viewed on appointment in the Tate Britain (Folio 21 Recto 'Five Sketches: Two Views on the Col du Bonhomme; Mont Blanc from the Col de la Seigne, and Two Views of Arvier in the Val d'Aosta', D29072; the page concerned can also be seen on the Tate's website).

Envoi

The lines by Victor Hugo are from the last of his 'Soleils Couchants' poems published in 1831 in the collection *Les Feuilles d'Automne.*

Bibliography

Alain-Fournier (1966) *Le Grand Meaulnes* (translated by Frank Davison), London: Penguin Books.

Ardagh, J. (1982) *France in the 1980s*, London: Penguin Books.

Ashdown, P. (2014) *The Cruel Victory: The French Resistance, D-Day and the Battle for the Vercors 1944*, London: HarperCollins.

Atkinson, A. B. and Harrison, A. (1978) *Distribution of Personal Wealth in Britain, 1923–1972*, Cambridge: Cambridge University Press.

Aubenas, F. (2010) *The Night Cleaner* (translated by Andrew Brown), Cambridge: Polity Press.

Aubert, J. (1939) 'Historique de la navigation sur le Haut-Rhône français', *Les Études Rhodaniennes*, 15 (1–3): 181–90.

Avenas, P. and Walter, H. (2007) *La Mystérieuse Histoire du Nom des Oiseaux*. Paris: Robert Laffont Éditions.

'B. B.' (1944) *Brendon Chase*, London: Hollis and Carter.

Baker, A. R. H. (1968) 'A modern French revolution', *The Geographical Magazine*, 40: 833–41.

Ball, J. (ed.) (1859) *Peaks, Passes, and Glaciers. A Series of Excursions by Members of the Alpine Club*, London: Longman, Brown, Green, Longmans and Roberts.

Ball, J. (1866) *A Guide to the Western Alps*, London: Longmans, Green & Co.

Bardon, G. (2011) *Reflets de Sologne*, Romorantin: Communication-Presse-Édition.

Barkham, P. (2010) *The Butterfly Isles*, London: Granta Books.

Barot, S. and Knapp, A. (2014) 'Les oubliés du 6 juin 1944', *Le Monde*, May 30.

Beevor, A. (2010) *D-Day: The Battle for Normandy*, London: Penguin Viking.

Behaghel, L. (2008) *Poverty and Social Exclusion in Rural Areas. Final Report – Annex I. Country Studies: France*, Brussels: European Commission.

Belloc, H. (1902) *The Path to Rome*, Woking and London: Unwin Brothers.

Belloc, H. (1909) *The Pyrenees*, London: Methuen.

Bocca, G. (2006) *Le Mie Montagne: Gli Anni della Neve e del Fuoco*, Milano: Feltrinelli Editore.

Boogaart, R. (2016) 'Monumental *lavoirs* and *fontaines* in France', additional material to *Follies in France III*, follies.org.uk (website of The Folly Fellowship).

Brown, R. (1994) *Overtones and Undertones: Reading Film Music*, Berkeley: University of California Press.

Brucy, G. and Velleret, R. (2016) *Un Fleuve, Deux Canaux*, Chatillon-sur-Loire: Association Castellio.

Bryson, B. (1998) *A Walk in the Woods*, London: Black Swan Books.

Buchan, J. (1925) *John Macnab*, London: Houghton Mifflin.

Buchan, J. (1935) *The House of the Four Winds*, London: Hodder & Stoughton.

Cameron, I. (1996) 'Poaching: crime and protest from the eighteenth to the twentieth century', *Parergon*, 14 (1): 241–55.

Chaix, P. (1855) 'Notes on the passage of Hannibal across the Alps; and on the valley of Beaufort, in Upper Savoy', *The Journal of the Royal Geographical Society of London*, 25: 182–91.

Champault, M. (1982) *Les Combats de Gien*, Gien: Société Historique et Archéologique du Giennois.

Chevallier, G. (1930) *La Peur*, Paris: Stock.

Chevallier, G. (1934) *Clochmerle*, Paris: Presses universitaires de France.

Clout, H. (1972) *The Geography of Post-War France: A Social and Economic Approach*, Oxford: Pergamon Press.

Clout, H. (1975) 'Timeless France', *The Geographical Magazine*, 48: 151–5.

Dearmer, P. (1904) *Highways and Byways in Normandy*, London: Macmillan.

de Beer, G. (1955) *Alps and Elephants: Hannibal's March*, London: Geoffrey Bles.

Diamond, H. (2007) *Fleeing Hitler: France 1940*, Oxford: Oxford University Press.

Dobson, M. (2010) *Contours of Death and Disease in Early Modern Britain*, Cambridge: Cambridge University Press.

Dodd, L. and Knapp, A. (2008) 'How many Frenchmen did you kill? British bombing policy towards France (1940-1945)', *French History*, 22 (4): 469–92.

DRJSCS Centre (2012) *Indicateurs statistiques de la politique de la ville. Département du Loir et Cher – Données localisées*, Direction Régionale de la Jeunesse, des Sports et de la Cohésion Sociale, Centre.

du Maurier, D. (1957) *The Scapegoat*, London: Gollancz.

Easterbrook, M. (2010) *Butterflies of Britain and Ireland: A Field and Site Guide*, London: A & C Black Publishers Ltd.

Edwards-May, D. (1984) *Inland Waterways of France* (5th ed.), Cambridgeshire: Imray Laurie Norie & Wilson.

Eisenhower, D. (1948) *Crusade in Europe*, London: William Heinemann Ltd.

Fleming, F. (2000) *Killing Dragons: The Conquest of the Alps*, London: Granta Books.

Genevoix, M. (1916) *Sous Verdun* (translated by H. Graham Richards as *'Neath Verdun* and published by Hutchinson, republished by Leonaur, 2010).

Genevoix, M. (1925) *Raboliot*, Paris: Grasset.

Gibbons, S. (1932) *Cold Comfort Farm*, London: Longman.

Girard E. and Daum, T. (2010) *La géographie n'est plus ce que vous croyez…* Éditions Codex.

Goldring, D. (1913) *The Loire; the Record of a Pilgrimage from Gerbier de Joncs to St Nazaire*, London: Constable & Company.

Grigg, D. (1980) *Population Growth and Agrarian Change. An Historical Perspective*, Cambridge: Cambridge University Press.

Grigson, G. (1970) *Notes from an Odd Country*, Basingstoke: Macmillan.

Grigson, G. (ed.) (1980) *The Faber Book of Poems and Places*, London: Faber and Faber.

Gros, F. (2014) *A Philosophy of Walking* (translated by John Howe), London: Verso.

Habel, J. C., Meyer, M. and Schmitt, T. (eds.) (2014) *Jewels in the Mist. A synopsis on the highly endangered butterfly species, the Violet Copper, Lycaena helle*, Sofia: Pensoft.

Hansen, P. (1995) 'Albert Smith, the Alpine Club, and the invention of mountaineering in mid-Victorian Britain', *Journal of British Studies*, 34 (3): 300–24.

Harrison, M. (2016) *Rain. Four Walks in English Weather*, London: Faber & Faber.

Harrsch, M. (2016) 'Hannibal's route over the Alps or just horse s***?', *Roman Times*, 13 April.

Hastings, M. (2014) *Catastrophe: Europe goes to War 1914*, London: William Collins.

Holt, C., Hewson, C., and Fuller, R. (2012) 'The Nightingale in Britain: Status, ecology and conservation needs', *British Birds*, 105 (April): 172–87.

Horne, E. (2015) *Zola and the Victorians: Censorship in the Age of Hypocrisy*, London: Quercus Publishing.

Hudson, W. H. (1909) *Afoot in England*, London: Hutchinson & Co.

Inglis, K. (1992) 'War memorials: Ten questions for historians', *Guerres Mondiales et Conflits Contemporains*, 167 (Juillet): 5–21.

James, H. (1884) *A Little Tour of France*, Boston: James R. Osgood and Company.

Judt, T. (1975) 'A society in stagnation', *The Geographical Magazine*, 48 (4): 236–40.

Knapp, A. and Wright, V. (2006) *The Government and Politics of France* (5th ed.), Abingdon: Routledge.

Lafon, A. (2014) 'War Losses (France)', in U. Daniel, P. Gatrell, O. Janz, H. Jones, J. Keene, A. Kramer, and B. Nasson (eds.) *1914-1918-online International Encyclopedia of the First World War*, Freie Universität Berlin, Berlin.

The Law Library of Congress (2014) *Inheritance Laws in the Nineteenth and Twentieth Centuries: France, Germany, United States*, Washington DC: The Law Library of Congress.

Leigh Fermor, P. (1979) *A Time of Gifts*, London: Penguin Books.

Leigh Fermor, P. (1987) *Between the Woods and the Water*, London: Penguin Books.

Leigh Fermor, P. (2013) *The Broken Road*, London: John Murray.

Le Sueur, B. (1989) *L'évolution de la navigation intérieure et de ses métiers, XIXe-XXe siècle*, Neuilly-sur-Seine: Centre de recherche sur la culture technique.

Lindert, P. (1986) 'Unequal English wealth since 1688', *Journal of Political Economy*, 94 (6): 1127–62.

Mabey, R. (1993) *Whistling in the Dark: In Pursuit of the Nightingale*, London: Sinclair-Stevenson.

Mabey, R. (2013) *The Ash and the Beech: The Drama of Woodland Change*, London: Vintage.

Macfarlane, R. (2003) *Mountains of the Mind: A History of a Fascination*, London: Granta Books.

Mahaney, W. and twenty-five co-authors (2017) 'Biostratigraphic evidence relating to the age-old question of Hannibal's invasion of Italy, I: History and geological reconstruction', *Archaeometry*, 59 (1): 164–78.

Manceron, V. (2006) 'Le pays de Dombes et ses mises en image: jeu sur les frontières et quête de reconnaissance', *Ruralia*, 18/19: 2–17.

Marren, P. (2015) *Rainbow Dust. Three Centuries of Delight in British Butterflies*, London: Vintage.

Mauret Cribellier, V. (1996) *Pont-Canal de Briare*, Orleans: AREP Centre Éditions.

McDonald, A. (1956) 'Hannibal's passage of the Alps', *The Alpine Journal*, 61 (292): 93–101.

McKnight, H. (2005) *Cruising French Waterways* (4th ed.), London: Adlard Coles Nautical.

McNee, A. (2015) *The Cockney Who Sold the Alps*, Brighton: Victorian Secrets.

Moore, W. (2011) *Free France's Lion: The Life of Philippe Leclerc, de Gaulle's Greatest General*, Newbury: Casemate Publishers.

Moorehead, C. (2015) *Village of Secrets: Defying the Nazis in Vichy France*, London: Vintage.

Moulin, A. (1991) *Peasantry and Society in France since 1789*, Cambridge: Cambridge University Press.

Neiertz, N. (1999) *La Coordination des Transports en France de 1918 à Nos Jours*, Paris: Imprimerie nationale/Comité pour l'histoire économique et financière de la France.

Némirovsky, I. (2004) *Suite Française*, London: Chatto & Windus.

Newson, S., Johnston, A., Renwick, A., Baillie, S., and Fuller, R. (2012) 'Modelling large-scale relationships between changes in woodland deer and bird populations', *Journal of Applied Ecology*, 49 (1): 278–86.

Oates, M. (2015) *In Pursuit of Butterflies: A Fifty-Year Affair*, London: Bloomsbury.

Oates, M. (2020) *His Imperial Majesty: A Natural History of the Purple Emperor*, London: Bloomsbury.

Packe, C. (1867) *A Guide to the Pyrenees: Especially Intended for the use of Mountaineers* (2nd ed.), London: Longmans, Green & Co.

Peterson, R., Mountfort, G., and Hollom, P. (1954) *A Field Guide to the Birds of Britain and Europe*, London: Collins.

Philippe, M-A. and Polombo, N. (2009) 'Soixante années de remembrement: essai de bilan critique de l'aménagement foncier en France', *Études foncières*, ADEF, 43–9.

Piketty, T. (2014) *Capital in the Twenty-First Century* (translated by Arthur Goldhammer), Cambridge: Harvard University Press.

Pillard, A. (1949) *La Bataille de Gien: 15-19 juin 1940. Témoignages et souvenirs*, Gien: Impr. Jeanne-d'Arc.

Poitou, C. (1978) 'La mortalité en Sologne orléanaise de 1670 à 1870', *Annales de démographie historique* ('La mortalité du passé'), 235–64.

Postel-Vinay, G. and Sahn, D. (2010) 'Explaining stunting in nineteenth-century France', *The Economic History Review*, 63 (2): 315–34.

Pringle, G. and Schaefer, H. (2012) *Rocks to Riches. Time, Change, and Ochre in a Village in the Vaucluse*, Bloomington IN: Xlibris.

Pritchard, S. (2011) *Confluence: The Nature of Technology and the Remaking of the Rhône*, Cambridge, MA: Harvard University Press.

Prost, A. (2014) 'War Losses', in U. Daniel, P. Gatrell, O. Janz, H. Jones, J. Keene, A. Kramer, and B. Nasson (eds.), 1914-1918-online *International Encyclopedia of the First World War*, Freie Universität Berlin, Berlin.

Robb, G. (2007) *The Discovery of France*, London: Picador.

Roche, L. (1951) 'Les aspects essentiels du remembrement rural en France', *Bulletin de la Société Française d'Économie Rurale*, 3(4): 157–66.

Roddier, M. (2003) *Lavoirs: Washhouses of Rural France*, New York: Princeton Architectural Press.

Rozental, A. (1956) 'The enclosure movement in France', *The American Journal of Economics and Sociology*, 16 (1): 55–71.

Scates, B. and Wheatley, R. (2014) 'War memorials', in J. Winter (ed.) *The Cambridge History of the First World War*, Cambridge: Cambridge University Press.

Scheck, R. (2006) *Hitler's African Victims. The German Army Massacres of Black French Soldiers in 1940*, Cambridge: Cambridge University Press.

Schiff, J-C. (1936) 'La fin de la navigation sur le Haut-Rhône', *Les Études Rhodaniennes*, 12 (2): 259–72.

Sherman, D. (1994) 'Art, commerce and the production of memory in France after World War I', in J. Gillis (ed.), *Commemorations: The Politics of National Identity*, Princeton NJ: Princeton University Press.

Shlaim, A. (1974) 'Prelude to downfall: The British offer of union to France, June 1940', *Journal of Contemporary History*, 9 (3): 27–63.

Simenon, G. (1932) *Le Port des Brumes*, Paris: A. Fayard.

Smith, P. (1975) *Arctic Victory. The Story of Convoy PQ18*, London: William Kimber.

Smythe, F. (1934) *An Alpine Journey*, London: Victor Gollancz.

South, R. (1906) *The Butterflies of the British Isles*, London and New York: Frederick Warne & Co.

Speaight, R. (ed.) (1958) *Letters from Hilaire Belloc*, London: Hollis and Carter.

Stephen, L. (1871) *The Playground of Europe*, London: Longmans, Green & Co.

Stevenson, R. L. (1878) *An Inland Voyage*, London: C. Kegan Paul & Co.

Stevenson, R. L. (1879) *Travels with a Donkey in the Cévennes*, London: C. Kegan Paul & Co.

Stevenson, R. L. (1881) *Virginibus Puerisque, and Other Papers*, London: C. Kegan Paul & Co.

Streit, C. (1958) 'De Gaulle urged federal union on Churchill in 1940', *Freedom & Union*, 13 (7–8): 14–6.

Sutcliffe, T. (1976) 'A nation of reluctant townsfolk', *The Geographical Magazine*, 48 (5): 290–6.

Wade, R. (1979) *The Companion Guide to the Loire*, London: Collins.

Walbank, F. (1956) 'Some reflections on Hannibal's pass', *The Journal of Roman Studies*, 46 (1 and 2): 37–45.

Weber, E. (1977) *Peasants into Frenchmen: The Modernisation of Rural France 1870-1914*, London: Chatto & Windus.

White, G. (1789) *The Natural History and Antiquities of Selborne*, London: B. White & Son.

Wright, G. (1964) *Rural Revolution in France: The Peasantry in the Twentieth Century*, California: Stanford University Press.

Wylie, L. (1974) *Village in the Vaucluse* (3rd ed.), Cambridge MA and London: Harvard University Press.

Young, A. (1929) *Travels in France and Italy during the years 1787,*

1788 and 1789, Cambridge: Cambridge University Press (based on the 2nd edition published in 1794 by W. Richardson, Royal Exchange, London).

Zdatny, S. (2006) *Fashion, Work, and Politics in Modern France*, Basingstoke: Palgrave Macmillan.

Zola, É. (1973) *La Débâcle* (translated by Leonard Tancock with the title *The Debacle*), London: Penguin Books.

Zola, É. (1980) *La Terre* (translated by Douglas Parmée with the title *The Earth*), London: Penguin Books.

Zola, É. (1995) *L'Assommoir* (translated by Margaret Mauldon), Oxford: Oxford University Press.

Acknowledgements

When I set off across France, it had not been my intention to write a book (or I would have taken the job of diary-keeping more seriously). The first people I am grateful to are the friends who commented on the blog I kept up at the time, which helped give birth to the idea after my return to England of carrying on writing.

A career of academic writing meant that the job of producing a book-length number of words was not so daunting. But of course those words needed to be very different – as my wife, Tina, put it pithily: 'it has to be interesting this time.' Some re-training was clearly needed and I took Guardian masterclasses in Nature Writing and Travel Writing, taught respectively by Patrick Barkham and Mike Carter from whom I learned a lot.

I next want to thank the people I stayed with along the way, especially the B&B hosts who welcomed me into their homes and encouraged me in my progress of whom I have written less than might be expected in a travelogue – that was not the deal in putting me up for the night. Likewise, I have written little of those who joined me for parts of the journey; I thank them for all their companionship and enthusiasm, which meant a great deal to me – Andrew, Jay, Tina, Honi, Riccardo, Judy, Patrick, and Richard.

Friends and family commented on drafts of parts of the book, or the whole manuscript, or discussed particular issues with me, or made suggestions – and they did so to considerable effect. I am forever grateful to Tina Gericke, my sternest critic, who encouraged and supported me all the way from when I first mentioned the idea of the journey to her through to the final production of the finished book, and to Tony Atkinson, Richard Barrie, Elodie Bellarbre, Isobel Butters, Sarah Caro, Alan Duffield, Jane Elliott, Sue Gordon, Jay Greenwood, Jon Harding, Simon Hill, Stephen Jenkins, Maryse Le Roux, Honi Loudon, Joe Loudon, Andrew McMorrin, Sarah Micklewright, Charles Mills, Judy Routledge, Joëlle Sabin, Yves Sabin, Beryl Steeden, James Todd, and Patrick Vandamme.

I thank daughter Charlotte for drawing the map, the sketches that form the chapter heads, and for the illustration for the cover; and her and daughter Harriet for all their support. And the last person I must thank is another family member: my late father, David, who managed to pass on much.

Index

Agriculture, 40
    employment, 9–10, 69
    farm size, 10
    field size, 69–71
    remembrement, 71, 134
    subsistence farming, 9, 134,
      224
    tractors, 9, 69
    vines (*see also* wine), 65, 116–8
Aix-les-Bains, 183
Alain-Fournier, 84, 93, 96, 225–6
    and Maurice Genevoix, 93,
      226
    Le Grand Meaulnes, 84–5, 96
Albertville, 186–7, 195–9, 212
Alderney, 1, 3
Alençon, 34–7, 42, 51, 61, 67, 75,
    123, 162, 185
Allier *département*, 229
Allier (river) 122, 147
Alpine Club, the, 214
    Peaks, Passes and Glaciers,
      197–8
Alps, 2, 5–6, 24, 133, 171, 174,
    176, 182–6, 188, 196–220
    Beaufortain, 197, 204, 206,
      210, 214
    Hannibal's crossing, 204–5,
      230–1
    Little St Bernard pass, 205,
      209, 230

    Prealps, 187–8, 191, 196
    skiing, 2, 196–7
    see also Mont Blanc
ancien régime, 75, 92, 142
Angeville, Adolphe d', 133, 228
Apennines *see under* Italy
Ardagh, John, *France in the 1980s*,
    134, 141–2
Ardant, Fanny, 36, 75
Armorican Massif, 22
Aron (river), 123–4
Aubenas, Florence, *Le Quai de
    Ouistreham*, 16
Auvergne, 128, 133–5, 139, 144

Ball, John, 214
Balzac, Honoré de, 9, 67
Barkham, Patrick, *The Butterfly Isles*,
    167
Bastille Day, 206, 210
Baudelaire, Charles, 79
B. B. (Watkins-Pitchford, Denys),
    Brendon Chase, 167–8
Beauce plateau, 67–71, 73, 78, 134
Beaufortain *see under* Alps
Belloc, Hilaire, 11, 35, 74, 77, 83,
    185–6
    The Path to Rome, 4–5, 11-2
    The Pyrenees, 24, 33, 198
bells, cow and sheep, 191, 208
Beuvron (river), 89

binoculars, 44
birds, 8, 17, 40, 42–4, 55, 157,
    173, 175, 220
    *A Field Guide to the Birds of
        Britain and Europe*, 112
    bee-eater, 108–9
    black-headed gull, 72
    black kite, 173
    cuckoo, 32
    goshawk, 111
    honey buzzard, 111
    hoopoe, 111–2
    house martin, 154
    nightingale, 8, 56–7
    nightjar, 163–4
    quail, 56, 130
    skylark, 50
    stork, 119–20
    swallow, 46
    swift, 67
    tern, 72, 94, 119
    turtle dove, 17, 46
    wood warbler, 32
Blois, 6, 41, 62, 72–83, 90, 95,
    98–9, 105, 117, 122, 158–9,
    175, 199
Bocca, Giorgio, 212
boredom, 40
boules (*pétanque*), 114
Boulogne, 2
Bourbon monarchy, 27, 76, 86,
    104, 142
Bourbon-Lancy, 125–6
Bourdelle, Antoine, 63
Braye (river), 61–2
Briare, 100–1, 110, 120, 124–5,
    147, 227
    pont-canal, 103-8
Bryson, Bill, *A Walk in the Woods*,
    83
Buchan, John, 3
    John Macnab, 94

The House of the Four Winds,
    3–5, 12, 20, 25, 219–20
Burgundy, 109, 117, 130, 171–2
Burke, Edmund, 198
butterflies, 44, 220
    differences from moths, 153
    French names, 45–6
    Apollo (*apollon*), 218–9
    Black-Veined White (*gazé*),
        199–200
    Brimstone (*citron*), 45
    Chalkhill Blue (*argus bleu-
        nacré*), 218
    Comma (*Robert-le-Diable*),
        120-1
    Common Blue (*azuré
        commun*), 55
    Dark Green Fritillary (*grand
        nacré*), 200, 217
    Granville Fritillary (*damier du
        plantain*), 66
    Great Sooty Satyr (*grande
        coronide*), 218
    Heath Fritillary (*damier
        athalie*), 66
    Holly Blue, (*azuré des
        nerpruns*), 55
    Large Skipper (*sylvaine*), 152
    Marbled White (*demi-deuil*),
        120
    Mountain Ringlet (*moiré de la
        canche*), 152, 189
    Painted Lady (*belle-dame*), 45
    Purple Emperor (*grand mars
        changeant*), 166–8
    Scarce Swallowtail (*flambé*),
        189
    Scotch Argus (*moiré sylvicole*),
        189
    Speckled Wood (*tircis*), 45
    Spotted Fritillary (*damier
        orangé*), 217

Small Heath (*fadet commun*), 45
Swallowtail (*machaon*), 65
Violet Copper (*cuivré de la bistorte*), 151–2
White Admiral (*petit sylvain*), 88, 111, 113, 166

Caen, 6, 14–16, 19–22, 26, 29, 34–5, 220
Calvados *département*, 50
Camino de Santiago ('The Way'), 4, 118, 125
canals, 104–7, 172
    Canal de Briare, 104–8, 123
    Canal de Caen à la Mer, 15, 17, 19, 220
    Canal de la Sauldre, 90–1, 124
    Canal de Roanne à Digoin, 124, 159
    Canal du Centre, 104, 110, 172
    Canal du Nivernais, 123–4
    Canal Lateral à la Loire, 105–8, 120, 124, 127
    Freycinet gauge, 106–7, 226–7
    and walking, 124, 148
Cévennes, 10, 144, 146, 165
Châlon, 104, 110
Chambéry, 6, 182–8, 190, 196, 217
Chambord, 82
Chamonix, 200, 202–3, 220
Chartres, 54, 68–9
cheese, 28, 32–4, 48, 149, 189–90, 196, 205–6, 208
Cher (river), 85
Cherbourg, 1, 63
Chevallier, Gabriel
    Clochemerle, 170–1
    La Peur, 170–1
churches
    architecture, 9, 23–4, 98, 114, 122–3, 132, 143, 146

modern stained glass, 98–9, 122–3
votive offerings, 31, 36
Churchill, Winston, 100–1
Civil Code (Napoleonic), 70, 141
Clare, John, 54, 57, 164
Clermont-Ferrand, 130, 148
    poverty, 134
cobwebs, 54
Col de la Seigne *see under* Mont Blanc
Coleridge, Samuel Taylor, 57, 203
communes, 58
    commune isolée, 135, 138
    merger, 138, 227–8
    number of, 136, 227
    powers, 138
    small size, 136–7
Cosson (river), 89
counties, English names, 51
Courmayeur *see under* Italy
crosses, wayside, 52–3

dawn, 50, 158, 165
Decize, 123–4, 151
de Gaulle, Charles (General), 37, 100–3, 190
départements, 80–1, 133
    naming of, 50–1, 73, 159
    overseas, 227
    powers of the *préfet*, 136
    see also individual names
Dickens, Charles, 69
Digoin, 104–6, 124, 159, 172
dogs, 13, 110, 181
Dombes, la, 172–4
Dorset, 33, 57, 121, 164, 199
du Maurier, Daphne, *The Scapegoat*, 141

Écouché, 28, 30
Eden, Anthony, 100–1

Eisenhower, Dwight (General), 29
éoliennes (wind turbines), 151, 162
European Union, 103
Exode, l' (the Exodus) *see* Second
    World War, Fall of France

Falaise, 29
Fédération Française de la Randonée
    Pédestre (*see also* GRs), 26
Féjoz, Henri (Chanoine), 230
Fête de la Musique, 125–6
films
    César awards, 144, 172, 177
    Days of Glory, 177–8
    Elizabeth, 36
    Être et Avoir, 144
    La Bataille de France, 226
    La Mort du Duc de Guise, 75–6
    La Vie Moderne, 144
    Raboliot, 93–4
    Ridicule, 172–3
    Suite Française, 226
First World War, 5, 17, 32, 58, 93,
    142, 170–1
    Battle of the Frontiers, 60
    Battle of the Somme, 60
    deaths, 60–1
    Paris, 96
    Verdun, 66, 137
    war memorials, 58–61
flâneur, 79–80
Florence *see under* Italy
Franco-Prussian war (1870-1),
    96–7
François I, 75, 82
Fréjus road tunnel, 183

Galt, Jaikie *see* Buchan, John, *The
    House of the Four Winds*
Geneva, 133, 200–1, 220
Geneva, Lake, 171, 175, 177, 202,
    206

Genevoix, Maurice, 93, 123
    and Alain-Fournier, 93, 226
    Raboliot, 93–4
Gibbons, Stella, *Cold Comfort Farm*,
    51
Gide, André, 216
Gien, 6, 83, 94–100, 123, 137, 159
Goldring, Douglas, 97, 115, 119, 160
Grigson, Geoffrey, *Notes from an
    Odd Country*, 62–6, 68, 76, 82,
    131–2
Gros, Frédéric, *A Philosophy of
    Walking*, vii, 2, 40, 79, 125, 188,
    219
GRs (footpaths), 5–6, 24–6, 51,
    161, 172–3, 206
guidebooks, 7, 19, 29, 35, 122, 176,
    196
Guiers (river), 181
Guise
    Hôtel de (Alençon), 36, 75
    Mary of, 36, 75
    Duke Henri of, 75–6, 104

Hampshire, 6, 112, 219
Hardy, Thomas, 57, 69
Harrison, Melissa, *Rain*, 157
Hastings, Max, *Catastrophe*, 61
Henri III, 75–6
Henri IV, 76, 104
hitch-hiking, 2, 19–20, 47, 49
holloways, 52, 103
Hook of Holland, 12
Hudson (river), 77
Hudson, W. H., *Afoot in England*,
    7, 121
Hugo, Victor, 88–9, 216
Huguenots *see* Wars of Religion
Hundred Years War, 54
hunting, 27, 87, 92–3
    see also poaching
Hyatt Huntington, Anna, 77

Institut Géographique National
(IGN), 6, 25, 222
Institut National de la Statistique
et des Études Économiques
(INSEE), 224–5, 227–8
Isère (river), 187, 196–7
Italy, 2, 4, 6–7, 34, 75, 89, 113,
116, 200
    Apennines, 98, 139, 149, 192
    casa Savoia, 185
    Courmayeur, 6, 200, 202,
        204–5, 214, 216–7, 220
    Florence, 2, 146
    invasion of France (1940),
        212–3
    Italian and French national
        characters, 216–7
    nocino (walnut liqueur), 146
    number of communes, 136
    partisans (1944), 192
    Po (river), 217
    Rome, 4
    Val d'Aosta, 200–2, 214, 217

James, Henry, *A Little Tour in
France*, 74-6, 82
Joan of Arc, 77, 98, 113
Judt, Tony, 9
Jura mountains, 171, 174, 179,
182–3

Keats, John, 57, 229

La Charité-sur-Loire, 118–9
La Fontaine, Jean de, 46
Land's End to John o' Groats, 7
Landes, les, 87, 225
Lang, Jack, 126
lavoirs, 23–4, 131–3, 140
Le Havre, 14–5, 17, 19, 29
Le Mans, 51–2, 54

Le Pen, Marine, 78
Leclerc, Philippe (General), 37
Leigh Fermor, Patrick, 40, 63, 120
    A Time of Gifts, 11–2
les trente glorieuses, 9, 71
Linnaeus, Carl, 65
Lisieux, 35
Loir (river), 62–8, 108, 131
Loir-et-Cher, *département*, 80
Loire, *département*, 159
Loire (river), 6–7, 15, 41, 62,
    72–83, 85, 94, 97–110, 113–26,
    128, 130, 147, 150, 158–9
    arrival at and leaving, 72,
        159–61
    catchment area, 73, 162
    and *département* names, 73, 159
    nature of, 72–3, 105, 119,
        175–6
    navigation, 105–6, 124, 159
    Second World War, 96–7, 225
    source, 146
Loiret, *département*, 225
Louis XII, 74
Lyon, 6, 106, 130, 147, 171–8,
    183, 205

Mabey, Richard, 57
Maison de la Magie (Blois), 74
Maison du Braconnage (Chaon),
    91–2
maps, 6–7, 21, 41–2, 45, 52, 61–2,
    109, 161, 171–4, 177, 180, 195,
    198
    Angeville, Adolphe d', 1836
        essai, 133, 228
    information included, 24–6,
        52–3, 58, 81–2, 84, 105,
        113, 125, 187, 220
Mary, Queen of Scots, 36, 75
Massif Central, 6, 8, 10, 40, 72, 83,
    102, 112, 125, 128–54, 171

Massif de la Chartreuse, 187–8,
  191, 199
Massif des Bauges, 187–96, 199,
  204, 207–8, 217
Massif du Vercors, 191–2
Meuse (river), 226
Micklewright, David
  advice, 19
  and the Alps, 24, 197–9
  and the Beauce, 68
  and birds, 8, 17, 42, 50, 56–7,
    164, 220
  and churches, 23, 122, 132
  diary keeping, 7–9, 17
  first visit to France, 1, 5, 8–10
  and the Massif Central, 8, 10,
    40, 148–9
  and the Pyrenees, 2, 24, 33,
    40, 188, 197–8
  and the Sologne, 84, 89
  Second World War, 17–8,
    42–3, 164, 223
  views on lunch, 33–4
  walking alone, 40
Mont Blanc, 150, 196–7, 200–4,
  214–7
  Col de la Seigne, 6, 186,
    204–5, 209–17, 230
  glaciers, 203, 214–5, 217
  'mania', 203
  my first sighting, 195
  and the Romantic movement,
    203
  sunset, 201–2
  Tour du, 204, 210
  Tunnel, 5–6, 200, 202–3, 217,
    220
  Val Veni, 214–6
Montoire-sur-le-Loir, 66–7, 102,
  108
Monts de la Madeleine, 125,
  127–8, 136, 146–54, 159–62,

188–9, 213
moon *see* night sky
Morvan, 134
moths
  burnet family, 218
  differences from butterflies,
    153
  Chimney Sweeper (*ramoneur*),
    153
  Humming Bird Hawk-moth
    (*moro-sphinx*), 153
  Speckled Yellow (*panthère*),
    200

Napoleon Bonaparte, 70, 211, 230
Napoleon III, 68, 86, 133, 206
Némirovsky, Irène, *Suite Française*,
  96, 127, 226
Nevers, 122–3, 147
New York (city), 77
New York Times, The, 13
night sky, 12–3, 48–9, 62, 82, 145,
  164–5, 194
North Downs, 164

Occitan language, 45, 144
Office National des Fôrets, 31
Orléans, 6, 77, 82, 106
orc morals, 167
Orne *département*, 30, 50
Orne (river), 14–6, 18–22, 27–30
Orwell, George, *The Road to Wigan
  Pier*, 16
Ouistreham, 5, 6, 14–7, 41, 211,
  218, 220

Packe, Charles, 198
Paris, 9, 36, 67, 74–5, 80, 132–3,
  136, 147, 160, 220
  and *autoroutes*, 7, 21, 130
  banlieues, 79
  and canals, 104–6

First World War, 96
Franco-Prussian War, 95–6
Second World War, 29, 37,
    95–6, 100, 126–7, 178
    and the Sologne, 86, 89–90,
    92, 94
Pétain, Phillipe (Marshal), 66–7,
    95, 100–2
Piketty, Thomas, *Capital in the
    Twenty-First Century*, 142–3
planets *see* night sky
PMU (*Pari Mutuel Urbain*), 23
Po (river) *see under* Italy
poaching, 91–4
Pont de Normandie, 15
population of France, 135
    rural depopulation, 9–10, 59,
    129–31, 135, 138–9, 143,
    148
    size, 24, 59–60
    urban share, 9
Portsmouth, 5, 16
Pouilly-sur-Loire, 115–7
poverty, 85–6, 128, 131–6
    definition, 134–5
    in the *régions*, 134
    rural vs. urban, 135
Prix Goncourt, 93
provinces (pre-Revolution), 81,
    115, 122, 128, 144
Puisaye, 109–13
Puy de Dôme, 130, 148
Pyat, Félix, 86
Pyrenees, 24, 33, 40, 118, 134,
    197–8
    walking with my father, 2, 12,
    33, 188, 196

railways, 22, 92, 106, 133, 160
    and bombing of France, 28–9,
    97, 187
    TGV (*train à grande vitesse*),

52, 220
rain, 116–7, 157–8, 183
râpées de St-Étienne, 161
régions, 34, 81, 134, 144
remembrement, see under agriculture
Revolution (1789), 37, 67, 76, 85,
    104, 136, 172, 174
    abolition of provinces, 81
    calendar (new), 22, 46, 120,
    156
    and the communes, 136
    and the *départements*, 50–1, 81
    impact on distribution of
    wealth, 141–2
    milliard des émigrés (1825), 142
    and partible inheritance, 70,
    141
    and poaching, 92
    storming of the Bastille, 92
Reynaud, Paul, 95, 100–2
Rhône (river), 6, 117, 124, 134,
    150, 161, 169, 171–2, 181–3,
    185, 197, 218
    my arrival at, 174–5
    navigation, 105, 107, 110,
    175–7
    Second World War, 177–9,
    211
rivers *see individual names*
roads
    autoroutes, 7, 51–2, 130, 182
    road signs, 30, 173
    Roman, 109–10
    routes nationales, 5, 147
    tarred, 5, 161, 211
    unsealed, 5, 10, 30, 145–6
Roanne, 6, 124–5, 150–1, 154,
    158–61
Robb, Graham, *The Discovery of
    France*, 50
Rodin, Auguste, 63
Ronsard, Pierre de, 62–4

Rouen, 20–1
Rousseau, Jean-Jacques, 186
rucksack weight, 11, 35
rural living standards *see* poverty

saints, 35–6, 54
    Hubert, 93
    John the Baptist, 30–1, 35,
      146
    Joseph, 36
    Thérèse of Lisieux, 35–6
Saint-Saëns, Camille, 75
Sancerre, 115, 117, 119, 146
Santiago de Compostela *see* Camino
  de Santiago ('The Way')
Saône (river), 6, 114, 150, 161,
  168, 171–4, 178
    navigation, 104, 110, 172,
      175, 177
Sarthe *département*, 37, 42, 50–1,
  55, 57, 91, 163
Sarthe (river), 37
Sauldre (river), 90
Savoie *département*, 50, 185
Savoyard state, 184–5, 206
Second Empire (1852–70), 37, 68,
  86, 96, 133, 160
Second Republic (1848–51), 86
Second World War, 9, 14, 57
    Arctic convoy (PQ18), 42–3,
      223
    atrocities, 179, 191–2
    Battle of Normandy, 29
    bombing of France, 19, 28–30,
      67, 95–100, 122, 186
    D-Day, 17–8, 22, 28–9, 95
    Fall of France, 95–7, 100–3,
      108, 126
    Franco-British Union, 100–3
    Italian invasion of France,
      211–3
    maquis (resistance), 191–2

Ranville cemetery, 18–9
Stalingrad, 43
Tirailleurs Sénégalais, 178–9,
  211
Seine (river), 14–5, 27, 68, 124,
  172
    navigation, 104, 107
sentiers de Grande Randonée see GRs
Sgùrr na Ciche (Knoydart), 44
Shelley, Percy Bysshe, 57, 203
signs, wayside, 27, 89
Simenon, Georges, *Le Port des
  Brumes*, 16
sleeping in the open, 12–3, 46–50,
  52, 62, 145, 163–5, 193–4
Smythe, Frank, *An Alpine Journey*,
  197–8
Sologne, 83–94, 108, 124, 137,
  152
  canal, 90–1
  colonisation, 86–7
  étangs (lakes), 84, 88–9, 172–3
  poaching, 91–4
  poverty, 85–6
  rivers, 85, 89–90
  villages, 87–8, 90
South Downs, 12
St Bartholomew's Day massacre, 75
  see also Wars of Religion
stars *see* night sky
Stephen, Leslie (Sir), 202
Stevenson, Robert Louis, 39–40, 157
  An Inland Voyage, 36
  Travels with a Donkey, 46, 50,
    165
stick, uses of, 13, 110, 188, 195
Sublime, the, 198–9, 203
Suisse Normande, 22–8
Switzerland, 4, 171, 197–8, 204,
  212

tartiflette, 205

teurgoule, 28
Third Republic (1870-1940),
    142–3, 206
Thomas, Edward, 32
Times, The, 203
Tocqueville, Alexis de, 70
Tolstoy, Leo
    War and Peace, 11–2, 42–3,
        119, 211, 221
Toul, 4, 11–2
Tour de France, 209
Trôo, 62–4, 68, 76, 131–2
Turner, J. M. W., 203, 214, 217

urban inequality, 79, 134

Vendôme, 67–8, 102
Via Francigena, 4
Vibraye, 59, 61, 227
Vichy regime, 66, 95, 102, 126,
    179
    treatment of Jews, 127
Victor Emmanuel II, 185–6
vines, *see under* agriculture
Vizetelly, Henry, 69

Wars of Religion, 31, 75, 118–9
Weygand, Maxime (General),
    100–2
White, Gilbert, *The Natural History
    of Selborne*, 32, 111–2
wildlife (*see also* birds, butterflies,
    and moths)
    badger, 52
    bear, 47
    fox, 111
    marmot, 214
    mole, 52
    red squirrel, 52, 111

viper, 54
William the Conqueror, 19
wine (see also *vines*), 11, 104, 117,
    134, 163
    Beaujolais, 154, 168–70
    Côte Roannaise, 154
    Côtes du Rhône, 117
    Mondeuse, 190
    Pouilly-Fumé, 115–7
    Sancerre, 115, 117
woods
    California redwoods, 47–8
    Fôret d'Écouves, 30–2, 35,
        37, 162
    Fôret de Gâtines, 64
    Fôret de Perseigne, 42–6
    Mirkwood (Tolkein), 47
    Puisaye, 109, 111
    sleeping in, 46–9, 193–4
    Sologne, 85–7
    walking in, 83, 87, 111
    Wild Wood, the (Grahame),
        47
Wordsworth, William, 57, 203, 229
Wylie, Laurence, *Village in the
    Vaucluse*, 138–9

Yeats, W. B., 62–3
Young, Arthur, *Travels in France*,
    51, 86, 92, 122, 159, 186, 198

Zola, Émile
    L'Assommoir, 132
    La Débâcle, 96
    La Terre, 68–70, 142
ZUP (*zone à urbaniser en priorité*),
    78-9, 95
ZUS (*zone urbaine sensible*), 79, 95,
    122